Jews & Sex

Jews & Sex

Edited by
Nathan Abrams

Five Leaves Publications
www.fiveleaves.co.uk

Jews and Sex
Edited by Nathan Abrams

Published in 2008 by
Five Leaves Publications,
PO Box 8786, Nottingham NG1 9AW
info@fiveleaves.co.uk
www.fiveleaves.co.uk

Cover photograph of Annie Sprinkle by Richard Sylvarnes,
courtesy of Annie Sprinkle

ISBN: 978 1 905512 34 8

Five Leaves acknowledges financial support
from Arts Council England

Five Leaves is a member of Inpress
(www.inpressbooks.co.uk),
representing independent publishers

Typeset and designed by Four Sheets Design and Print
Printed in Great Britain

Acknowledgements

I would like to thank Matthew Reisz who, as editor of *The Jewish Quarterly*, took a chance and published an essay of mine about Jews in the porn industry in the Winter 2004/2005 issue entitled, "Triple Exthnics". This was followed by the Limmud programming team which, that December, allowed me to present a talk called, "Porn Again Jews: Jewish Involvement in the Adult Film Industry". The reaction to my talk, held at 11pm at night to a packed audience of young Jews of both sexes, was so universally positive, that I decided to continue with this research. Meanwhile, having read my piece in *The Jewish Quarterly*, Ross Bradshaw contacted me about editing this collection. I would like to thank Ross for not only having the initial idea, but also for approaching me and for his editorial abilities which made this book possible. The contributors deserve praise, too, for without them there would not be such a long, interesting and varied book. I hope the readers find as much pleasure in this book as I have had editing it. Some of it has been a real eye-opener!

Contents

Introduction
Nathan Abrams

What is the relationship between Jews and sex? What is Jewish sexuality? In seeking to answer those questions this anthology represents a wide-ranging selection of thought-provoking and sometimes challenging essays. Although it is by no means comprehensive or exhaustive, *Jews & Sex* is intended to provide an overview of new and contemporary writing on a diverse number of topics from a range of perspectives: historical, theological, literary, artistic and filmic. The scope of the collection is broad, covering erotic theology in the Bible through to Jews and sex in the contemporary film industries in the United States, Israel and Britain. It covers many countries during different periods. The contributors are even broader: England, Wales, Ireland, the United States, Israel and Australia are all represented.

The collection begins where it seems most appropriate, with the Biblical and other texts that intimate a sexual relationship between God and the Jewish people. Sex and sexual behaviour are of major concern both to the Hebrew Bible, from the first commandment given to Adam and Eve to go forth and multiply, to the sexual purity laws of Leviticus. Thus, in the opening chapter, Rabbi Geoffrey Dennis explores the motif of the people of Israel as the emotional and sexual "partner" of God. This idea begins in Biblical literature and is reiterated and expanded throughout rabbinic and esoteric literature, especially in the corpus of medieval Kabbalah, becoming one of the central themes of Jewish mystical theosophy. While the "sexual" implications of this imagery are always present in this idea, it is only in the works of Kabbalah, such as *Sefer Zohar*, that this theme is developed in such frankly sexual terms that it amounts to a very elaborate metaphysics of sex. This theme has had implications beyond the theological and folkloric, for it has been used in various ways by religious Jews as a paradigm for shaping their own sexual ethics and evaluation of human sexuality.

Continuing with the theological theme, Jay Michaelson considers the religious significance of liberated sexuality and whether certain behaviours, primarily homosexual, extra-marital sex and non-procreative sex of various kinds, are permitted or forbidden by Jewish religious law. His particular focus is that of queer sexuality and where it fits, since it transgresses conventional gender categories, into the Biblical insistence on order. He seeks to provide answers to questions surrounding the role of queer people and theologies within Judaism. In doing so, he uncovers some interesting ideas; for example, that the halachic system includes multiple gender and sex categories and isn't merely restricted to that of male and female, straight and gay.

While still on the subject of homosexuality, Hinde Burstin's chapter provides a striking contrast by exploring lesbianism in Yiddish poetry. Taking three different Yiddish poets in different eras (the 1920s, 1960s and 1990s), and in three different continents (America, South Africa and Australia), she discusses the issues confronting the writers in writing and publishing work with lesbian themes such as lesbian longing, internal dreams and hidden desires versus external realities, the closet versus openness, knowledge versus constraints imposed by social structures, and women's preparedness to place their desire above societal expectations. It is rare to find published Yiddish poems that express sexual feelings or relationships between women. But in these unusual examples, a great deal is revealed about the women themselves and their surrounding societies. In addressing lesbian themes in Yiddish poetry, Burstin hopes to break down stereotypes of Jewish women, the Jewish community and Yiddish poetry. She also debunks the myth that same-sex attraction was not a feature of Jewish community or Jewish life. The fact that these poems were written in different continents and time periods underlines the universal nature of Jewish women's attraction to other women, both Jewish and non-Jewish.

Continuing with the theme of homosexuality, Nir Cohen shifts the focus to Israel. One of the most remarkable developments within Israeli society in the past three decades, he argues, is the rise of the local gay community. The shift in the status of gay men, lesbians and transsexuals from the margins of society into the mainstream has been a symbol of liberalism and secularity both in and outside of Israel. The success of gay artists such as Dana International, for example, and "gay" films such as *Yossi and Jagger* (Eytan Fox, 2002), which is at the centre of his essay, have contributed to the new image of Israel as a pluralistic and progressive state, at least on these issues.

10

Despite the late arrival of gay consciousness to Israel in the mid-1970s, it has been on the rise ever since and has gradually lifted the legal restrictions that the state had imposed on its gay citizens for many years. The changing representations of the members of the gay community in the media and the frequent references to it in popular culture led to a juridical revolution, which took place between 1988 and 1993, and secured gay men and lesbians an (almost) equal standing in society. The community's wish to assimilate, however, has had its price. Aiming at integration and acceptance rather than social change, the members of the gay community have internalised the heterosexist, militaristic cultural norms they were originally set to challenge. More than the "feminine", effete "queer" Jew of the Diaspora, it is the "Muscle Jew" of the Zionist movement, and his later incarnation into the soldier of the Israeli Defence Force (IDF) that has captured Israeli gay men's imaginations. The Israeli gay community thus favours its militarist, straight-acting men with the consequence, Cohen argues, that gayness in Israel nowadays is acceptable and even desirable as long as it does not transgress the rigid boundaries of Zionist masculinity. Cohen explores these issues by taking a close focus on the representation of male homosexuality in *Yossi and Jagger*.

Sandra Meiri and Yael Munk maintain the filmic and Israeli context. In their reading of the film *Gift from Heaven* (Dover Kosashvilli, 2003), they explore the most intimate sexual representations of the male Jew, in particular, the two old anti-Semitic concepts that sustained the notion of the sexual degeneracy of the male Jew in the Diaspora, namely the myth of the hypersexual exotic Jew and, by contrast, the notion of the effeminate, "castrated" Jew. In doing so, they argue that the film tackles the hegemonic model of sexuality still prevalent in Israeli society — that of the male, military, Ashkenazi, secular *Sabra*, which has its roots in the "New Jew" model of the Zionist movement, and which was designed to erase all traces of the exiled, effeminate Jew.

Jyoti Daniels takes another Israeli film as the subject of her essay. However, rather than examining Israeli male homosexuality, Daniels looks at what might be perceived as its polar opposite: the heterosexual female body in Hasidic Judaism. Daniels explores how *Kadosh* (Amos Gitai, 1999) represents gender, ritual and the belief system of Hasidism. She argues that the domesticated female body, which is denied active participation in public space in Hasidic Judaism, has become a site for manipulation by patriarchal authority and political intent in order to promote an idealised version of the "Hasidic Woman". This "Hasidic Woman" has been constructed as the ideal daughter, mother, and wife whose very *raison d'être* is reproduction. Furthermore, she shows how the Hasidic female body is marked as impure, weak and profane. A particularly interesting insight is how hair becomes the focus of the Hasidic woman's sexuality, thus redirecting attention from the traditional foci of female sexuality, namely the genitalia.

Like Daniels, Judith Lewin discusses the representation of Jewish female sexuality in film but her essay explores nineteenth-century Britain through the prism of Sandra Goldbacher's 1988 film *The Governess*. Lewin introduces us to the French Jewish actress La Rachel, and since acting was then conventionally associated with Jewish women, by association Jewish women were framed as prostitutes. The film's protagonist, Rosina, would love to act but instead she pursues a career as a governess and ultimately a single, female professional photographer. In doing so, Rosina provides an alternative model of Jewish femininity as she embraces her art and sexuality, chooses independence and creativity, and most importantly, claims her subjectivity.

Remaining on British turf, but a century later, Gavin Schaffer examines images of Jewish sex but this time in the non-Jewish British imagination. He argues that they do not paint any kind of monolithic picture as Jews have been labelled at different moments as sexually pure and sexually immoral, as corrupted and as hygienic, as predatory and as clannish. These conflicting and often contradictory sexual discourses managed to operate in the same period, and none could be described as ever having become dominant in Jewish representations. Probing these attitudes towards Jewish and non-Jewish sexual mixing, Schaffer recognises that the issue of sexual assimilation has been a thorny one in Jewish/non-Jewish relations in Britain.

Peter Lawson brings the British context up to date with his chapter on sex in the work of recent British Jewish novelists such as Linda Grant and Howard Jacobson. He argues that such authors are concerned to depict Jewish sexual desires as challenges to mainstream British constructions of sexuality. But where Grant has romantic notion of Jewish gender roles,

Jacobson's writing borders on the pornographic, particularly in its invocation of the Holocaust. Lawson ends his essay by examining the work of younger Jewish novelists like Naomi Alderman whose debut novel was a surprising hit in its depiction of a lesbian relationship in the Orthodox Jewish community of Hendon, North London. Taken together, Lewin, Schaffer and Lawson trace the construction and perception of Jewish sexuality in Britain over a period of one hundred and fifty years.

Lisa Bloom's essay provides a fitting bridge between the British and American contexts. She explores contemporary feminist artists in both countries and looks at how their art seeks to represent and explode traditional and even anti-Semitic characterisations of Jewish femininity and sexual identity emerging from both within and without the Jewish community. Her chapter raises questions about the regulation of Jewish women's, and, in some cases, gay men's bodies and sexualities through anti-Semitic discourses and the visual strategies that artists employ to articulate Jewish self-consciousness and engage with aesthetic questions. One surprising item is that she mentions the story that Barbie was invented by a Jewish woman, Ruth Handler, and was named after her daughter Barbara.

The final five essays all explore aspects of Jews and sex in the United States. Returning to the literary theme, Alan Gibbs' chapter examines Henry Roth's construction of a complex set of links between sex, guilt and Jewishness in his autobiographical novel series, *Mercy of a Rude Stream*. Roth wrote the series over a protracted period towards the end of his life, and used it to address his long silence as a novelist and to confess to adolescent and incestuous sexual relationships with both his sister and a cousin. The four volumes of the sequence grant rich insights into Roth's sexual guilt, and the ways in which this distorted both his feelings about his Jewishness and his ability to write. Gibbs examines the diverse ways in which the links between sex, guilt and Jewishness are made in the novels. He illuminates, for example, the way in which a motif using the colour green is constructed in order to link sex and Jewishness with associations of guilt in the young Ira, the protagonist of the series. Above all, Gibbs argues that the complex nexus of associations between sex, Jewishness and guilt is predicated upon the two Iras in the *Mercy* series: the narrated adolescent and the narrating old man. The former rejects his Jewish heritage as a source of weakness, and

13

therefore links it to his sexual guilt. By contrast, the mature Ira re-embraces Judaism as a source of strength, and now realises that his adolescent transgressions were quite inimical to his Jewish background.

In contrast, Ben Furnish surveys sex on the stage in a century of predominantly American Jewish theatre. Jewish theatre, though not far behind in the late 1870s, had to move quickly to catch up with centuries of development in European drama. But catch up it did, so that Jewish artists were soon using the stage — and Jewish audiences looking to it — to depict modernity's greatest conundrums. Among these was the psychology of sexual desire itself, which probably first entered Yiddish drama in 1906 in David Pinski's *Yankl der Shmid* (*Yankl the Blacksmith*). Non-marital sexual conflicts soon followed as central motifs in such works as Peretz Hirschbein's *Miriam* (1908) and Sholem Asch's now-famous *Got fun Nekomah* (*God of Vengeance*) in 1907, which dealt with sexual slavery, prostitution, and lesbianism. By the end of the twentieth century, American Jewish dramatists writing in English confronted sexuality directly. Plays such as Harvey Fierstein's *Torch Song Trilogy* (1981), Martin Sherman's *Bent* (1979), Larry Kramer's *The Normal Heart* (1985), and Tony Kushner's *Angels in America* (1991) highlight sexual issues amid such major twentieth-century concerns as the Holocaust, AIDS, and the analogous civil rights concerns of gays and Jews.

Sustaining the notion of performance, but in a very different arena, Roberta Mock's chapter focuses on the work of Annie Sprinkle and Marisa Carnesky, Jewish performance artists who use their bodies as cultural canvases which respond to and exploit the eroticised stereotypes of Jewish women that were consolidated in the late nineteenth century in the figure of *la belle juive*. Sprinkle is an ex-prostitute and pornographic film star who has performed her sexuality with men, women and transsexuals. In her work, she both exploits and dispels myths of the vagina dentata. Carnesky, on the other hand, a stripper and burlesque artist and (in her own words) has been the "girl from nowhere". Both work in a long tradition of sex-positive female Jewish performance, and their work which emphasises autobiography and nudity draws attention to and celebrates the relationship between Jewishness, femininity and sexuality.

My own chapter ties in with Mock's in that it also explores Jewish sexual performance. I examine not only the role that Jews have played in the adult film industry in the United States, particularly in front of the camera, but also how that role has been written about, most notably on the internet. The area isn't only under-studied, but those who have written about it have tended to fit the story of Jews in porn into narratives which either advance a thesis of Jewish sexual liberation or one of Jewish sexual corruption. In that latter respect, the essay mirrors some of what Schaffer discusses in his chapter about Jews in the British imagination. Furthermore, many of the female Jewish performers in porn provide/d an alternative model of Jewish sexuality and femininity that in some ways echoes that of Rosina in *The Governess*, as discussed by Lewin. At the same time, they also suggest an interesting contrast with the topic of the following chapter, the so-called "Jewish American Princess" (JAP).

In his chapter David Weinfeld explores the ways in which American Jewish popular culture treated the Jewish woman, often vilified as a JAP. The stereotype had emerged in the mid-1950s in novels such as *Marjorie Morningstar* (1955) and *Goodbye, Columbus* (1959) but it was not until the late 1960s that the character's new name become recognizable. The JAP stereotype evolved and crystallised around the image of a spoiled, whiny, materialistic and sexually frigid Jewish woman. Jokes, novels and other texts contrasted her with the exotic non-Jewish woman, or *shiksa*, depicted as both saint and whore, who showered her Jewish lover/husband with kindness and sexual pleasures. Unfortunately, the demon of the JAP was used to explain the increasing phenomenon of intermarriage in the United States in the 1960s and 1970s. Popular culture and imagery, specifically films like *The Heartbreak Kid* (1972), as well as jokes, implicitly blamed the JAP for Jewish male intermarriage. Occasionally, writers blamed her explicitly, in articles and books about the JAP in the early and mid-1970s. They frequently described or depicted Jewish men as fleeing in droves from the JAPs embracing instead *shiksas*.

The final essay in this section, and the book, by Thomas Grochowski, switches the focus back to Jewish masculinity, in particular that model presented by Woody Allen. Like those men discussed in the preceding chapter, Allen also exoticises the polymorphously perverse *shiksa*, which he contrasts — in his nightclub act, his fiction and drama, and most famously his films — to his small, inconsequential physical appearance, the *nebbish,* and his own descriptions of himself as a sexual stud (observable in his nightclub routines and in *Play it Again, Sam* [1972], among other films). At the same time, however, Jewish masculinity is frequently lampooned as Allen also uses discourses of sex to target a number of Jewish taboos such as kashrut, most famously in the "What's My Perversion" sketch from *Everything You Always Wanted to Know About Sex* (1972), but also in some of his prose works, such as his "Kaiser Lupowitz" detective stories. "Jewish guilt" and sex also feature in Allen's work.

Of course, there is much more work to be done beyond the limits of the essays presented here. However, I hope that this collection will inspire scholars and others to undertake this research into Jews and sex.

Chapter One
The Bride of God: Jewish Erotic Theology
Geoffrey W. Dennis

Introduction

The term "erotic theology" is not commonly heard in Jewish religious discourse. Generally, if a modern Jew even attempts to engage in sustained theology reflection, what Arthur Cohen defines as the study of "…the nature, person, and manifestation of God, the relation between God and history, evil and freedom, redemption and eschatology",[1] issues of sex or Eros simply do not come up. In this regard, most Jews today are thorough-going disciples of the twelfth-century philosopher Maimonides, whose argument that God has neither body nor passion — is in fact devoid any quality that can be construed as "human" — has come to permeate subsequent philosophic thinking.[2] Consequently most modern Jews would describe God — if they attempted to describe divinity at all — as a purely spiritual entity that transcends gender, without a hint of anything that can be remotely associated with sexuality.[3]

Yet even a casual examination of the full scope of Jewish writings about God reveals this attitude to be but one rather selective reading of all that Jews have had to say about God and God's relationship to creation, humanity, and Jews in particular. In reality, Jews have used erotic metaphors and the language of sexuality to describe their God, and have done so with considerable consistency across time. Broadly speaking, the term "erotic theology" is most often associated with the particular religious phenomenon known as mysticism. For some scholars, eroticising divinity is the very definition of what mysticism is.[4] And, as we will learn, much of the sexual language and imagery applied to God in Judaism appears in texts which are characterised as "esoteric" and/or "mystical". But hardly all of it; much more of this erotic discourse is hiding in plain sight, appearing in the Hebrew Scriptures, the Talmud, the Midrash, and other fundamental and authoritative Jewish sources.

Divine Sexuality in the Ancient Near East

To understand the particular way Judaism develops themes of the sexuality of its God, it is useful to consider the mythic and religious milieu in which Israelite religion and monotheism emerged.

For virtually all peoples of the Ancient Near East, divinity was envisioned in gendered terms — gods and goddesses. Moreover, gender and sex were cosmic, meta-divine realities; the gods did not select or control their gender, it was assigned to them by a higher fate.[5] That being said, the partnership of the gods was fundamental to the Cosmos, either creating or sustaining it. Sometimes called a *syzygy* (a "yoked pair"), or in more expressly sexual form a *heiros gamos* ("sacred coupling"), this union within divinity that gives birth to the world, perpetuates the seasons and fructifies the earth, was an important mythic element in all the known religions of the ancient Mediterranean basin and the Near East. The particularly sexual aspect of the gods' syzygy was often forefront and explicit in pagan religious literature, as it is in this Akkadian account of the god El and his consort goddesses conceiving the twins Dusk and Dawn:

> [El walks] the shore of the sea, and strides the shore of the deep…
> Now they are low, now they rise, now they cry "Daddy, Daddy",
> And they cry "Mama, Mama".
> El's "Hand" grows long as the sea, El's "hand" as the flood,
> Long is El's "hand" as the sea, El's "hand" as the flood.
> El, his rod sinks, El his rod sinks.
> El, his love-staff droops, he raises, he shoots skyward.
> He shoots a bird in the sky; he plucks and puts it on the coals.
> El would seduce the women. Lo, the women explain:
> "O mate, mate, your rod sinks, your love-staff droops….
> The women are El's wives, El's wives forever…[6]

Logically, this kind of sexual theology requires a polytheistic context: intercourse takes at least two (though this passage intimates a kind of divine *ménage à trois*). This being so, it is intuitive to think, as many readers of the Bible have, that once the Israelites settled upon the proposition that "…our God is one" (Deut. 6:4), any notion of God engaging in cosmic sexual acts to perpetuate creation would be rendered nonsensical; in the absence of a corresponding consort goddess, divine asexuality would seem to be the logical corollary of monotheism. Yet a careful reading of the Hebrew Scriptures reveal that even in the monotheistic context of Israelite religion, the concept of *heiros gamos,* of cosmos-sustaining sacred sexuality, is actually displaced rather then dispensed with.

To understand how the sexual life of the God of Israel was reconceptualised in Israelite thought, we begin with a text that is itself consciously absent of erotic overtones, but one familiar to most of us: the Israelite creation narrative of Genesis 1:1-2:3. In it, God forms the cosmos via a series speech-acts, progressively dividing up the watery primordial chaos into binary groupings: heaven and earth, sea and dry land, plants and animals. At the conclusion of this project, following the creation of humanity, whom He declares to be made in His image, God takes time to rest and designates that day of rest, the Shabbat, a sacred day. In contrast to many polytheistic cosmogonies, where some aspect of the universe is formed by means of divine birth, the God of Israel creates only via words. Any notion of cosmic partnership, let alone sexuality, seems to be utterly absent in this account; sex is a feature of creation ("Be fruitful and multiply...") but not of the Creator.

Here is where a sense the cultural and literary context of Scripture becomes critical, even though neither Genesis nor *Enuma Elish* have any sexual dimension. Scholars of the Ancient Near East have argued for nearly a century now that the creation account in Genesis is partly a monotheistic reworking of a Babylonian creation myth, the *Enuma Elish*. In this myth, the world is created, not by birth, nor by divine fiat, but as the aftermath of a cosmic battle. The god Marduk is offered dominance in the divine syzygy by the other gods if he will do battle against the sea/chaos monster Tiamat. Marduk defeats the creature and then divvies up its corpse to construct the cosmos, in a pattern similar to the one described in Genesis. At the culmination of the process, Marduk creates humanity from Tiamat's blood with the express purpose that man will "bear the god's burden that those [the gods] may rest". The gods who sided with Marduk enjoy through him the privilege of cosmic governance and conclude the process of creation in festive relaxation.[7] This feature of the *Enuma Elish,* the syzygistic theme of a supremely powerful deity being in partnership with other, lesser powers, is the feature that is of interest to us, while the idea of "rest" is the key to understanding it.

For the Babylonian account, "rest," one of the privileges of cosmic authority, is vouchsafed only to divine things: Marduk and his partner gods and goddesses. In the Genesis account, by contrast, the lone God rests alone — but only for a while. For when God chooses Israel to be "His people" at Mount Sinai, He includes this commandment to the Israelites, to "remember the Sabbath and keep it holy. Six days you shall labour and do all your work, but the seventh day is a Sabbath of the Lord your God... For in six days the Lord made heaven and earth and sea, and all that is in them, and He rested on the seventh day..." (Ex. 20:9-11, NJPS translation). In essence, by bringing Israel into covenant with Him, God elevates the collectivity of the people to a status analogous to that of a minor deity in *Enuma Elish*. While it is subtle, it is none the less the case that the Biblical writers revived and reworked the pagan theme of syzygy, of divine partnerships, to assert that Israel has become God's consort; this move exalts Israel over other mortals by making it alone God's sacred partner in "holiness".

While the texts we've discussed so far remain bereft of any erotic connotations, elsewhere in the Scriptures it becomes abundantly clear that this partnership, the covenant at Sinai, is understood as more than a mere contract between a patron god and His vassal; it is a wedding covenant and Israel has become God's bride. Thus the prophetic writers repeatedly speak of the relationship of God and Israel as that of a husband and wife: "I accounted your favour, the devotion of your youth, your love as a bride ..." (Jer. 2:2). Israel's lack of devotion to the exclusive worship of God is likened to marital infidelity: "Now you have whored with many lovers, can you return to Me?" (Jer. 3:1). Marriage also stands as the metaphor for describing Israel's reconciliation with God:

> On that day, declares the Lord, you will call me *Ishi* [literally, "my man" but idiomatically, "my husband"] and no more will you call me *Baali* [another term for "my husband," but one that is related to the word "Baal", an alien god]... And I will betroth you unto Me forever; Yes, I will betroth you unto Me in righteousness and in justice, and in loving kindness and in compassion. And I will betroth you unto Me in faithfulness. And you shall know [The Hebrew verb translated here as "know", *yud-dalet-ayin*, also carries the denotation of "have intercourse", a double-entendre that the Biblical writer consciously deploys] the Lord (Hosea 21:18; 22).

In deploying this image of God and Israel as partners in a sacred marriage, the Biblical authors generally eschew the kind of raw, explicitly sexual like imagery that we saw in the story of El and his wives. But as the Hosea passage demonstrates, the sexual dimension of this relationship is never far below the surface, and in one place, the book of Ezekiel, overtly sexual rhetoric bursts forth in a vivid and startling passage:

> Your [speaking of Israel] breasts became firm and your [pubic] hair sprouted. You were still naked and bare. Again I passed by you and saw that you were now old enough for love. So I [God] spread the corner of my cloak over you to cover your nakedness; I swore an oath to you and entered into a covenant with you; you became mine, says the Lord God (16: 6).

Here all the graphic sexual elements (exposed breasts, pubic hair) are associated with Israel, the divine bride, yet the overall sexual implications are just as explicit, with God even claiming exclusive sexual access (the act of a man spreading his cloak over a woman signified his "honorable intentions", that the coitus about to be initiated is for the purpose of marriage).[8] The point is made: the love that God has for Israel is a kind of erotic love. Israel is expected to reciprocate that love with equal passion and desire.

Post-Biblical Developments

While the prophets envisioned Israel as God's love partner, even to the point of comparing God's desire for a relationship as analogous to that of a sexual partner, what we do not see in the Hebrew Scriptures is a fully developed theology of *heiros gamos*; the idea that the harmonious "union" of God and Israel is a matter of creative/cosmic import in a way analogous to the pagan theologies we have already mentioned. It remains a matter of speculation whether this lacuna is a result of Israelite writers refusing to make this connection, or whether later editors of the Scriptures, offended by this erotic strain of Israelite theology, censored it.

Yet use of sex as a theological metaphor continues in later Jewish thought, especially within the purview of what has been dubbed "mysticism" by modern scholars. The Jewish mystical project probably emerged in part with the decision that the book *Shir ha-Shirim* [Song of Songs] be included in the Biblical canon.[9] According to the Talmud, Rabbi Akiba, a rabbinic figure widely identified with the esoteric, was shocked when he learned that the inclusion of that book had once been controversial to earlier Sages. He is said to have remarked, "Heaven forbid that any man in Israel ever disputed that the Song of Songs is holy. For the whole world is not worth the day on which the Song of Songs was given to Israel, for all the Writings are holy and the Song of Songs is holy of holies" (Mishnah Yadayim 3:5). Akiba could assert this because the early Jewish mystics understood that book, which poetically narrates the often lusty love felt between a woman and a man, to be the internal musings of God; the book lays bare divine desires for Israel during the Exodus. For Akiba and those who thought like him, no conception of the covenant was more central that this one.

The canonisation of Song of Songs — its acceptance as authoritative — served to affirm and reinforce the trope that characterises God and Israel's relationship as that of lovers (Babylonian Talmud, Eruvin 21b; Song of Songs Rabbah 3:15-19). The dominant tenor of this characterisation is emotional. But the Song of Songs' extravagant imagery of the lover's world and its constant use of metaphors from nature also invites the interpreter to see God's universe as sexually-charged. In such a cosmos, it is easy to imagine that sexual union is indispensable to the balance and harmony of all things. Male and female come to symbolise the polarities of existence that live in constant tension, while sex is the recurrent mechanism that reintegrates those polarities into a unity. What eventually emerged (or re-emerged) from this within Judaism was a belief that sexuality is the mechanism that sustains existence at all levels. For the Jewish mystics, being male and female come to be regarded as more then merely part of the divine plan, they become the essential dynamo of the universal order and unpacking these conjugal mysteries reveals the mind of God.

Still, this notion of an engendered universe is only rarely alluded to in Talmud, Midrash, or the medieval commentators. There are certainly multiple reiterations of the motif that collective Israel (*Knesset Israel*) is the "bride of God": "The groom, the Eternal of Hosts, is betrothed to the bride, the community of Israel, arrayed in beauty" (Babylonian Talmud, Pesachim 106b). Moses at Sinai is envisioned as a kind of match-maker or wedding officiant:

> [At Sinai] Moses went forth and came to the Israelite camp and aroused the Israelites from their sleep, saying to them: Arise from

your sleep, for your God desires to give you the Torah. Already
the bridegroom wishes to lead the bride and to enter the bridal
chamber.... And the Holy Blessed One went forth to meet them
like a bridegroom who goes forth to meet the bride, so the Holy
One went forth to meet them and give them the Torah (Midrash
Pirkei de Rabbi Eliezer 41).

A meeting that culminates in a spiritual consummation: "God
became wedded to the Jewish people at the time of the Exodus
and through the giving of the Torah. The consummation took
place when God's Presence enveloped them" (Comment of
Eliezer ha-Rokeach, on Talmud, Kiddushin). This schema of
Israel as the consort to God also involved extending the motif to
the principal symbols and institutions of Judaism. Thus, the
Torah comes to be characterised as a *ketubah* [marriage contract]
(Exodus Rabbah 46:1), the Sabbath is a reiteration of the wedding (Genesis Rabbah 11:8; PR 23:6), and while it stood, the
Temple in Jerusalem was perceived as the bridal chamber
(Lamentations Rabbah 4:11) where Israel and God enjoy their
most perfect union, further evidenced by this comment on a verse
from *Shir ha-Shirim*: "'His bed (Song of Songs 3:7)' This [refers
to] the Temple. And why is the Temple compared to a bed? Just
as this bed serves fruitfulness and multiplication, so too the
Temple, everything in it was fruitful and multiplied" [Tanhuma
(Buber) Numbers 17a].[10]

Yet like the Bible, rabbinic literature rarely elaborated on this
motif in an expressly sexual fashion. One of the few examples
that approaches a fully articulated theology of *heiros gamos* is
this Talmudic passage discussing the meaning of the two
cherubs [sphinx-angels] that decorated the Ark of the Covenant
kept inside the Holy of Holies [the innermost chamber] of the
Temple:

> R, Katina said: When Israel would ascend [to the Temple] on the
> Festival, they [the priests] would open the curtain for them, and
> show them the cherubs, who were entwined in [sexual] embrace.
> They would then tell them, "Behold how beloved you are of God,
> like the love of man and woman".

Here one Sage describes the two cherubs, one apparently representing God, the other Israel, as actually coupling like two lovers.
In the subsequent narrative, his colleagues were scandalised by

this story. Then another Sage, Resh Lakish, rallies in defence of this claim, remarking:

> When the Babylonians entered the sanctuary, they saw the cherubs embracing one another, they took them out to the market and said: "Is Israel, whose blessings are blessings and curses are curses, involved in such things?" They immediately denigrated them, as the verse explains, "All their valuables were denigrated for they saw her nakedness" [Lam. 1:8] (Babylonian Talmud, Yoma 54a-b).

This startling passage has been given little interpretive attention, even in esoteric literature, but early mystical traditions do attest to their own understanding that the Cherubs in the Temple were representations of the *Merkavah*, the "chariot" of God, an idiom derived from the book of Ezekiel, chapters 1 and 10, which was taken to embody the divine order. It was apparently left to the disciple to connect the dots and realise the cherubs personified the sexual nature of the universe. So for many centuries this erotic theology was truly occult in the sense that it was not subjected to sustained analysis by most Jewish commentators, and therefore hidden from general view. That is, until the great Kabbalistic flowering of the thirteenth century.

The Cosmic Dimension of Sexuality

It is only in *Iggeret ha-Kodesh*, a mystical-medieval sex manual, that the metaphysical significance of coitus in Judaism is fully articulated: "Such is the secret of man and woman in the ways of Kabbalah. Thus, this [human sexual] union is a matter most elevated, [when] it is done properly, and the greater secret is that the *merkavot* [also] unite, this one to that, in the manner of male and female" (*Iggeret ha-Kodesh* I, 49). As said earlier, the *merkavot* [chariots] mentioned in this passage is a Jewish mystical term for the structure of the godhead. So what the author of the *Iggeret ha-Kodesh* is conveying is that our bi-sexual nature (that is, our division into male and female) is a reflection of the larger cosmic structure and when humans unite in sex, the act is a mimesis of what happens within the divine realms (*Sefer ha-Yihud*, 33c-d; *Or ha-Hammah*, I:186a). Just as important, human sexuality becomes, in a sense, a substitute for the function of the ancient Temple in maintaining cosmic harmony. As Moshe Idel writes,

> It seems as if the religious function of the cherubim, according to
> some rabbis, has been transferred to human pairs... the logic of
> this transfer seems to be as follows: when the Temple was
> destroyed, its cultic function [of sustaining the cosmos] was par-
> tially preserved by the human sexual activity when performed in
> purity. In fact the association between Temple and paradise as
> place of sexual bliss and procreation has already been suggested,
> on the basis of many other sources.[11]

According to *ha-Iggeret* the reality that human sexual union
ensures cosmic harmony is the *ha-sod ha-gadol*, [the great secret]
of Jewish mysticism. It is only in the thirteenth-century master-
work of classic Kabbalah, *Sefer Zohar* (the *Book of Splendour*),
that this notion of a sexual dynamic operating *within* the godhead is made fully explicit.

Even more revealing is the Zoharic model of the *Sefirot*, a flow
chart of ten divine emanations. In the classic model of how these ten
divine forces interact, they are divided into male and female quanti-
ties, and it is the ongoing union of these attributes that enlivens and
sustains our material universe. In particular, the Zohar emphasises
the importance that two particular sefirot, *Tiferet*, representing
transcendent (masculine) deity and *Shekhinah,* signifying the
immanent (feminine) divine presence in creation, be constantly
brought together. At first glance, the role of *Shekhinah* seems to displace the Jewish people as the consort of God, but in fact it is a
distinction without much difference, for *Shekhinah*'s alternate mystical identity is *Knesset Israel* (Assembly of Israel). So rather then
theologically replacing Israel with a female divine entity, exotic and
strange as that might have been, Jewish mysticism takes the equally
radical step of further elevating an abstracted, idealised notion of
Jewish peoplehood to quasi-divine status.[12]

From the time of the Zohar on, this conjugal theology became
more visible, aspects of it became well known, and were expan-
sively applied to other aspects of Jewish ritual praxis, as
exemplified in this eighteenth-century Hasidic commentary on
prayer:

> Prayer is union with the Divine Presence. Just as two people will
> move their bodies back and forth as they begin the act of love, so
> must a person accompany the beginning of prayer with the rhyth-
> mic swaying of the body. But as one reaches the height of union
> with the Presence, the movement of the body ceases (Tzava'at
> RIVaSH, 43b).[13]

Implications for Contemporary Jewry

The consequence of such a complicated mystical theology is that human sexuality becomes an especially exalted, sanctified, and potentially enlightening aspect of the human experience. More than that, it potentially takes on divine qualities — we are deeply integrated into the causality of the universe and how we use our sexuality has cosmic consequences, effecting the larger creation, and even divinity itself. This mystic theology of conjugal mysteries reverberates in complex ways on Jewish attitudes toward the concrete realities of sex. On one hand, it celebrates and elevates the status of the human body:

> Let no one think that there is anything shameful or ugly in such union, God forbid! The right kind of [sexual] union is called *yada*, "knowing" ...we who possess the holy Torah, believe that God created everything as divine wisdom decreed. God creates nothing shameful or ugly. If sex is shameful, then the genitals are too. Yet God created them! How could God create something blemished, disgraceful, or deficient? ...When sexual union is for the sake of heaven, there is nothing as holy or pure. The union of man and woman, when it is right, is the secret of civilization. Thereby one becomes a partner with God in the act of Creation (*Iggeret ha-Kodesh* I, 6).

On the other hand, having raised the status of sex so high, it also means that sexual behaviour that is considered transgressive is much more consequential. Permitted sex, performed with the correct intention, is a conduit of divine blessing, it harmonises divine forces, and even enhances divine power. Conversely, inappropriate sexuality (generally coinciding with the Biblical and rabbinic categories of forbidden unions and acts) undermines the cosmic order and weakens divine power in creation. Jewish mysticism consequently views human sexuality as a portal to both holy and demonic realms. Indeed, the linking of sexual transgression with evil spirits began in antiquity (Babylonian Talmud, Eruvin 18b, Sotah 9b, and Shabbat 196a; Genesis Rabbah 20:11; Avot deRabi Natan 1:4) and became a prominent feature in the sexual ethics of Kabbalistic works such as the Zohar (I:55a, 57a; II 231b; III 76b).[14]

Yet this erotic theology has been lost and unknown to most Jews. The bulk of Jewish thought that has undergone the crucible of modernity has cleaved to the rational philosophic tradition which eschews ascribing any "human" qualities to God. Partly as a consequence of this, and partly as a consequence of the larger compartmentalization of religion in the West, sexuality has been both thoroughly secularised and radically privatised, to the point where the suggestion that religious norms might delimit sexual behaviour is seen as either quaint or inappropriate by most Jews.

To the degree that Jews of different persuasions discuss such matters, there exists a vast intellectual dissonance between traditionalists and modernists. This tension, even polarity, about the meaning of sex itself contributes to contemporary conflicts when it comes to sexual mores. For those who cleave to these traditions, who regard Israel as truly the Bride of God, the contemporary disregard of such customs as *niddah* (family purity rules), sexual continence outside of marriage, or the tolerance of homosexuality, are matters of grave consequence. For those Jews who have largely secularised the meaning of sex, who are either ignorant or indifferent to Jewish traditions of sacred sexuality — even, perhaps especially, if they have a more generalised sense of Judaism's positive perception of sex — the strictures and prudishness of traditional Jewish communities are both stifling and incomprehensible. Both sides value sexuality, but for very different reasons.

It does not have to be so, of course. The Talmud generally treated the pragmatics of human coitus and the erotic relationship of God and Israel as complimentary, not conflicting subjects. And there are ample ways in which individual contemporary Jews can and have negotiated between radically spiritual and radically secular approaches to sexuality. Still, it is this intersection between tradition and modernity, between the poles of the reconditely mystical and the utterly utilitarian, which at times discordantly reverberates in contemporary intra-Jewish discourse about sex.

Chapter Two
Boundaries and the Boundless:
Homosexuality, Liminality, Judaism
Jay Michaelson

Is sexuality religiously significant?

What is the religious significance of liberated sexuality? Most of the last quarter century's wrestling with this question has revolved around whether certain behaviours (chiefly homosexual sex, but also extra-marital sex and non-procreative sex of various kinds) are permitted or forbidden by religious law, and the status of Biblical text in the context of a modern sexual and political ethic.[1] Especially in the political sphere, the categories are familiar ones: liberal values and traditional values, society and autonomy, acts and identities, morality and equality. Yet these categories are both overbroad and anachronistic — particularly "homosexuality" and "heterosexuality", coined in 1869, and often used to refer to sexual identity, a concept not found in Biblical text.[2] Nor is Leviticus' agenda our own; Biblical scholars have long observed that the Levitical prohibitions are more concerned with ritual purity,[3] ancient gender roles and the shame of "making a woman out of a man",[4] as well as proscriptions against "foreign" cultic practices,[5] than with contemporary notions of "family values", "nature", or "personal dignity".[6] For Biblical text, the religious significance of sexuality has less to do with nature and freedom than with questions of purity, boundary, and pleasure.

This chapter addresses one such question, taking up the claim that queer sexuality is a form of erotic liminality which transgresses conventional gender categories, investigating how this liminality intersects with the Biblical insistence on order, and concluding with strategies of reading religious text in the context of the dissonance between the two. As a threshold matter, I take as a premise that sexuality[7] exists, and that how desire and love are expressed is religiously significant. Sex and sexual behaviour are of paramount concern both to the Hebrew Bible, from the first commandment given to Adam and Eve to the patrimony of the Israelite kings, and religious consciousness, law, myth, poetry, and mysticism. *How* homosexuality matters to Judaism

28

and Christianity is quite complex; *that* it matters is, I believe, irrefutable. I also take as a premise that this significance extends beyond issues of liberation to a host of other questions. For example, what distinctive roles, if any, do queer people play in religious communities? What do queer theologies look like in Jewish and Christian traditions? What are the relationships between pleasure, eros, and ethos in normative religious structures and the reality or fantasy of the so-called "sexual cults" of the Ancient Near East, to which some Biblical texts are said to be responding? These and many more questions spring from the premise that sexuality in general, and homosexuality in particular, is theologically and religiously significant. How one construes one's love for other people affects how one construes one's relationship to God, Torah, and Israel. All the rest is commentary, of which this chapter is, it is hoped, one example.[8]

Is the Liminal Sacred, or Terrifying?

Of the many iterations of religious queer identity proposed in recent years, some of the most interesting connect homosexuality with liminality and an upsetting of categories of sexual binarism and dimorphism. Curiously, in both contemporary queer theory and contemporary gay spirituality — two discourses which almost never interact with one another, and which in many ways are diametrically opposed — binaries are the problem and queerness is the remedy. In queer theory, gender and sexual dimorphisms are social constructions which invariably efface difference, administer power to the powerful, and subject the weak/disfavoured to the rule of the strong/favoured.[9] Dyads such as them/us, black/white, and female/male both oversimplify actual experience and invariably subordinate one side to the other. Many contemporary philosophers such as Emmanuel Levinas and Jacques Derrida have argued that even the basic dualisms of self/other and presence/absence contain within them the seed of oppression, marginalization, and subjugation; as soon as we divide, we begin to conquer.[10] Queer sexuality, by eluding the heteronormative expectations of gender and sexual role, can serve as "a potentially privileged site for the criticism and analysis of cultural discourses".[11]

Likewise, though in a rather different intellectual key, for the leading writers of the half-anthropological, half-fantastical literature of "gay spirituality", who seek to reclaim for queer people (primarily gay men) the ancient roles of "those who walk between", gender-variant people who often served as shamans, healers, and other intercessors with the infinite.[12] These writers draw on diverse traditions, from the gender-variant Galli of the classical world[13] to the one hundred and fifty-seven Native American traditions which held that people we would now label as gay or lesbian possessed two spirits, one masculine and one feminine, and accorded them special significance in society (medicine men/women, shamans, warriors, etc.).[14] Of course, our understanding of these "third-gendered" and "two-spirited" people remains greatly attenuated, but the evidence is considerable, ranging from the gender-variant *berdache*s or *winkte*s of the Plains Indians (including Omaha, Sioux, Iban, and Hidatsa people), to shamans of Siberia (including the Chukchi, Yakut, and Koryak tribes), the *basir* of Borneo, and the male *isangoma* of the Zulu.

Yet in these traditions and in nearly all others, the liminal is sacred precisely because it is terrifying. Rites primitive and modern imbue times and spaces of transition with holiness precisely to sanctify what would otherwise be a foretaste of death. In the moment of in-between, that point of inflection between what was and what is becoming, there is a potentially terrifying liminality, a taste of extinction. And precisely for that reason, because such moments occasion brief transverses of the ineffable, the liminal is sacralised by ritual, symbol, and myth. Symbolically, ordinary life is the place of distinctions; therefore, those who transcend distinctions likewise transcend ordinary life.

There are, however, multiple strategies for negotiating the relationship of boundary and the boundless. On the one hand, there are those who regard journeys into the boundless as sacred — shamanic traditions, perhaps, and chiliastic ritual which joins the Dionysian to the Divine. On the other hand, there are those which seek to demarcate zones of domesticity around the chaotic, or even to bury the forces of chaos, like the Furies entombed beneath Athens at the conclusion of Aeschylus' *Oresteia*. The former movement sacralises death and the one who walks into its unbounded realms; the latter one seeks to place it in a zone of confinement. The former rejoices in the power of the orgiastic, when boundaries are effaced; the latter carefully circumscribes that power within a taboo which is never transgressed.[15]

If it is possible to speak broadly, surely the dominant traditions within the Jewish and Christian religions tend toward the latter approach; these are religions of civilization. These traditions did not invent the idea — Marduk's defeat and division of Tiamat in the *Enuma Elish*, as well as other Babylonian and Sumerian texts, is a founding moment of civilization, and, like the battles depicted in the metopes of the Parthenon, represents the victory of order over chaos (and, often with a phallic symbolic structure, patriarchy over femininity).[16] Nor is the rejection of the Dionysian absolute; David dancing before the Ark (2 Sam. 6:1-23), folk festivals of orgiastic love, and, arguably, the blood rituals of the priestly cult, are but three examples of its persistence. But in general, Biblical Judaism sanctifies not the ecstatic but the formal, not the chaotic but the ordered. Jewish Biblical narrative favours the tablets of the law, not the golden calf; Moses' descent to the people, not his ascent to the ineffable; the precise rules and regulations of Leviticus, not the "strange fire" of Nadav and Avihu. Even amid the majestic theophany of the godhead at Sinai, the Biblical text spends less time on the power and glory of revelation than on what God tells Moses about tort law and damages.

Yet this is how it must be, for in a religion of civilization, the notion of boundary is essential. One does not organise clans, tribes, and nations without a healthy respect for hierarchy, law, and propriety — and within the Jewish tradition, the respect reaches its apotheosis. God mandates civil and ritual law, and, notwithstanding the tendency of Biblical narrative to complicate the simplifying tendency of Biblical legislation, the overwhelming emphasis is on the need for order and boundary. Binaries of pure and impure, male and female, dark and night, Israelite and foreigner, and sacred and profane, are the essence of the Levitical writings, both in the body of Leviticus and in the "Holiness Code". Indeed, the injunction "to discern between impure and pure" is repeated over and over again: in Leviticus 10: 10-11 ("discern between holy and secular, and between impure and pure"); 11:47 ("to discern between impure and pure") and Leviticus 15:31 ("thus shall you separate the children of Israel from their impurity").

Taking a cue from the Mary Douglas of *Purity and Danger*, we can see these concerns as reflecting the idealised plan of Genesis itself. Dietary laws divide water creatures from air creatures, air

31

creatures from earth's, and abhor transgression of the boundary.[17] God saw that it was good — because now it was ordered, where before it was not. Or, taking a cue from the Mary Douglas of *Leviticus as Literature*, we can see the precision of the sacrificial offerings as mirroring the precision of the design of the tabernacle, and even the structure of the Biblical text itself.[18] Indeed the prohibitions, and the symbolism, extend even to garments: *shatnez*, the Biblically-proscribed blending of wool and linen was prohibited both because it was sacred to the Egyptians (perhaps like Leviticus's forbidden sexual unions), and because it is an improper blending.

The borders drawn around sexual behaviour are of the same type. It is not known whether the Levitical prohibitions, like the ban on *kedeshim*, referred to actual chiliastic ritual present in the Ancient Near East, or whether, particularly in light of the essential identity of Israelites and Canaanites, and the fact that, in Ken Stone's words, "the binary opposition between 'Israelite' and 'Canaanite' turns out, in large part, to be an effect of particular biblical discourses",[19] the sexual distinctions were invented by Biblical authors seeking to demarcate pseudo-ethnic, rather than ethical-sexual, boundaries.[20] Whatever the historical facts regarding these practices, however, Israelite "border anxiety" (Stone's term again) clearly leads to a rigid creation and enforcement of sexual boundaries. Indeed, the very Hebrew word for holiness, *kadosh* (etymologically related to *kedeshah*), carries the meaning of "separate". In the Biblical system, binaries are necessary; they are needed; they are holy.

Quite clearly, there is a flat contradiction between civilising boundaries on the one hand, and queered or otherwise effaced binarisms on the other (though obviously, this structure is itself a binarism that is susceptible to critique). Nor is the tension restricted to the margins of sexual differentiation: not only men who have sex with other men, but inter-religious couples, single parents, and anyone following (or creating) alternative models of Jewish sexual-social life find themselves astride the boundaries of the halachic mainstream.[21] So does anyone who sees himself/herself/themselves as both/and rather than either/or. The Levitical understanding of liminality is squarely opposed, perhaps even deliberately, to the sacralization of boundary-crossing found in certain shamanic cultures, hypothesised in the Ancient Near East, and celebrated by latter-day spiritual thinkers, many of whom are themselves constructing their views in deliberate opposition to "Judeo-Christian" religious thought. Obviously, as discussed below, these structures are symbolic, not literal; poetic, not political. Yet to the extent they inform not merely the superficial details of religious praxis but its very form and structure, the binary-disrupting queer finds "hirself" in, ironically, a binary opposition to the Biblical ideal.

Notwithstanding the hysteria of the homophobes, there are not enough queer Jews in the world to threaten the foundations of the Jewish community. But in terms of personal identity, one is enough. If the act of boundary-crossing, at once the formative move of the Hebrew (*ivri*, crossing-over) people and the antithesis of normative Jewish life, is to be admitted as an act of devotion to God, then what becomes of the prescribed codes of worship, or the sense of security that comes from fidelity to the permitted? The *nomos* gives meaning, and security — what is lost when it is compromised, not merely in practice (as, of course, it is all the time) but at the core of its theoretical foundation? Is it inauthentic to adhere, say, to the dietary laws, with all their arcane details and historical accidents, if one understands one's sexuality not merely as an exception to a particular, misinterpreted rule of the Levitical holiness code, but as an expression of boundary-crossing itself? Of course, one may maintain the folkways of the Jewish tradition for many reasons, not merely those stated by the philosophers of halacha. But the idealised vision of a sacred society constituted by law and boundary is in irreducible tension with a (non-) identity of liminality and blending.

Queerness and Multivocality

What strategies are available, then, for the queer Jew seeking both a spiritual/religious life that includes Biblical consciousness, and an erotic self-conception that includes some notion of liminality?

First, of course, it bears repeating that such a self-conception is optional, not essential; probably only a small minority of GLBT people see themselves as third-gendered or liminal, and to claim that "virtually normal" identities are inauthentic (as some have claimed) defeats the whole purpose of sexual (or other) anti-essentialism. Moreover, assimilationist language arguably ought to remain predominant politically, not merely because it's convenient for lesbian couples to file joint tax returns, or because moments of intimacy are not the business of the secular state, but because privilege, however constructed or artificial it may be, should still be allotted to all who'd like to seek it, rather than restricted only to some. To put the matter simply, maybe marriage is dyadic, limiting, and intrinsically heteronormative — but let me have it too if I want it.

If we do take liminal sexual identity seriously, however, it implicates the deeper question of how Judaism itself is to be understood. If "Judaism" means the normative practices of the rabbis, interpreting the Bible and explicating revelation for all, then the options are, indeed, assimilation or alterity: either finding accommodationist textual readings that remove the problem (in a time-honoured rabbinic move), or constructing alternative Jewishnesses beyond the agreed-upon pale of Jewish culture. If, on the other hand, one conceives of "Judaism" as describing the practices of the Jewish people — describing, not merely prescribing — then the agenda shifts. Now the question is not how gays can be accepted into the traditional Jewish world, but how to recover (or half-invent) suppressed Jewish voices to complement the norms of the priestly/rabbinic elite with the lived experience of the Jewish people. Of course, our direct knowledge of the lives of marginalised and suppressed groups is extremely attenuated. Was there a class of *kedeshim,* of Israelite sex-priests who offered experiences of Divine communion to men and women alike? Were there Israelite spiritualities maintained by marginal women who lived outside of the familial structure, and in congregations of their own? We may never know for certain, but at the very least we may take a view of "Judaism" that is broader than the norms of priestly elites.

Third, and enlarging the context a step further, liminal sexuality informs religious consciousness is in its questioning of sexual and national boundaries. What would it be like for a practicing Jew to, as Stone suggests, "identify with, rather than over against, the Canaanites"? Sexuality may be the site of such an identification, if the deeper meaning of Jewish boundary-patrol is assimilation into other nations — if, as Stone says, "the 'Canaanite' is arguably positioned with respect to the 'Israelite' in something like the same way that the 'homosexual' is positioned with respect to the 'heterosexual'",[22] i.e., as a sexualised, projected Other, seen as outside but actually interior to the "norm". Sexual pluralism thus leads to a deeper pluralism that can be a much-needed corrective to parochialism and ethnocentrism, because in problematising the rhetoric of social construction in the area of sexuality, it questions the same lines drawn, often with the same brushstrokes, between us/them, gay/straight, Canaanite/Israelite, even female/male.

Fourth, all the foregoing discourse of boundary and boundary-crossing should be understood within the context of Biblical multivocality on sexuality. Theodore Jennings has shown that the Bible had much more to say about same-sex relationships than two verses in Leviticus, including the tale of David and Jonathan and the homoerotically inflected stories of Jacob, Joseph, and others. The story of David and Jonathan, of course, has been a resource for gay readers of the Bible for generations.[23] But Jennings persuasively argues that there is a deeper, theological significance to these relationships — they mirror the ultimate same-sex partnership between YHWH and Israel, in which YHWH is the permanent "top", the *erastes* to Israel's *eromenos* — and that the Priestly writer of Leviticus should not be given more authority than the writers of these other texts.[24] And while clearly the Bible does not approve of the behaviour of all its characters, Jennings convincingly shows that homoeroticism is not itself denigrated by these texts; indeed, it is utilised as a resource for exploring the dynamic between YHWH and Israel itself.

Jennings' view fulfils what Biblical scholar Nanette Stahl calls "the most common construction of the generic tension between law and narrative in the Bible [:] that the law is undermined by the narrative that enacts it". Perhaps, following Stahl's suggestion, one might see the tension between law and narrative as itself reflecting an ethos of multivocality and disruption. For Stahl, "law is both the agent of divine order and the locus of an underlying theological tension. Through law, God attempts yet again to set the world right. Yet the very wording and structure of the law, and the interactions of legal units with the narrative frame, reveal that law is also an agent of disruption and destabilization".[25] Such a view, particularly when augmented with a midrashic consciousness which sees Biblical law and narrative as fonts for an infinite number of interpretive and fantastical elaborations, would suggest that a queering of halacha is not diametrically opposed to the *nomos* but a fulfilment of its inherent instability. In this way, the queer plays her archetypal role of

trickster and holy fool, productively fulfilling the inherent instability of religious law, a trope echoed in texts such as Midrash
Psalms 12:5, which says that a qualified rabbi can rule forty nine
ways on each side on a legal question, and the famous "Oven of
Achnai" passage in Baba Metzia 59a in which the rabbis' legal
reasoning overrules a Divine voice.

Finally, beyond the Biblical shadows but within a conception of
Biblical consciousness, there are mystical approaches to sacred
text which provide alternatives to the exoteric ones. Perhaps sur-
prisingly at first, but less so if we consider closely the nature of
its project, the Kabbalah, the great body of Jewish mystical and
esoteric traditions, is replete with resources for a queer recon-
struction of boundary and liminality. In a recent study, for
example, I have provided a queer reading of Kabbalistic gender
dimorphism, interpreting Kabbalistic discourse on circumcision
as an inscription of the feminine within the masculine.[26] Charles
Mopsik has uncovered medieval and early Modern Kabbalistic
texts on transgendered souls, which, while repeating certain
clichés about homosexuality, nonetheless recognise that sexuality
and gender variance is a quality of the soul that does not confirm
to simple dimorphisms.[27] The homoerotic Jewish poetry of the
medieval period, written at the same time and in the same place
as the early schools of Kabbalah, still largely awaits translation
and interpretation.[28] And the sexual teachings of Sabbateanism,
which often explicitly include homoerotic and proto-feminist language and theology, have barely been described in English-
language scholarship.[29] These are all potential resources for finding oneself in history, and constructing from the very "burnt
books" of the Jewish tradition itself a self-understanding of queer
consciousness that denies neither the strands of that tradition
nor the liminal potentiality of queer sexual identity.

It is no coincidence that these resources exist within the mystical tradition specifically; mystical thought permutes the
expected categories of gender and sexuality just as it permutes
the structures of God, Torah, and Israel. Eros and mystical practice are so carefully patrolled by law because, blessed by the
simplicity of love or holy desire, it is easy to efface distinctions.
Labels, categories, genders and even transgressions matter little
when, in the throes of love, ecstasy, or passion, eros in its multiple permutations is the most natural thing in the world.
Whether mystical or otherwise (if there is an otherwise), ecstasy

is the ultimate liminality, for it explodes out of history seemingly without context, referent, or frame. Such interstitial moments of innocence — delightful but infantile, as they are without connection to ethics, history, text, or community — play in the liminal and the sacred, and deny the coherence of form and substance. Thus the erotic is a metonym for the mystical — not merely a metaphor, but an embodiment, a reflection, and even an actualization of the necessarily transient unions with the transcendent. If it is for this reason the normative structures of religion seek to contain and contextualise the disruptive moments of eros and thanatos, then perhaps the undressing of the contextual frame is, itself, a necessary step in its redemption.

Chapter Three
Female Fantasies from the Other Side of the Wall: Twentieth Century Lesbo-Sensuous Yiddish poetry
Hinde Ena Burstin

It is rare to find published Yiddish poems portraying sexual relationships between women. Even poems expressing sexual desires between women have seldom appeared in twentieth century Yiddish literature. While such poems are scarce and difficult to access, they do exist. This essay explores three lesbo-sensuous Yiddish poems, written by three poets, on three continents (Europe, Africa and Australasia) in three different decades of the twentieth century (the 1920s, the 1960s and the 1990s). Since the poems I have examined were more sensuous than explicitly erotic, I have coined the term "lesbo-sensuous" to describe these expressions of sensuousness between women rather than the more widely-used term "lesbo-erotic". This chapter is unique in exposing and highlighting published lesbo-sensuous Yiddish poetry by women. Previously, on the rare occasions when lesbian themes in Yiddish literature have been raised, the discussion has focussed on writing by men. For example, Rebecca Alpert's encyclopaedia entry on "Lesbianism" in *Jewish Women: A Comprehensive Historical Encyclopedia* mentions two literary sources between 1700-1945, both Yiddish (Sholem Asch and I B Singer), but both men.[1] To date, there has been no documented discussion of lesbian Yiddish poetry by women.

It should perhaps not be surprising that women's writing on this essentially female theme has been underrepresented in both publication and literary analysis. Women writing on this theme in Yiddish have been subject to significant barriers to publication. Like other female writers, many Yiddish poets have borne the primary responsibility for raising children, maintaining households and often financially supporting their families, leaving them little time for writing. The impact of these pressures and the deadening effect that they have on creativity has been documented.[2] Further, women writing Yiddish poetry often lacked parental and societal support, and experienced negative, even punitive responses to their work. Those women who managed to

38

overcome these obstacles and had the courage to send their work out for publication still struggled for legitimacy as men were the literary critics and largely controlled the Yiddish press. The dominance of male editors and publishers has been widely recognised as easing male poets' path to publication, while making it far more difficult for female poets to be published.[3] Irena Klepfisz claims, "Yiddish women writers were trapped by the conflicting motives of the men who exercised power and control over Yiddish journals, newspapers and presses".[4] At times, women confronted outright hostility from male writers and editors, who sought to undermine and discredit talented female writers.[5]

Given these constraints, it can be assumed that women writing on non-mainstream themes had a particularly difficult time publishing their work. For women who dared to write of their own desire for other women, the issues were exacerbated. Lesbo-sensuous writing by women has had to contend with both sexism and heterosexism. The impact of these forms of prejudice cannot be overstated, in both stifling creativity and limiting publication opportunities. The general reluctance to publish lesbian works is reflected in the Jewish community. As Rebecca Alpert advises, "For most of its three-thousand-year history, lesbianism has been a subject of little interest in Jewish texts or societies".[6] Yet, it is simplistic to assume that publishing lesbo-sensuous poetry is more difficult in the Jewish — and hence Yiddish — community. It can be argued that the reverse is true. Yiddish writing was at the vanguard of cultural expression about lesbianism in Europe and the United States in the early twentieth century. Sholem Asch's 1907 play *Got fun Nekome* (*God of Vengeance*) opened in Berlin in 1910, and was translated into Hebrew, Polish, Russian, German, Czech, Italian and Norwegian. "This play was the first with a lesbian theme to be performed on the American stage"[7] when it appeared in English translation on Broadway in 1923. Unsurprisingly, the performance of *God of Vengeance* was not without controversy. The play was closed down by the police and the judiciary, who charged and prosecuted every cast member for obscenity. Asch's play has many merits; however, it is still writing by a man about what is women's domain. It is essential to examine how women envisage, experience and express desire for one another, as opposed to how men imagine such desire to be. This chapter examines three such examples.

Dina Libkes' *On the Other Side of the Wall*

Dina Libkes *(Dine Libkes)* was born in 1900 in Slovetshna, District of Volin, Ukraine. She completed her school education in the *shtetl*, but left soon afterwards. She writes, "In 1920, in the pogrom-period, [I] ran away from my parents' loving but constraining clutches, to Kiev".[8] Libkes completed pedagogic courses and worked in a children's home with child-survivors of pogroms. She then taught at a secondary school before becoming an assistant librarian. In Kiev, she began to write, with her work first published in 1922 in the Kiev paper *Komunistisher Fon* *(Communist Flag)*. Several of her sensuous poems to, for and about women appear in Korman's *Yidishe Dikhterins Antalogye* *(Anthology of Yiddish Poetesses)*, among them, her poem, *Fun Yener Zayt Vant (On the Other Side of the Wall)*.[9]

Fun Yener Zayt Vant
Dine Libkes

gevidmet L.R.

Fun yener zayt fun mayn kheyder vant
Shloft a yunge mit mir baynand,
Veys ikh, veyst zi,
Az fun yener zayt vant!...

Treft amol in kholem,
Rukt zikh op di vant,
Derfil ikh ir naketn varem —
Ir hant —

Broyzt in mir mayn yugnt oyf,
Ikh khap zikh oyf —
A vant!
Vert toyt-fardrosik far ventisher altkayt,
Far shteynener kelt...

Fun yener zayt vant,
Shloft a yunge mit mir baynand,
Veys ikh, veyst zi,
Az fun yener zayt vant...

On the Other Side of the Wall[10]
Dina Libkes

Dedicated to L.R.

On the other side of my bedroom wall,
A young woman sleeps beside me, enthralled[11]
I know, she knows,
That on the other side of the wall!...

Sometimes, in my dream,
The wall slides away and
I can feel her naked warmth,
Her hand —

My youth bubbles up in me,
I wake up and see —
A wall!

Deathly-detestable
Is this walled oldness,
This stony cold...

On the other side of my bedroom wall,
A young woman sleeps beside me, enthralled
I know, she knows,
That on the other side of the wall!...

It is no coincidence that Libkes uses a metaphor of a wall in her poem. The wall is often a symbol of societal structures sealing people either in or out. Even in the supposedly liberated 1920s, when *Fun Yener Zayt Vant* was published, there were still many social institutions and community controls to keep lesbians apart. But society cannot wall in or close off consciousness. As Libkes writes: "I know, she knows/That on the other side of the wall..." Although neither can see or feel the woman who calls out her desire, they are both aware. Libkes writes further, "Sometimes, in my dream,/The wall slides away". It is Libkes' dream that the wall between her and the young woman will shatter, crumble, disintegrate. But it happens only in her dream because it cannot occur in reality. To Libkes, the wall really does move away, as she muses movingly, "I feel her naked warmth –/Her hand — ". These lines entwine their way into the imagination, enticing and exciting similar feelings in the reader. Libkes uses spaces, ellipses and dashes as pauses, so that the reader stops for a moment to catch her breath between feeling the naked warmth and the young woman's hand.

The poet portrays herself as "bubbling up" with "youth" and energy. When she suddenly wakes up and realises she is caressing a wall, her resentment is so bitter that she describes it as "deathly-detestable". The contrast between the young, warm, naked dream and the old, cold reality is strong. The dream is full of desire; the reality — full of despair. The old structures, the authoritarian walls are as cold as stone, again contrasting with the naked heat of the young woman. Libkes completes her cycle by repeating the first verse. The poem's conclusion is positive and powerful. The poet reminds us that even the tallest, strongest walls cannot destroy awareness or desire. That is perhaps the purpose of the poem. After all, Libkes does not address the poem to the young woman on the other side of the wall, but to the reader, whom she tells of the wall and what it can and cannot keep apart. The poem is rebellious and gives courage to Libkes herself, L.R. — to whom the poem is dedicated (possibly the young woman on the other side of the wall), and all those readers who recognise their situations in Libkes' lyrics.

Sarah Aisen's *Young Sprouts*

Compared with Libkes' poems, Sarah Aisen's *Yunge Shprotsn* (*Young Sprouts*) is less open and obvious. Sarah Aisen (*Sore Ayzn*) was born in 1910 in Kaunas, Lithuania. She completed a Hebrew *gymnasye*, the European equivalent of secondary school and junior college, before studying at a Lithuanian university. She became a Yiddish teacher in Kaunas. Her first book, *Meydl Lider* (*Maiden Poems*) was published there in 1937. Arriving in South Africa in 1938, she taught at the Johannesburg *Talmud Toyre*, an after-hours Hebrew school established and run by the Jewish community to provide free education for children from the poorest sectors of the community. Later, she settled in Cape Town, where her second book, *Geklibene Lider un Poemes* (*Selected Poems and Odes*) was published in 1965. Aisen is a passionate writer who describes her desire vividly. Her poem *Yunge Shprotsn* (*Young Sprouts*) powerfully portrays a young woman's yearnings.[12]

Yunge Shprotsn
Sore Ayzn

Shoyn gut azoy tsi zitsn shtil
Tsvishn khavertes in letstn bank
Dikh onkukn durkh shirtsl-tyul
Un foyl zikh tsuhern tsum lerers gang,

42

Fun tovl biz tsum vant,
Un vider biz tsum tish,
Un dan tsetrogn un in aylenish
Derklern romantizm in lirik,
Un vider zetsn zikh tsurik.
Un onkukn dikh lang,
Tsvishn khavertes oyf ershtn bank.

Young Sprouts[13]
Sarah Aisen

How good it is to sit quietly now
Among girlfriends in the back row
To gaze at you through a veil somehow,
And listen lazily to the teacher go
From the blackboard to the wall
And back to the desk again.
I blush when I'm asked to explain[14]
Romanticism and lyric,
I sit back down so quick
And stare at you long and slow
Among girlfriends in the front row.

Yunge Shprotsn is about first attraction opening up the senses, whispering of possibilities that one didn't know were possible, or knew were not possible. It is a quiet, subtle poem. For Aisen, it is important to be discreet about her feelings. As she writes in the first line of the poem, it is good to sit quietly. The author is alone with her feelings, but she is not alone. She is "among girlfriends", sitting at the back of the class, where she can stare, unseen, at that which she desires. Her gazing is not open or sharp. It is hidden. Aisen peers through a veil so that others will not notice. She has clearly already learnt that she should and must hide her desires. Further, when looking through tulle (as the veil is described in the original Yiddish), contours become hazy. If one wants what one cannot have, or should not want, boundaries also become blurred.

The contrast between the writer's inner and outer worlds is striking. In the outside world, the teacher paces the room in constant, visible motion. But the teacher is in the background, making little impact. The author listens, lazily, not to his words, but to his footsteps. Her inner world is disturbed when the teacher wants her to explain "romanticism" and lyric poetry. It is ironic that that is the subject being taught. But the subject doesn't capture her attention; it intrudes on the true romanticism of her gazing. When the student must explain, she becomes unnerved and speaks quickly. This is a contrast in tempo and pace, compared with when she is watching quietly and covertly. The cycle returns to the beginning when she sits and gazes again. Now, the staring is "long". The attraction is drawn out, and the reader tastes the deliciousness of her desire. But it is the last line, "among girlfriends in the front row" which arouses the reader from the dreamy fantasy. This is the first indication that the poem is to a young woman. It is unexpected, a surprise, like the feelings themselves are. It is also a symbol of the covertness of her desire.

Yunge Shprotsn is a quiet, yet powerful poem about desire, when desire alone is enough. Its subtlety is subversive. The feelings that Aisen expresses are instantly recognizable for those who have experienced such feelings themselves. The poem's title, *Young Sprouts* hints at a future blossoming.

Hinde Ena Burstin's *Miriyam's Song*

The third and final poem in this essay, *Miriyam's Lid* (*Miriyam's Song*) is an openly lesbian poem. The author, Hinde Ena Burstin (*Hinde Burshtin*), is also the author of this paper. I was born in 1962 in Melbourne, Australia and was raised in a Yiddish-speaking home. Yiddish is my mother-tongue. I teach Yiddish language and literature, having taught children and adults in Australia and abroad. I am also a community worker with marginalised communities, including lesbians. I have been writing Yiddish poetry since childhood. My early poems appeared in school publications and the SKIF (*Sotsyalistisher kinder farband* or Union of Socialist Children) magazine, *Chavershaft*. My publishing debut was in 1992 in the Jewish lesbian anthology, *The Chosen of the Chosen*.[15] Since then, more than fifty of my Yiddish and English poems, essays, articles, stories and translations have been published in anthologies, journals, newspapers and encyclopaedias in USA, Canada, Israel and Australia.

Miriyam's Lid, along with my translation, *Miriyam's Song*,[16] was published in the 1990s in a time of relative freedom. But the poem describes a time and a situation that were not so free.

Miriyam's Lid
Hinde Burshtin
far Shaunelen

O, Miriyam, mayn malke fun midber
On dir iz mayn harts ful mit payn.
Tref mikh farnakht bay dem brunem:
Veyst shoyn vu ikh vel bahaltn zayn.

Ze az man zol dikh nisht nokhgeyn
K'hob moyre, vayl s'drot a gefar
Zey zogn s'iz nisht normal undzer libe-
Zey kenen undz teytn derfar.

Nor ikh hunger dikh tsu haltn un haldzn
Mit libe dayn layb tsu mir drukn
Mit veykhkayt dikh vider tsu vign
Tsuzamen dem zun fargang ontsukukn.

Ven du bist a zikhere in mayne orems
Veln mir zikh tseflamen vi shkiye royt
Kh'vel dir lekn dos zamd fun di viyes
Kh'vel dir lekn dos zalts fun der hoyt.

Undzer libe brent heyser vi der midber
S'brit vi zamd vos derzet nisht keyn shotn
Hobn gepasknt di velkhe hobn keyn anung
Az s'iz undzer libe farbotn.

Zey zogn az tsvey froyen torn nisht libn
Galik zaynen di gezetsn oysgeklerte.
Ven es trefn zikh nor undzere lipn
Veyst dos himl az du bist mayn basherte.

Ikh bin greyt far yeder sakone
Vayl mayn oazis, mayn tayve bistu.
Biz ikh vel vider in dayne shvartse oygn zinken
Farzink ikh in umetiker umru.

Gib akhtung, o hit zikh mayn honik.
Shushke zikh tsu mir geshvind.
Ze az men zol dikh nisht khapn
S'iz dokh undzer libe keyn zind.

O Miriyam, mayn malke fun midber,
Az vest shoyn onkumen, vet mir zayn beser.
Yo, groys iz take di sakone
Nor s'iz dokh undzer libe nokh greser.

45

Miriyam's Song[17]
for Shauna

Oh Miriyam, my queen of the desert —
Without you, my heart's filled with pain.
Meet me at twilight by the well:
I'll be hiding where we arranged.

Make sure that you are not followed.
I'm frightened, for the danger is great.
They say that our love isn't normal —
They will kill us if they find out.

But I hunger to hold you and hug you
To press your body to mine with love,
To rock you gently once more
As together, we watch the sun set.

When you are safe in my arms again,
We'll burst aflame like the dusk desert sky.
I will lick the sand from your eyelashes,
I will lick the salt from your skin.

Our love burns hotter than the desert.
It scalds like sand that sees no shade.
But those who have no idea
Have ruled that our love is forbidden.

They say that two women must not love.
Bitter as bile are their made-up laws.
All it takes is for our lips to meet
And the Heavens know you are my *basherte*.[18]

I'm prepared to face every danger
For my oasis, my passion is you.
Until I can sink into your dark eyes again,
I slip down into lonely unease.

Oh Miriyam, my queen of the desert.
When I hold you, I'll feel so much better.
Though the risk we take is great,
Our love is even greater.

Miriyam's Lid uses biblical motifs to recall a time that was not so free. It is a poem about women who have already tasted their love, and want to, need to eat of this pleasure again. Once again, this poem has a theme of hiding, as is evident in the lines: "Meet me at twilight at the well,/I'll be hiding where we arranged". It is clear from these words that this is not the first time the two women are meeting. The words, "I am frightened for the danger is great" and then "They will kill us if they find out" underline the vital importance of remaining hidden. But they also highlight the preparedness of both women to meet, even if they must remain hidden, even if meeting could cost them their lives. There is a demonstrable division — on one side, the two women, Miriyam and her *basherte*, and on the other side, "Them", those who have power, who dictate that such love is "not normal". But those who have power cannot control the feelings between the two women. The poem tells: "I hunger to hold you and hug you". The hunger is stronger than the danger. All the disapproval, dangers and decrees cannot keep apart those who desire to be together. The poem reminds the reader that those who make laws, those who pass judgement, are not those who feel the feelings. The rule-makers forbid that which is foreign to them, and which they themselves do not understand.

The lines "All it takes is for our lips to meet/And the Heavens know you are my *basherte*" show that the Heavens understand what society does not. The Heavens ally with the women, in their battle against society's hostility. Echoes of nature as an ally are also evident in the description of Miriyam as an oasis. The sensual fantasies in the poem involve images of heat, like in Libkes' poem. But this poem describes the sensual activities between the women more openly — a sign of the times in which the work was published. The poem concludes: "Though the risk that we take is great,/Our love is even greater." As in the two previous poems, the conclusion here is strong and defiant. It lauds the power of a love that is stronger than the danger, a love that that no risk and no rules can restrain.

Geographic and temporal contexts

All three poems address themes of lesbian longing and hidden desires versus external realities; the closet versus openness; knowledge versus constraints imposed by social structures, and women's preparedness to place their desire above societal expectations. These poems have a more positive perspective and resolution of lesbian attraction than Yiddish writing on lesbianism by men.

Though sharing common themes, the poems must be considered in their geographic and temporal contexts. Libkes published a number of lesbo-sensuous poems in the 1920s, an adventurous time both in the open-mindedness of society and in the innovative approaches explored in Yiddish literature. Women in particular began expressing themselves explicitly, publishing evocative, even provocative poems, full of intimate images. Yet these writers were exceptional, for as Norma Fain Pratt advises, "...well into the second and even third decades of the twentieth century, Yiddish women writers were considered by literary critics to be rare phenomena".[19]

Young Yiddish poetesses from Ukraine, such as Libkes, created fresh, new writing with distinctive themes.[20] Even so, Libkes' poems are bold and radical. Life and literature were not so open in Ukraine. Under Soviet rule, all writing was subject to censorship, and sexuality was considered taboo. It is therefore not surprising that "in the literary and intellectual spheres [homosexuality] was mentioned less and less, and was all but unmentionable by 1930".[21] This makes Libkes' writing and publication even more audacious and remarkable. While Libkes is a pseudonym, her biography in Korman's book makes her true identity clear by naming her brother, who was a well-known Yiddish writer.[22]

Though Aisen was born only ten years after Libkes, she published on lesbo-sensuous themes under vastly different circumstances. Aisen was already a recognised Yiddish writer in Lithuania and South Africa, with a long-standing and wide-ranging record of publication in newspapers, journals and anthologies, when her poem *Yunge Shprotsn* appeared. She was fifty-five years old, compared with Libkes, who was in her early twenties when her lesbo-sensuous poems were first printed. Aisen's *Yunge Shprotsn* was published in the 1960s, a time associated with free love and sexual experimentation. Yet what people felt free to do between the bed sheets is different to what they felt free to put between the sheets of journals and books.[23] This was even more the case in South Africa. While the South African constitution today is unique in explicitly banning discrimination against lesbians and gays, in the 1960s when Aisen's poem was published, there was a lack of openness about divergent sexualities, and no organised gay or lesbian community.[24] In this context, it is not surprising that Aisen took a secretive approach to her same-sex attraction. It is significant that Aisen's poem does not include a dedication, unlike the other two poems discussed here.

48

Publishing lesbo-sensuous poetry in the 1990s was an entirely different undertaking. The poem, *Miriyam's Lid* was published in the United States along with two other, more explicitly erotic lesbian poems, at a time when identity politics were at the fore in literature, and queer culture had emerged in all manner of creative expression, including Yiddish literature. Though I was unaware at the time, the then eighty-two year old Blanche (*Blume*) Lempl had recently published her story *Korospondentn (Correspondents)*[25] with "its allusions to contemporary lesbian life".[26]

Australian society was becoming more open and tolerant in the 1990s, but discrimination against non-heterosexuals was still enshrined in some aspects of the law. For example, I could have lost my job without legal recourse, had the school where I taught known the true nature of my publications. (In a deliciously ironic twist, an enlarged copy of a notice in *Der Bay* International Yiddish Newsletter, recommending that readers buy the latest issue of *Bridges* journal for my three poems, was displayed on the school's front door. My colleagues, who had surprised me with this proud promotion, were not aware of the subject matter of my poems, as this had not been mentioned in *Der Bay*'s notice.) Around the same time, local Jewish lesbian visibility and activism increased. The Jewish Lesbian Group of Victoria (JLGV), of which I was a founding member, had gathered momentum in the three years since its inception, and now began actively challenging the Jewish community's heterosexism. The spread of the Queer Yiddishist movement, along with JLGV, gave me a sense of strength and safety. Particularly in the New York Yiddish community, and even in Australian Yiddish communities, it has been possible (if not always easy) for me to be open about my sexual identity. That is not the same as being open about my sexuality.

Publishing erotically-charged poetry within the Yiddish community is not without anxious anticipation. How many other lesbo-sensuous Yiddish poems have not been submitted for publication because their authors have harboured similar concerns? It is noteworthy that none of the three poems discussed was published in the birthplace of the author. As with their distinct geographical history, the three poems appeared in three different types of publications, reflecting the various avenues available for Jewish lesbian publishing. Libkes' work appears in an anthology, among other Yiddish writing by women. This was the most obvious place to begin my search for lesbo-sensuous Yiddish writing.

In a sense, Libkes' publication is the most noteworthy, because her work appears in a mainstream Yiddish collection. Aisen's poem was published in her own book of selected poetry. She chose to include *Yunge Shprotsn* in her collection, suggesting that she was not completely closeted. Perhaps she felt that the subtext would be understood by those "in the know" and not noticed by those with a more naïve or narrow concept of sexual attraction. In the lesbian community, like other marginalised communities, code markers are clear to insiders, but not necessarily to outsiders. *Miriyam's Lid* was not published in a Yiddish-language journal, but in the Jewish feminist journal, *Bridges*, thus emerging in a Jewish feminist milieu rather than a Yiddish one. Yiddish publishing is considerably constricted today, with fewer publications, and thus fewer editors and publishers deciding what is publishable. In this context, it is not surprising that I chose to submit lesbo-sensuous Yiddish poems to a Jewish feminist journal with a commitment to publishing Yiddish writing, as opposed to a Yiddish publication, that probably has no commitment, and perhaps no desire, to publish lesbian writing.

At the time that I published these poems, I believed them to be the first lesbo-sensuous Yiddish poems in print. I am thrilled to learn otherwise. Discovering other Yiddish poems by women depicting their same-sex desire is the fruit of an extensive search. Yiddish poetry by women has been dispersed in journals, newspapers and other regional publications, with very few published in book form. Even fewer have been anthologised in Yiddish poetry collections. This was already of concern to Ezra Korman when he compiled *Yidishe Dikhterins Antalogye* in the 1920s. Even then, he felt many talented Yiddish poets would be condemned to obscurity due to this obstacle in locating Yiddish writing by women.[27] Mass migrations of Jews since then, and particularly the wanton destruction of countless Yiddish publications by the Nazis, has further exacerbated the difficulties in accessing women's lesbo-sensuous Yiddish poetry, along with other Yiddish writing.

Though the physical dispersion of published Yiddish poetry by women makes research challenging and time-consuming, it is vital if we are to have a fuller picture of Yiddish women's writing and women's desire for one another. Little is known about lesbo-sensuous Yiddish poetry, and the women who penned these works. More needs to be uncovered. My research is just the beginning. The three lesbo-sensuous Yiddish poems I have introduced and discussed break down stereotypes of Jewish women, Jewish community and Yiddish poetry. They also debunk the myth that same-sex attraction was not a feature of Jewish life. The fact that these poems were written in different continents and different time periods underlines the universal nature of Jewish women's attraction to women.

On the surface, it appears that these poems are about concealment. But hidden in the lines of all three poems is the message that women's fantasies cannot be destroyed, love and sensuality between women cannot be decimated. Nor can society silence women's desire to shout and write about their love and lust. In current times, it shouldn't be just a fantasy to read in Yiddish about this love and desire. Let us hope that more Yiddish poems will be uncovered and published that joyfully celebrate lesbo-sensuous fantasies from this side of the wall.

Chapter Four
The Return of the Sissy Jew:
Gayness and the National Israeli Discourse
in Eytan Fox's *Yossi and Jagger*
Nir Cohen

Introduction

On 9 May 1998, Dana International, an Israeli transsexual of a Yemenite origin, won the Eurovision song contest for Israel with her song "Diva". Her victory performance in Birmingham, England, dressed in a colourful parrot dress, was then followed by a spontaneous gathering of thousands of people, trans, gay and straight, in Tel Aviv's Rabin Square. This unplanned celebration, which went on until early morning, was an unprecedented display of non-normative sexualities, one that could have not been imagined only ten years earlier. Voting for a transsexual to represent Israel in an international musical competition was an impressive achievement in itself; winning this competition was a whole different story. It meant not only a national victory, but also a victory for all sexual minorities.

Dana's success was, at the time, the perfect epitome of the Israeli gay community's long battle against prejudice and ignorance in a hetero-normative society. Interestingly, Dana was not only a gay icon. Soon enough she was appropriated by mainstream culture. She was formally received in the Knesset (Israel's parliament), congratulated by the prime minister and was appointed "ambassador at large".[1] This was quite an achievement for someone, who, only a few years back, would be destined to life in the margins of Israeli society.

As her adopted stage name (Dana International was born with the Jewish-Israeli name Yaron Cohen) and life story suggest, Dana has been continuously breaking barriers. She has built her career by boldly crossing gender, ethnic, national and sexual lines, constantly deconstructing categories and binaries. While she has identified herself with many of these categories, she has committed herself to none. Shortly after her victory she declared, "I represent gays and lesbians from all over the world... I represent the regular Israelis, all the Arabs, the Christians... Everyone who wants to be represented by me".[2]

52

Dana's fame was made possible by a growing tolerance to gays, lesbians and transgenders in Israel. Gay consciousness has been on the rise since its arrival to Israel in the mid-1970s, a period of time in which most of the legal restrictions that the state has imposed on its gay subjects have been gradually lifted. The changing representations of the members of the community in the media and the frequent references to it in popular culture led to a juridical revolution, which took place mostly between 1988 and 1993, and secured gay men and women an almost equal standing in society.

Granted, in terms of visibility and legalization, the gay community in Israel has acquired itself a stable place in hegemonic Israel. Yet, Dana International is an exceptional, unique example. Life outside the hetero-normative order in Israel is not as diverse as Dana's story may suggest. Some of the oppressing practices in Israeli mainstream society have been endorsed by the gay community, as part of its quest to produce a clean-cut, wholesome picture of homosexual life. Thus, most of the representations of homosexuality focus on a limited gay experience, namely, that of a middle class, Ashkenazi (of European origin, read in Israel as "white") man. Ignoring large groups within the community and turning its back to burning issues like the AIDS epidemic, the gay community has created a homogenised, exclusionist model of gay life. In this respect, Dana's success seems almost like a footnote in the community's history books.

The community's wish to assimilate has had its price. Aiming at integration and acceptance rather than social change, the members of the community have internalised the heterosexist, militaristic cultural norms they were originally set to challenge. As a consequence, gayness, male homosexuality in particular, is perceived nowadays as legitimate and even desirable as long as it does not transgress the rigid boundaries of Israeli hegemonic culture. Emphasising the likeness of the community's members to everybody else, the meaning of gay identity in contemporary Israel has been reduced to a mere sexual orientation. The gay community has been described as "the minority everyone loves" and Israel as "one of the loveliest places in the world to be gay"[3] but does a distinct Israeli gay identity actually exist?

Focusing on the representation of male homosexuality in Eytan Fox's 2002 film *Yossi and Jagger*, I would like to suggest in this essay that more than the effeminate, homosexualised Jew of the Diaspora, or queer politics, it is the "muscle Jew" of the Zionist movement, and his later incarnation, the valorous Israeli Defence Forces (IDF) soldier, that has captured Israeli gay men's imagination. Like the Jewish *Yishuv* (the pre-state Jewish community in Palestine) and hegemonic Israeli society, the Israeli gay community is organised in a hierarchical way, and favours its white, Ashkenazi militarist men.

My choice of *Yossi and Jagger* is not accidental. Originally produced for Israeli TV, *Yossi and Jagger* became one of the most popular Israeli films of 2002. It garnered mostly favorable reviews, and was shown in 2003 in numerous film festivals around the world, including the Berlin International Film Festival and the London Lesbian and Gay Film Festival. The film's huge success in Israel and abroad has highlighted the limited gay experience, which is at its core, as the only acceptable model. The film best exemplifies Fox's credo as a filmmaker and a gay public figure in Israel. Being one of Israel's most prominent filmmakers, Fox, whose films and TV productions tend to focus or at least touch upon gay issues, has the power to either set or break cultural limits. The way he uses this power, as the case of *Yossi and Jagger* suggests, is often unsettling.

The Unknown (Queer) Soldier

Yossi and Jagger, set in an outpost near the Lebanese border in the late 1990s, narrates the secret love affair between Yossi (Ohad Knoller), a young company commander, and his deputy Lior (Yehuda Levi), nicknamed Jagger, "because he looks like a rock star", as explained in the film. Following the unexpected visit of Yoel, their chauvinistic colonel (Sharon Raginiano), Yossi learns that he and his soldiers will launch another ambush the same night, the third in a row. Yossi's attempts to change the colonel's decision fail, and his fears are fulfilled: the ambush ends fatally at dawn, with the death of Jagger.

Even though the film was released into a relatively receptive social climate (the outcome of a series of legal battles in the previous two decades), it was largely perceived as breaking new ground as it gave the marginalised the right to rewrite their role in Israeli culture from which they have been excluded. The portrayal of a gay love story between two men, who happen to be IDF officers, was perceived as controversial. Subsequently, the

IDF authorities refused to assist the filmmakers with the production.

The filmmakers were taking a step further the implied homoerotic feelings that often characterise male bonding, "feelings of desire and affection between members of the same sex, but not necessarily their physical expression".[4] Although homoerotic relationships had been portrayed in earlier Israeli films as an immanent part of the military experience, actual gay relationships in this environment were seldom explored, probably because of the army's official anti-gay policy, which was finally changed only a few years ago. Even though Israeli gays and lesbians have never been officially restricted from serving in the army they could not serve in certain "sensitive" positions, in which their sexual orientation was considered a security risk.

The film, however, reinforces the existing power structure: as I shall argue, *Yossi and Jagger*'s covert message reaffirms the old regime, which oppresses gay men, and constructs them as the "other" of a heterosexist society. Although the spectator may tend to read it at first as a subversive work, the film actually rules out a real possibility of gay existence, both in military and civilian life.

The IDF serves as a quintessential symbol of a male-dominated, homophobic society. The army is more than a functional organisation; it is the people's army, an all-Israeli cultural signifier. As Baruch Kimmerling observes, the military has become an inseparable part of civilian life in Israel, as large portions of the hegemonic political culture have a military-minded orientation.[5] Thus, the prohibition of gayness in *Yossi and Jagger* should be seen as a statement about the position of gay men in contemporary Israeli society in general, rather than about the particular circumstances of the military. It is probably for this reason that Fox chooses not to take a clear stand on the actions of the Israeli military: it is the cultural significance of the military within Israeli society that he wishes to explore more than the orders it carries out.

It is important to note, however, that the lack of explanation of the fighting can be read as a statement against the occupation and Israeli policy. The naming of the outpost *Havatselet* (Hebrew for lily) and using the word *Perach* (flower) to describe a casualty in a code language, as well as the unflattering portrayal of the colonel (a point I will discuss in detail shortly), are ironic comments on the horror of an unnecessary war and the attempt to

55

euphemise it with propaganda. Furthermore, Jagger's death is rendered superfluous, as the piece of land the soldiers are protecting was returned to Lebanese control after the time represented in the film. In many of the heroic-nationalist genre films, which were very popular in the first two decades after the establishment of the state of Israel, as Ella Shohat has suggested, the concluding Israeli triumph was a result of "numerous heroic acts of individuals whose death was necessary for the birth of the nation".[6] In *Yossi and Jagger*, Jagger's death does not lead to a triumph, but quite the opposite, it delineates an unnecessary loss that is followed by an admission of a failure, namely Israel's withdrawal from Lebanon. At the same time *Yossi and Jagger* adopts the one-sided, agitprop view of the prolonged Israeli-Arab struggle that was explored in previous heroic-nationalist films. As in *Give Me Ten Desperate Men* (*Havu Li Asara Anashim Meyuashim*, Pierre Zimmer, 1964), for instance, so too in *Yossi and Jagger*: "the Arabs do not appear in the film but perform the narrative role of abstract agent of death, since it is an Arab mine that kills the hero's beloved".[7] This confusion indicates not only the uncertain position of the film concerning state-politics issues but also its lack of clarity on political sexual issues. Just as Fox does not take a clear stand on Israel's contribution to the escalating situation, he is torn between his wish to challenge existing sexual norms and the impossibility of escaping them.

When it is not silenced, the love affair between the two protagonists in the film adopts the hetero-normative model. The gay voice and body are stereotypically constructed in the film, and they are eventually eliminated, both literally and metaphorically. Thus, the controversial display of intimacy between two men does not fulfil the promise for a progressive view of gayness. Two pivotal scenes in the film best exemplify the tension between what is seen on the screen and what is actually implied. In the first scene, which I shall refer to as the snow scene, the two lovers, Yossi and Jagger, leave the compound for an isolated area where they consummate their desire.

The Snow Scene: Love with Borders
It is only outside the borders of the military compound, hence metaphorically outside the borders of society, that Yossi and Jagger's love can thrive. Their isolation from Israeli society is symbolised by the white snow, which is not a typical sight in

Israel, better known for its warm weather and desert landscapes. The place where they are lying is not only an alien landscape, but in fact it is not occupied by Israel any more. The IDF had withdrawn from these territories two years before the film was produced. Even if it is just a coincidence, it nonetheless intensifies the feeling that these two lovers do not belong in the Israeli narrative or the Israeli landscape. Furthermore, the fact that this particular scene, like most of the film, takes place in an area that the IDF had occupied, an act that was widely condemned as immoral and wrong, both inside and outside Israeli society, implies that Yossi and Jagger's love, parallel to the act of occupation, may be perceived in the same way. The film does not provide a "safe" locus for gay love/desire. It is dangerous to be or act gay within the boundaries of the consensus (the military compound) but it is also highly dangerous to cross them. The place where Yossi and Jagger consummate their love is not the peaceful haven it seems to be but a part of a battle zone, not too far from where Jagger eventually meets his death.

Although there are verbal references in the film to the alleged sexual potency of gay men, there are no explicit sex scenes. The close-up shot on the sperm stain on Jagger's uniform confirms the two had sex, off-screen. The boundary between what is seen and what is left off-screen is not unintended. In his analysis of Andy Warhol's 1964 film *Blow Job*, Roy Grundmann writes:

> the film's self-censorship separates not only the visible from the invisible but also the acceptable from the taboo. Thus, the frame's function can be considered a conceptual analogy to a guard patrolling the (metaphorical) border between civilization and barbarity, rigorously regulating its permeability, ardently stemming the tide of unregulated eros on behalf of civilization's course: Only what passes for "advanced" may cross over.[8]

The "metaphorical" border Grundmann mentions in regard to *Blow Job* becomes an actual border in *Yossi and Jagger*: their sexual act is external to the border of the frame as well as to the border of the State of Israel. The area where they make love is the place of the uncivilised, with a rabbit, which the two lovers spot, as a symbol of wild nature and the lurking terrorists, who are not seen in the film, and whom the spectator becomes aware of through the events that follow, as a symbol of barbarity.

The moderate and suggestive love scene is another reason for questioning the presumed controversial nature of the film. It is reasonable to assume that had the film dealt with heterosexual lovers more graphic scenes would have been included. Nonetheless, this scene delineates the strict gender role division that is to be found in Yossi and Jagger's relationship. This division is an adoption of a linear, generic model of sexual identity formation, which cannot accommodate the dynamic and fluid nature of sexuality that queer politics aims to explore, and as such is also heavily based upon a stereotypical, hetero-centred outlook on gay men: Jagger is the "femme", Yossi is the "butch", in the tradition of the seventies' gay macho "clone" look, "whereby gay men", as Richard Dyer has argued, "no longer saw themselves as intrinsically different from their objects of desire but made themselves into those objects of desire".[9] By sticking to this hetero-normative portrait, the filmmakers reaffirm Dyer's claim that

> even where no gender inflection or exaggeration is involved, no sissiness or man-manliness, relations between men always take place in a world where distinctions are drawn between men and women — it is virtually impossible to live, imagine or represent sexuality between men as if it is not informed by awareness of the difference between men and women.[10]

The role-oriented division between the two — Yossi the muscular, rational commander versus Jagger, his effeminate, sensitive, and irrational deputy — is meticulously constructed throughout the film. Although far from being explicit, the snow scene implies the protagonists' sexual roles: Yossi is the "top", the active lover, whereas Jagger is the "bottom", the passive one, traditionally perceived as connoting femininity and powerlessness. In his analysis of Rainer Werner Fassbinder's *Querelle* (1982), Richard Dyer observes how social sex-power is embodied in homosexual intercourse:

> the person who fucks is powerful and the person who is fucked is powerless. Fucking and being fucked are the means by which power is asserted or relinquished. Both may provide pleasure, but the pleasure of being fucked is the pleasure of humiliation. It is in the fucking that the social realities of sex power — of gender, of heterosexual status — enter into gay desire.[11]

Dyer also points out the marking of the characters in the film "in terms of masculinity/femininity, above all through the

58

equation fucker=male, fuckee=female".[12] This clear-cut division is heightened by Jagger, who, while his body is under Yossi's, asks ironically, "is this rape, sir?" The spectator's gaze is mediated through Yossi's gaze, which symbolises the power Yossi is exercising over Jagger. Yossi knows, however, that he will lose his status in the army if he comes out. His power as a commander is granted to him as long as he keeps pretending to be someone he is not. He trades his true self for his position. Gay power is not allowed in the film: as Jagger attempts to force his wishes on his long-time partner, namely that they both come out, he is punished and dies.

As has been stated, gay intercourse is not present in *Yossi and Jagger*, but the strict division described by Dyer is reflected in that scene in which Yossi is physically on top of Jagger, unzipping Jagger's coat, discovering he is not wearing his uniform underneath and telling him that he (Yossi) usually puts his men in jail for less than that. Even though this remark is spoken light-heartedly, just before they start kissing, it comes as an affirmation of Yossi's dominant and masculine character compared with the feminine Jagger, who is at his mercy. Both positions serve as stereotypes fashioned by hetero-social norms, debasing the efforts to expand the concept of "gayness" and sexuality in general.

By playing the role of the masculine, heterosexual soldier, Yossi reflects the national discourse. His masculine traits are even encapsulated in his typical Israeli name. In comparison, Lior's nickname, Jagger, a non-Israeli name, refers to Mick Jagger's ambiguous sexual persona. On the surface, the character of Yossi is the manifestation of the ideal muscular Jew, envisioned by Zionist Max Nordau, and, cinematically, a link in a long chain of characters that convey, in the words of Yosefa Loshitzky, "a powerful eroticised counter-image to the diasporic Jew".[13] His character embodies the eternal connection of the warrior, muscle and heterosexual Jew to his ancient land.

By contrast, Jagger is represented as an irrational and impulsive character who, in insisting on coming out and therefore on putting his own needs and ambitions before the interests of the state, violates the normative, heterosexist power balance. Jagger's gestures and good looks (one of the soldiers tells him "you are beautiful like a girl") suggest that he is more stereotypically gay than Yossi, and contribute to the reading of his body as feminine, an outcome of an ideology that, in the words of Lee Edelman, "throughout the twentieth century, has insisted on the necessity of 'reading' the body as a signifier of sexual orientation".[14] The marking of Jagger's body as "different" is a result of "the homophobic insistence upon the social importance of codifying and registering sexual identities".[15] Even though not necessarily suspected of being gay (he is not humiliated by his fellow soldiers, but it might be his higher position that prevents the others from questioning his sexuality in public), Jagger is perceived as the "other" from the beginning, and his otherness will eventually lead to his death.

Yossi manages to avoid being so marked. He masks his homosexuality and becomes his own self-oppressor. This is illustrated in the scene where he blackens his face, camouflaging himself, before setting out on the ambush. As he examines his reflection in a broken mirror, a symbol of his fragmented, homosexual self, he adds even more camouflaging paint, although his face is completely blackened already. The uniform and rituals that create the ethos of the military as the ultimate melting pot experience by blurring any racial, socio-economic or educational differences between soldiers are also a device to blur his homosexuality and to produce "a flawless surface of conventional masculinity".[16]

Dressed in his uniform, putting on an act as the straight commander, Yossi is "safe" in as much as he reveals the undisputable connection between performativity and masculinity. He passes for straight, that is, only because of his clothes and acquired gestures. This performativity is emphasised at one point in the film, in which Jagger — angry with Yossi after the latter refuses to come out with him and blames him for not caring about their militaristic, nationalist cause — mocks Yossi, declaiming dramatically anachronistic macho phrases like "yes sir, let's kill some charlies, sir!"

The fear of being marked leads Yossi to play down his homosexuality to the extent of total non-visibility and even absurdity: Yossi, whose secret is known only to his lover, is threatened even by the presence of a rabbit that is watching him and Jagger. The rabbit symbolises both cowardice (the Hebrew word for "rabbit", *shafan*, also means "coward") and unbridled sexuality at the same time, implying Yossi's internal conflict between his gay sexual drive and his fear of fully accepting it.

Yossi's masculine traits, as opposed to Jagger's "femininity", are manifested mainly when the latter insists that they come out together. This option is unacceptable for Yossi, who wishes to pursue a career in the military. His determined refusal suggests that gay love is an irresponsible act that may jeopardise his career. By demanding that they come out together and then celebrate in a hotel room with one "queen-size bed", Jagger establishes the domestic-familial space, stereotypically related to femininity and therefore, gayness, that stands in contrast to the militaristic-masculine space Yossi occupies, a space that cannot accommodate his non-normative sexuality. Thus Yossi tells Jagger they can either keep going on his terms, discreetly, that is, or break up: "I am sorry I don't surprise you with a ring, it is not an American movie", he says. His gayness is a dream or a fantasy, and just like a Hollywood film it differs from reality.

The two lovers are aware of the role division between them, and they refer to it throughout the film. As they lie in the snow, Jagger starts singing along to his favourite song, which happens to be playing on a small portable radio he has brought. The song "Your Soul" is sung by Rita, whose dramatic pop music and ultra-feminine appearance made her one of the most successful female singers in Israel and a gay icon. As the viewer expects, Yossi does not share his partner's love for Rita: "your musical taste is so gay", he tells him. Jagger then accuses him of preferring Meir Ariel to Rita. Ariel, the late Israeli singer, was an archetype of the Sabra, who made derogatory comments about homosexuals in an interview in September 1998.[17]

The connection between Yossi and the homophobic Ariel stresses his self-hatred. In this sense, the lyrics of Rita's song — which bear an even more explicit gay connotation because Hebrew, as opposed to English, for instance, marks gender explicitly — and which are sung loudly by Jagger and addressed to Yossi, are the essence of how Jagger sees his lover. The lyrics describe a life of lies as a dark and lonely experience, encouraging the addressee in the song to come to terms with his own "true" self:

Let's dispel the foggy curtain
Let's stand in the light, not in the shadow
Until when will you keep on running?
To games of power.

You can cry sometimes,
When you break inside.
Tell me about your moments of fear;
It is much easier to be afraid together.
When cold winds will storm outside,
I will send hot fire through you.
One day you may stop running
Between the shadows
In your soul.

It is no wonder that two versions of the song — the original and a cover version recorded by Ivri Lider, a popular and openly gay Israeli singer — are played several times, in addition to the two times it is sung by Jagger. The latter alters the lyrics, changing them into "it is much easier to stick it up the rear", and by doing so, emphasises the original lyrics' covert gay meaning.

The Death Scene: The Very Sad Ending of *Yossi and Jagger*

The first and last time Yossi softens is when he realises that Jagger has been injured, and is dying. Jagger's death, the emotional climax of the film, enables Yossi to come to terms with his own sexual identity, implying a possible fissure in the wall of silence. In these moments, while waiting for rescue, he tells Jagger things he never dared say before. He declares his unconditional love, not the least bothered by the presence of another officer, who, for the first time, realises the two officers are lovers.

This self-realization follows a prevalent universal pattern in gay narratives, in which, in the words of David M. Halperin, "the weaker or less favored friend dies... Death is the climax of the friendship... and it weds them forever... death is to friendship what marriage is to romance".[18] Thomas Waugh reinforces Halperin's claim by arguing that death is a narrative device used to make sure the gay romance will not last:

> the same-sex imaginary preserves and even heightens the structures of sexual difference inherent in Western (hetero) patriarchal culture but usually stops short of those structures' customary dissolution in narrative closure. In other words, the protagonists of this alternative gay rendering of the conjugal drive, unlike their hetero counterparts, seldom end up coming together. We don't establish families — we just wander off looking horny, solitary, sad, or dead... gay closures are seldom happy endings.[19]

This pattern is especially prominent in Israeli films that deal with homosexuality. According to Raz Yosef, the disposal of the homosexual body is inevitable, in order to keep Israeli heterosexual hegemony intact. [20]

Jagger's death is the first time Yossi adopts some of Jagger's "reckless" behaviour, as he breaks the barrier between the public and the private, the domestic and the military, by rushing to Jagger not as the latter's commander but as his grieving partner. This gesture could be read as an irrational and emotional, and therefore feminine, reaction, at odds with what the spectator has learnt to expect from Yossi. Unfortunately, this moment of self-realization can only be experienced at Jagger's death.

However, it is important to note that the film defines a gay identity, not so much by portraying homosexuality as natural and neutral, but rather by denouncing heterosexual courtship and relationships as hollow and abusive, employing the same arguments usually made against gay men. The two gay lovers in the film are ironically shown to be more committed than their fellow soldiers. The latter either replace intimacy with abusive sex, as is shown in the power-oriented sexual relationship between Goldie (Hani Furstenberg), one of the female soldiers, and the married colonel (her declared refusal to commit herself to a relationship — "I am here to have fun, not to get married" — is probably more a protection against hurt than a sign of liberation); or else they cannot reach their love objects: Yaeli (Aya Steinovitz), the other female soldier in the film, who is desperately in love with Jagger, remains blind to the fact that he is gay. Like the others, she can read the signifiers, describing him as "gentle" and "different from all the other men", but fails to interpret them. As a gay couple, Yossi and Jagger adjust themselves to the hetero-normative model, and they succeed in doing so more than their heterosexual counterparts. The latter are conventionally stereotyped: the colonel abuses his power and the female soldiers are either whores or virgins. Thus, they become a grotesque representation of chauvinistic norms.

Reversing the norm in Hollywood films, it is the straight characters in *Yossi and Jagger* who illuminate the gay protagonists and are used as a critical reflection of heterosexual, militaristic morals. Being the primary target, the colonel not only cheats on his wife with one of his soldiers, but also abuses his power in order to do so. At one point in the film he orders his sex partner to move her "fat ass to the car". The colonel refers to the news about the upcoming ambush as good news, stressing how much he likes "the action and the smell of burnt flesh in the morning" although he is not there with the soldiers to smell the burnt flesh the following morning.[21] When Yossi tries to change the colonel's decision, the latter accuses him of becoming a "homo" and a "sissy" and of worrying about his soldiers as if he was their mother (thus, stereotypically connecting homosexuality with cowardice and motherhood, hence femininity). In his reaction to what will prove to be justified concerns, the colonel reveals not only his unenlightened opinions regarding women and homosexuals but also his erroneous judgment.

The character of the colonel and the longing of the other soldiers for love that is not within their reach reflect the shortcomings of straight relationships compared to the stability and warmth that are to be found in the relationship of Yossi and Jagger. Furthermore, Yossi's judgment is proven to be better than the colonel's, suggesting that although Yossi is the misfit in a heterosexist system he can surpass those who are supposed to be superior to him in the military hierarchy. The film, therefore, inverts the balance of power between homosexuality and heterosexuality, in which the former is implicitly superior to the latter. This power struggle, however, takes place within a heteronormative domain and adopts heterosexist morals. The greatest achievement of Yossi in the film is his false attempt to play down his sexuality in order to pass for straight. It is Jagger who tries to break with his self-imposed silence, an act for which he is killed, and it is the disposal of his marked body that secures the existing power structure.

Jagger's death and the discretion that is an immanent part of Yossi and Jagger's partnership violate the idyll. In the end the militaristic and homophobic structure remains intact, and even Jagger's grieving parents, in the final scene of the film, are kept in the dark as to their son's sexuality. During the *shiva* (a period of seven days' mourning) Jagger's mother (Yael Pearl-Beker) says to her son's fellow soldiers that it is only now after his death, that she realises she did not know him at all. This saying may be interpreted as an expression of a remote feeling she might have that behind the "normative" appearance there was something different about him. The fact that only Yossi knows Jagger's favourite song implies a fracture in the concealed existence of both Yossi and Jagger. To seal this concealment of Jagger's true nature, Yaeli declares her love for Jagger, adding that she believes he felt the same for her, although they had never talked about it. Jagger's mother is left with the belief that her son had a girlfriend, that he was "normal" by society's standards. Although far from the truth, it is suggested that the parents are better off this way.

Conclusion

Disguised in their uniforms, suffering in silence until the death of Jagger, the two protagonists prove gay men can be a part of Israeli society as long as they accept the heteronormative order and keep their love a secret. The significance of "transplanting" a forbidden desire into the army is undermined by the realization that they surrender without a fight to heterosexist norms. More than anything, *Yossi and Jagger* attests to the difficulty for gay men in Israel to create a new, different vision. If the word "queer", as argued by Ellis Hanson, "invites an impassioned, even an angry resistance to normalization", and "is a rejection of the compulsory heterosexual code of masculine men desiring feminine women",[22] *Yossi and Jagger* is anything but a queer work. The film was made by a gay activist filmmaker, known for encouraging famous Israeli artists to make their sexuality public, yet it only shows how prevalent heterosexist norms are to the extent that they have become internalised by members of the Israeli gay community itself.

Chapter Five
The Return of the Repressed:
Sexual Stereotypes of the Old Jew
and the Case of *Gift from Heaven*
Sandra Meiri and Yael Munk

Dover Kosashvilli's *Gift from Heaven* (Israel/France, 2003) includes sex scenes unprecedented in Israeli cinema. The image of one of the male characters' penis with a sword ready to sever it from its body; the image of the female protagonist's genitalia exposed to the audience from the point of view of a young boy staring at it; as well as some very explicit episodes of sexual intercourse have resulted in the film being branded pornographic by both audiences and critics. In this essay we would like to suggest that by rendering visual the most intimate sexual apprehensions of the male Jew, Kosashvilli, an Israeli filmmaker of Georgian origin, revives on the Israeli screen two old anti-Semitic concepts that sustained the notion of the sexual degeneracy of the exilic male Jew, namely the myth of the hypersexual exotic Jew and, by contrast, the notion of the effeminate, "castrated" Jew. In doing so, he consciously confronts the Israeli audience with one of its last taboos — sex. In our opinion, this confrontation should be seen as an oppositional standpoint to an oppressive Zionist melting pot policy. Thus the sexual provocations of *Gift* — both visual and verbal — should be read within the context of the unresolved relation between sex and the Jews at large and their representations in Israeli cinema.

Gift tackles the hegemonic model of sexuality still prevalent in Israeli society — that of the male, military, Ashkenazi, secular *Sabra*, which has its roots in the "New Jew" model of the Zionist movement. This model was, to a large extent, an antithesis of the two most prevalent anti-Semitic notions about the sexuality of the male Jew as mentioned above. Indeed, the accumulated body of anti-Semitic notions regarding Jewish sexual practices embedded in the process of nation-building and immigration policy provides a key to understanding nationhood in terms of both Zionist ideology and the survival of the State of Israel. Given that the thinkers of Zionist ideology were deeply troubled by historical associations between certain images/notions and anti-Semitic stereotypes (which in the long run resulted in genocide), one of its main projects became the repression of the image of the Old Jew, concurrently generating a new type of Jew: a "political ideology [that] sought... to transform the Jewish body itself, and especially the *sexual* body".

According to David Biale, the idea that the Jews were especially degenerate was a favorite theme of modern anti-Semitism and it "was frequently linked to the accusation of Jewish male hyper-sexuality, which posed a purported threat to the purity of the 'Aryan' race".[1] But the Zionists adopted the discourse of degen-eration as a catalyst for solving the "Jewish Problem" in a land of their own, where a rural society was to be created through sex-ual moderation. The needs of the individual were cast aside in favor of the national effort required to build this utopian society, so that the overheated erotic drives of the Jews were now chan-neled into hard, physical, collective labour.[2]

The sexual stereotype of the effeminate Jew derives its power from the complicity between circumcision and castration. In his examination of the various ways Jews adopted the anti-Semitic, debasing and even pathological association of the Jewish man with femininity and homosexuality, Michael Gluzman explains how the male Jewish body, in the course of development of the discourse of sexuality, was perceived not only as feminine, but also as challenging the very anatomical distinction between male and female.[3] Daniel Boyarin traces the negative connotations associated with the effeminate Jew back to Freud: "Zionism is... a mode of repressing, of overcoming his [Freud's] Jewish homo-sexual effeminacy".[4] For Freud, as well as for Herzl, being a nation like any other ultimately means mimicking all *male* gen-tiles, being men like all other men — i.e. being manly (physical and heterosexual).

In its depiction of sexuality, Israeli cinema has had its own his-tory of complicity with this model. In *This Is the Land* (*Zot Hi Ha'Aretz*, Baruch Agadati, 1935), the heroes are shown "making love" to the earth, "penetrating" the dirt with their ploughs.[5] At the film's climax, one pioneer collapses from exhaustion and through a dissolve disappears into the field, suggesting that his dead body serves as a fertiliser. In later years, this eroticism demonstrated towards the land was displaced to military homo-eroticism. The homoeroticism prevalent in such films as *One of*

Us (*Echad Mishelanu*, Uri Barabash, 1989) is not outweighed even by the presence of a female soldier, who is the girlfriend of one of the two protagonists, Yotam; the film's real couple is Yotam and his beloved Rafa. Thus, in one memorable scene, Yotam pins his girlfriend to the wall, undresses and penetrates her. But her image fades away into the shadows of a large slide projected on the wall, showing Rafa and a group of other friends of his, so that her fading away conveys in fact the image of the two main male characters making love.

In some Israeli films women who are raped fall in love with their assailants. In almost every case they are objects of aggressive male sexuality, with no voice of their own. Even when a female heroine is the film's protagonist, her personal domestic tragedy (becoming a war widow) is depicted through male eyes. For example, in *Siege* (Gilberto Tofano, 1970) an IDF widow tries to get on with her life and starts a relationship with a man, but her late husband's friends, as well as the film's omniscient narrator, judge her harshly for her "unfaithfulness". Another example of this critical approach towards women's sexuality is Dan Wolman's adaptation of Amos Oz's novel *My Michael* (1974), where, unlike the case in the novel, the distress of the heroine is conveyed entirely through her sexually extravagant fantasies. Only in the late seventies, when women began to make their own films, a different feminine voice was heard in Israeli cinema, condemning such portrayals of female sexuality. These films paved the way for autobiographical women's films that criticised the violent and abusive Israeli cinematic initiation of women into sexuality. Finally, it is almost impossible not to mention here the director Amos Guttman who openly and courageously deals with the fate of homosexual characters in the macho society of Israel.[6]

By the end of the millennium, sexual representations in Israeli cinema reached a certain *modus vivendi* that corresponded more or less to western liberal norms of sexual representation. This status quo was shattered with the release of Kosashvilli's *Gift from Heaven*. Contrary to his previous and much acclaimed film, *Late Marriage* (Israel/France, 2001) which laid the ground for many of the themes which recur in *Gift,* the latter was heavily and uncompromisingly criticised for its unprecedented, graphic depiction of sexuality. Audiences and critics alike denounced the film and its director, finding it vulgar and debasing in its extreme portrayal of Georgian stereotypes.

In its depiction of sexuality *Gift* embodies the return of the repressed by restoring the two stereotypes of the old degenerate Jew: hypersexuality and effeminacy (castration). However, the finesse of the film lies in the way it interweaves the two notions, since the hypersexuality of its protagonists is connected throughout to their fear of castration. Thus, *Gift* uncovers that which was behind the constitution of the model of the new Jewish male sexuality: fear of castration. Furthermore it inscribes Zionism and its melting pot project as two forms of fetishism — two forms of veiling the ancient castration anxiety of the Jews. This is made explicit in the two key scenes to which we alluded at the outset.

The first occurs during the wedding ceremony of one of the protagonists of the film, Vaja (Yuval Segal). Vaja takes the heavy gambler Ponchika (Menashe Noy) aside and drags him into a cellar nearby, asking for the money he is owed. Vaja and his brother, Bakho (Rami Heuberger) are the principal organisers of a diamond robbery which they plan to pin on Ponchika, and hence to erase his debt. Vaja convinces Ponchika to take the blame for the robbery solely on himself and even to go to jail, by literally threatening him with castration. Ponchika pleas to be allowed to pay his debt monthly, but Vaja, without further hesitation, grabs a sword he has previously hidden in the cellar and holding it to Ponchika's throat, orders him to pull down his trousers, then his underwear. "Kill me, there's no money there," says Ponchika. "I told you before," Vaja replies, this time holding Ponchika's penis, "your ugly head is of no use to me." The next shot is a close-up of Vaja's left hand grasping Ponchika's penis while his right hand is holding the sword over it, as if getting ready to cut it off. Naturally, this convinces Ponchika to assume the blame for the robbery.

While this scene is solely concerned with the fear of castration, the second provides a key to the understanding of how the two stereotypes — hypersexuality (as a form of fetishism) and feminization (as castration) interact. The scene occurs in the middle of the film. It involves a little boy named Zaza (Hen Koren), who happens to be hiding under a table when his eyes are unintentionally confronted with the genitalia of the female protagonist. Zaza is sent by an older friend to deliver a message to his sweetheart who is this woman's daughter. The woman, Fira (Anastasia Kovlenko), who has just come out of the bathroom, sits down by the table, her naked body wrapped in a towel, and spreads her legs. The film adopts Zaza's gaze so as to offer a clear view which becomes even clearer when Fira lifts one of her legs in order to paint her toenails. The reaction shots of the shot/reverse-shot sequence show the little boy's astonished gaze several times. Having delivered his message he flees the room.

Linking this scene to the earlier Vaja/Ponchika one which specifically tackles the fear of castration one recalls Freud's description of the little boy who discovers that his mother or any other woman for that matter lacks a phallus. Inferring from what his eyes have just perceived that he too could be castrated, a defence mechanism develops in which different objects and even persons take on phallic value, a phenomenon which Freud calls fetishism.[7] Symbolically, fetishism is a way of disavowing lack, difference, heterogeneity. It is because of this disavowal — since the child does not really relinquish the idea that there is nothing in the place where there should be something — that Freud sees fetishism as a perversion. And this very same perversion is scrutinised in the film: the way many ethnic and cultural minorities are dismissed, ignored and debased, as they are forced to subscribe to one historical form of (male) Zionism, to one hegemonic sexual culture. In *Gift* the hypersexuality of the Georgian male characters is designed as a mode of coping with castration anxiety, becoming thus a form of fetishism. However, the ingenuity of the film consists in the way the concept of castration is understood and dealt with. Put in the context of Israel's multi-ethnic society, represented here by Georgian ethnicity, the film takes on the meaning of difference and heterogeneity — those aspects denied by the ideology of both Zionism at large and the melting pot ethos in particular. Thus, the film brings to the surface the deep fear of Israel's uniform hegemony in relation to its multi-ethnicity and multiculturalism.

We may now elaborate and say that in bringing together the two stereotypes *Gift* has a double effect. Firstly, it exposes the assimilation of the "castrated" Jew stereotype thus explaining the obsession of Zionism with healthy, masculine bodies. In other words, it renders the muscles of the "New Jew" into a form of fetishism — a Jewish male defence mechanism against the fear of castration: "[I]n Nordau's account... physical and erotic degeneracy were linked. Nordau... glorified the modern Jewish sportsmen... and contrasted them with those Jews in ancient times who would only engage in sports after surgically hiding their circumcisions".[8] Secondly, the hypersexual behaviour of the film's protagonists, their constant preoccupation with sexual matters — their philandering and sexual pursuits; confrontation with sexual taboos through direct allusions to incest — becomes a form of difference, a form of sexuality never seen before in Israeli cinema, thus introducing the notion of difference into what had till now been a homogeneous model of sexuality. In so doing *Gift* creates a most interesting and invigorating paradox. Sex seems to be a principal preoccupation of three generations of Georgian immigrants, men and women alike.

In fact, *Gift*'s evocation of old Jewish sexual stereotypes through the depiction of a Georgian community which directly refers to the exilic, exotic Jew with whom the stereotype of hyper-sexuality was associated, alludes not only to the role that the new model of Jewish sexuality played in the Zionist edifice at large, but also, specifically, to the role it played in the melting pot project, whose objective was the implementation of Zionism in the young State of Israel by requiring of Jews in their new land to give up, not only their sexual but also their cultural difference. Hence, the bringing together of the two old sexual stereotypes in an economy of fetishism declares that both Zionism and the melting pot were but two forms of fetishism, two projects designed to veil difference, intended to remove the need to contend with the Jewish inheritance of heterogeneity. In its place, these two monumental projects created a model of sexuality which was merely an antithesis to racial prejudices, with the purpose of subjecting sexual and cultural difference to a unified, male model.

In its insistence on portraying its male characters as a bunch of good-for-nothing bums, obsessed with sex, the film echoes Uri Zohar's *Peeping Toms* (1972), which presents an economy of voyeurism and fetishism.[9] However, unlike *Peeping Toms* whose protagonists are Israeli-born *Sabras*, Dover Kosashvili, who has assumed the role of spokesman for Georgian ethnicity in all his films — including the short film *With Rules* (1998) and the afore mentioned *Late Marriage* — adopts a more radical textual politics with *Gift*, which consists not only in its portrayal of sexuality but also in its critique of the Israeli absorption policy which brought thousands of Jews from Georgia into the country, there ending its role and leaving the new immigrants to deal with an unfamiliar and hostile culture — the hegemonic, homogenous culture of Israel. Just like Jews in the Diaspora, the Georgian community was left with no choice but to fence itself into "ghettos" within the

71

country's cities, in an attempt to preserve its unique tradition and culture, which remained foreign to the Israeli hegemony. It is within the walls of this internal exile that the sexual stereotype of the old Jew of the Diaspora is evoked in the film. *Gift*'s sexuality becomes an expression of internal exile through the hyperbolisation of that stereotype.

The robbery plot (or rather its planning) is a device designed to provide a rationale for dealing with the main theme of the film — the (hyper)sexuality of its protagonists. The strangeness of this mode of sexuality is further accentuated through the exaggeration of other Georgian stereotypes, thus reinforcing the notion of otherness, of difference, of heterogeneity. The film resists the ideological temptation to portray any members of this group in a positive light, thereby laying the cards of Zionist ideology on the table. The cracks in the Israeli/Zionist ideological edifice are exposed not through a critique of Israeli attributes, but rather through what the film portrays as Georgian characteristics: vulgar and violent behaviour, as well as all kinds of rituals and customs, such as the obligation on a man's part to marry a young girl after he has raped her. For example, Vaja is in love with Margo (Ronit Yudkevitch), a widow who repeatedly rebuts his relentless attempts to gain her affections. In order to be close to her, he spreads the rumour that he has raped her daughter, whom he is therefore now obliged to marry. The daughter, Ketto (Beki Griffin) is more than pleased to marry the young and handsome Vaja (she does not seem to be bothered at all by the rape rumour) and the three engage in a blissful Oedipal triangle.

Fira is a Russian physician, who is more concerned with her sexual than her professional life, thus hinting that not only men are fetishists; both genders are subject to the same ideology and policy. At the beginning of the film she carries on an affair with Jemali (played by the director of the film, Dover Kosashvilli). Jemali then passes her on to his friend, Bakho. One night Jemali comes to take Bakho to his mistress, and he finds him doing a jigsaw puzzle of the Statue of Liberty. The image of the puzzle, which is in the colours of the American flag, is the epitome of the film's complex, paradoxical politics, as expressed through its sexual economy. For those who have become the pariahs of the nation (Israel), America is the phantasmatic idealised object (in another corner of the house, Bakho keeps a person sized replica of the Statue of Liberty). The jigsaw, however, is missing quite a few pieces and has a huge hole in it. This hole is later displaced to the sexual triangle. Jemali comes to lure Bakho into having sex with his own mistress, whom he treats as a fetish, a trophy to be passed on to his friend, so that he may get a taste of what life will be like after they have stolen the diamonds, thus drawing an analogy between her and a precious stone. But as it turns out, she becomes very fond of Bakho, who reciprocates her feelings, and this development in the plot dissolves this other blissful oedipal triangle in which the three are engaged for a while.

These different holes deriving from one basic hole representing radical Otherness (as portrayed in the scene with the female genitalia and the little boy), are veiled, disavowed within the economy of Zionist discourse, by means of a basic distinction between "Us" and "Them". Rather than acknowledging the Other as a unique but integrated member of society, as part of a multi-ethnic/cultural nation, colonial discourse is very often based on visual differentiation with regard to traits and skin colour, as noted by Ella Shohat and Raz Yosef.[10] Kosashvilli is well aware of this principle and therefore tends to cast Israeli actors in the role of Georgian characters, a device whose function is to introduce a split into the film's diegesis. He transforms Israeli cinema's leading actors — Yuval Segal, Rami Heuberger, Lior Ashkenazi & Moni Moshonov — into authentic Georgians through the use of language, which in terms of the melting pot policy, reverses the very mechanism of adjustment: it is no longer the new immigrants who have to learn Hebrew in order to perform (at school, in the military, at work, etc.) but the Hebrew speaking *Sabras* who have to learn Georgian in order to perform (in the film). Given that almost all the dialogues are permeated with sexual discourse or sexual connotations, while the actors uttering them are *Sabras* playing Georgians, the effect is also a reversal of the normative sexual politics of Israeli cinema, as well as of Israeli society, whereby uncouth male sexual discourse is usually connected to the "authentic", military *Sabra*.

This sense of queerness/Otherness in *Gift* is further enhanced by a kind of folkloristic ambience which resonates with Emir Kusturica's films. For example, in the scene where Vaja comes to his father to confess his love for Margo, he finds him sitting in a steaming washing machine, as if it were a sauna. He wears a swimming cap and a plastic collar around his neck. Two pipes on the wall look as if they are attached to his cap, conveying thus the image of an alien from outer space. Gheorgei, the so-called Patriarch (Moni Moshonov) protests against the fact that Vaja has led everyone to believe that he raped Margo's daughter and therefore is now obliged to marry her. What bothers Gheorgei is that Vaja's oedipal triangle echoes the dynamic of the incestuous relationship with his own daughters. He rejects his eldest daughter's advances to sleep with him, but locks his youngest daughter in a closet because he does not approve of her boyfriend. This patriarch is a kind of Georgian Don at the sound of whose voice everyone in the film is supposed to tremble. The effect on the viewer, however, is somewhat different — queer in fact. The scene also alludes to Moshonov's drag persona from a television satire series during the 1980s (*Zehu-Ze*), in which he played the part of a female Polish character.

This queering effect recalls an earlier scene in the film, where another male character, Razzo (Alon Neuman) is caught by his wife wearing her skirt. When she asks what he is doing, he tells her that he is only trying to understand the humiliation she herself was exposed to in an earlier scene, when she met Jemali in the street. He had lifted her skirt and removed her underwear, publicly exposing her intimate parts. Razza asks his wife to show him how exactly her panties were taken off. She replies: "You're a pervert like your father" (the whole incident is actually initiated by Razza's father who makes a pass at Jemali's wife by attaching sexual connotations to the vegetables she is buying — the two also meet in the street). Then she pulls down the skirt and in the next shot we get a clear view of Razza's underwear with a big Mickey Mouse imprinted on the fabric.

Interestingly enough, the only authentic Israeli *Sabra* who appears as such in the film, without undergoing a process of "Georgianisation" or queering is the Prime Minister at the time the film was made, Bibi (Benjamin) Netanyahu. However, Netanyahu, the authentic *Sabra* who symbolises for many the dominant Zionist ideology, is not represented by an actor but by many portraits of Netanyahu himself, in various sizes, hanging on the walls alongside various decorative Georgian icons. One particularly large portrait hangs on one of Margo's walls. In contrast to the jigsaw with its missing pieces, Bibi's portrait, with its conspicuous silver frame, conveys indeed the notion of a fetish. In the scene where Vaja declares his love for Margo, the two face each other, their profiles to the camera, while the huge portrait in the background seems to be the only thing that brings them together — as if this fetishistic icon (reminiscent of Zionist ideology) is alone responsible for the bringing together of a whole community whose relationships are possible only amongst its members, without any possibility of breaking out of this situation. In another scene where Vaja comes to convince Margo to marry him, he addresses Netanyahu's portrait, stating boldly: "You don't scare me." The conversation which Margo and Vaja have (which revolves around the reasons for Margo's rejection of Vaja's courtship, mainly the rape rumour) focuses on Georgian customs and is permeated with sexual connotations. Vaja lures Margo into measuring him for a pair of trousers, as Margo is a seamstress. Another portrait of Prime Minister Netanyahu seen elsewhere is small, but decorated with a particularly ornamental frame, thus enhancing the sense of fetish.

Rather than offering a serious history of the Georgian community as responsible for various mafia organizations in Israel, the film offers what Teshome H. Gabriel, in reference to the concept of folklore in third-world cinema, has termed "popular memory" as distinct from "official history." According to Gabriel, official history, like hegemonic ideologies, inhibits people from constructing their own histories, while popular memory is wedded to constant change, considering the past as a political issue, ordering it not only as a reference point but also as a theme of struggle.[11] In *Gift*, through the hyperbolisation of the two old Jewish sexual stereotypes, we are forced to recognise that Israel today is a changed, multi-cultural society whose uniqueness lies in that it does/must not have one hegemonic ideology and one official history, but rather a multitude of sexual matrices. Some of these do not comply with the prevailing macho model of the militaristic *Sabra*. We see many cases in Israel of young male immigrants, who are made to believe that the only way they can be part of Israeli society is by proving their sexuality and manhood by enlisting in IDF combat units. Of course, many of them die for this belief.

In conclusion, the way sexuality is used and manipulated in *Gift* becomes a form of resistance to Zionism and its melting pot ideology, which has been consolidated over the years in Israeli society and culture through the sexuality of the military and of the Ashkenazi, male, secular *Sabra*. *Gift* reverses the equation of the need to redeem degenerate Jewish identity with the constitution of a uniform sexual identity, by displacing the concern, or rather, (male) obsession with sex, to the (real or imaginary) Georgian community. By bringing together the two old sexual stereotypes associated with Jews — hypersexuality and the castrated Jew — the film exposes the aftermath of an ideology which stemmed from their assimilation.

Chapter Six
Scripting the Jewish Body: The Sexualised Female Jewish Body in Amos Gitai's *Kadosh*
Jyoti Sarah Daniels

Drawing on scholarship from within the fields of religion, gender, culture, and film this chapter will outline how the female Jewish body is represented through mythic and ritual discourse and presented on the cinematic screen. Using the film *Kadosh* (1999), directed by Amos Gitai, I will indicate how the social manipulation of gender allows Hasidic women to play or act out certain roles and rituals, which are shaped by systems of belief. Gendered ritual performance, as played out on the cinematic screen, is a complex interaction of shaping and structuring, of presenting and selecting, certain gendered behaviours in order to represent masculine and feminine identities. It is evident from *Kadosh* that women's performance of ritual is a complex mix of symbols, actions, and ideologies that work to uphold a traditional Hasidic belief system that is grounded in part in a specific gendered ideology. Feminine images have arguably been tied to the body and motherhood in Hasidic Judaism. Within this chapter conceptions of female body as impure and sexual will be looked at as two separate but interlinking parts to a discussion on the ritual roles women play in Hasidic communities and how this is reflected on the cinematic screen.

Kadosh

Directed by Amos Gitai and released in Israel in 1999, *Kadosh*, meaning sacred or holy in Hebrew, is a story of two sisters' relationships with each other, and their husbands. This story takes place in a close-knit ultra-Orthodox neighbourhood in Jerusalem, known as Mea Shearim. The film begins with a long slow uninterrupted shot of the ritual lives of Hasidic Jews as Meir (Yoram Hattab) is shown chanting his morning prayers with reverence towards God. As soon as Meir chants his final few verses of prayer, the viewer begins to understand immediately the gender ideology present in the film and within the portrayed Hasidic culture. Meir recites the famous prayer, "Blessed are you, Lord, our God, ruler of the universe who has not created me a woman".

Herein lies the quintessential androcentric thought present in Hasidic Judaism. From here the camera slowly focuses on Rivka (Yaël Abecassis) waking up before her husband leaves for the Yeshiva. Meir looks at Rivka and proclaims, "I have such respect for you Rivka". As Gitai presents it, irony abounds this scene, for on the one hand Meir has just thanked God for not making him a woman, and yet at the same time seems to have so much respect for his wife Rivka.[1] The constant play and interaction between strict ritualised behaviour and intimate personal moments is a theme, which is reflected time and time again throughout the film.

The genuine love that Rivka and her husband Meir share with one another is threatened when Meir's father (Yussuf Abu-Warda) insists that Meir re-marry to ensure that the family line is continued, since after their marriage of ten years Rivka has still not been able to produce a child for Meir. Due to Rivka's seeming infertility she is deemed useless by her community, as her only role in life is to ensure the birth of Hasidic children. The major plot twist in the story is when the viewer finds out that it is not Rivka that it is barren but rather it is Meir who is sterile.

In contrast to the more traditional portrayal of Hasidic women exemplified in the character of Rivka, Malka (Meital Barda) the more aggressive and passionate sister exercises her individual will to a greater extent. The film follows Malka's affair with her long-time love Yaakov (Sami Huri), a rebellious young man who left the Hasidic community to join the Israeli army. He still considers himself a Jew and a believer in God; however, in the eyes of the Hasidic community he is considered a rebel and hence Malka is forced to marry another man. The irony is that the man chosen to marry her by her Hasidic community, Yossef (Uri Klauzner), ends up abusing her. The genuine love she has with Yaakov is replaced by an abusive relationship with a man who was deemed worthy enough by her own community to marry. The needs of the community and how they clash with those of the individual is a theme felt throughout the entire film.

The gender ideology presented in this film stems from the non-Hasidic director's interpretation of the lives of Hasidic women and men. This gender ideology is most prevalent in the themes of the female body being a source for impurity (represented in the *mikvah* ritual), the sexualised female body as seen through hair and clothing conventions and a woman's only worth located in motherhood, in which the themes of motherhood, impurity, and sexuality coalesce. For the purposes of this chapter I will focus on the sexualised female body as seen through hair and clothing conventions and the female body as being a source of impurity.

In making a film about Mea Shearim, Israeli director Amos Gitai gives the viewer a glimpse into a Hasidic community's way of life; a life which is rarely seen on the cinematic screen. He chose Mea Shearim to represent Jerusalem because, as he explained, "I had to touch on religion because Jerusalem is about religion — the city's beauty, its aristocratic way of looking at the rest of the planet is about religion". As I will show, however, it is evident from this film that Gitai's look at Mea Shearim serves as his criticism of Orthodox religion. As Gitai argues, "I didn't want to make a piece that indoctrinates... I feel the film is strong and critical, and I am critical of the way that the three great monotheistic religions — Judaism, Islam, and Christianity — treat women. The ideologies are constructed by men to insure their domination..."[2]

The Modest and Impure Female Body as Presented in *Kadosh*

The laws of *tznius* pertain to the Jewish modesty codes; most often the word is associated with clothing and patterns of behaviour. The notion of *tznius* drives Hasidism's expectation for girls and women. Hasidic women are to be modest at all times and following the laws of *tznius* attains this. This word incorporates ideas of modesty, sanctity, and purity; which becomes the basis for outlining "proper" female behaviour. Stephanie Wellen-Levine relates the complex play this idea of modesty has in the Hasidic community: "women who achieve a high level of *tznius* can expect abundant blessings, including wealth, children, and grandchildren. Beyond personal gain, behaving with proper *tznius* [also] unleashes sparks of holiness throughout the world and encourages the coming of the Messiah".[3] The most obvious signifier of modesty is related to dress. Women are prohibited from wearing clothing that may reveal the shape of their body thus they must wear dresses or skirts that are to be long enough to conceal the body at all times; shirts must cover the elbows and collarbone; trousers are forbidden.

In addition to clothing and patterns of behaviour, women must also cover their heads with either a wig or a scarf as a symbol of modesty. As seen in *Kadosh* a married woman must shave or cut her hair and don an appropriate wig. The reason for hair covering is because in those forms of Judaism such as Orthodoxy or Hasidism the hair of a married woman takes on an erotic connotation which has, for centuries, made it necessary for married women to cover their hair, except when in the company of their husbands and sometimes other women.[4] Carol Delaney's work is important to mention here. Although she deals primarily with Turkish village society and Islam, the same erotic connotation to hair can be seen.

> Like flowers of the field, a young girl's hair grows freely, representing the rampant fecundity, beauty, and seductiveness of the world as well as the entanglements by which men are ensnared. Around the time of menarche, when a girl's sexuality ripens, it must be enclosed; it is not free for the plucking. The hair and the girl must be domesticated. The headscarf binds and covers her hair and symbolically binds her sexuality, which is henceforth under the mantle of her father and brothers until conveyed to her husband at marriage.[5]

In Hasidic culture young girls do not wear scarves but are required to tie back their hair or to braid their hair, so as to ensure that it is not free flowing. However, when a woman marries her sexuality is bound by the headscarf, wig, or hat, and she is seen as under the mantle of her husband. Lynne Schreiber notes the majority of "observant" Jewish women today cover their hair with hats, snoods, scarves, and wigs, while a strong minority remain unconvinced that this practice is *actual* law.[6] The effects of cultural discourse are evident in a statement such as Schreiber's. One understands from Schreiber's work that in order to be an "observant" Jewish woman one must cover her hair. Operating within Schreiber's conceptualisation of proper female behaviour, it is not a great leap to view those women that do not wear a wig, shave their hair, or don a scarf as "inappropriate", "immodest", and "non-observant Jews". Schreiber argues, like all other *mitzvoth,* the covering of hair is a difficult task,

> ...hair covering is by no means as easy one to undertake. Whether a woman has been raised with the notion that she will cover her hair once she marries, or she is among the growing number of *ba'alei teshuvah* (newly religious) or modern Orthodox who were

not raised with such an absolute belief, most women go through self-defining transformations when taking on the *mitzvah* of covering hair.[7]

In understanding the portrayal of the female body in film most attention has been paid to women's bodies in their relation to reproduction and sexuality. Most work within the area of film studies and the female body has paid attention to the gendered female body in terms of sexuality, with emphasis paid to wombs, vaginas, and breasts. However, as Howard Eilberg-Schwartz argues, "…it would be a mistake to think that it is simply the reproductive or erotic parts of the female body which are at issue in the representation of femininity".[8] He further argues that the female head is an important site for the discussion of the symbolization of gender and how this is linked to particular belief systems. Hair has not received the attention it deserves. The covering of hair, the shaving of hair, and the uncovering of hair are all important sites to begin an investigation into how the head is sexualised in film and how this is further reflective of particular belief systems and values. According to Eilberg-Schwartz the covering of the female head highlights the eroticism of female hair.[9] Wig wearing in Hasidic culture can become a contested tradition as on the one hand women wear wigs to avoid sexual attraction from males. But, on the other hand, the covering of the hair often sexualises the hair, hence sexualising the female body. Karen Lang argues that, "the manner in which religious persons treat their hair can reveal something about their attitudes towards sexuality and about the means they choose for controlling the potent force of sexual desire".[10] Lang's argument can be applied to the representation of hair in *Kadosh*.

Turning attention to the film one sees that the play on the erotic faculties of hair is seen throughout *Kadosh*. Rivka never cuts her hair from which one can see why the community may see Rivka as impure. When she attends the *mikvah* she cannot ensure that all her hair is cleansed thoroughly, therefore contamination may still exist after attending. The *mikvah* attendant (Rivka's mother) calls attention to the fact that a woman may be barren if she has not followed the laws of *Taharat HaMischpachah* (family purity) diligently, thus providing a potential explanation for Rivka's failure to have children. As the film progresses much attention is paid through cinematic cues on the erotic power of her hair. When Rivka and Meir are intimate with each other, there is always a stress laid on Rivka's beautiful hair. Although Rivka most likely shaved her hair when she first got married, she has let it grow out and has chosen instead to wear a scarf to cover her hair when she is in public. In the home, her hair is always covered as well, with the exception of when she goes to sleep at night, and when she and Meir are sexually intimate with one another.

In direct contrast to this, is the wedding scene where Malka shaves her hair and then afterwards wears a wig in public. According to tradition, Malka is shown cutting off her hair. The scene is very powerful as Malka's emotions vary between crying and laughing. Malka cries for the potential independence and life that she has just lost, and she laughs as she is following social convention, rules and laws which she does not agree with. When Malka finally decides to leave Jerusalem and Mea Shearim she goes to the bar where Yaakov works. In the sex scene that follows Malka removes her wig in front of Yaakov prior to lovemaking, as a form of undress, hence we see the emphasis placed on hair and sexuality once again. As seen in the film, then, a transferral of notions takes place wherein the erotic symbolised by female genitals is transferred to the hair and this is further emphasised, as the naked female body itself is never shown. Thus, female hair takes on an erotic function and furthermore by covering the hair, Hasidic cultural gendered discourse as represented in film, implies that female sexuality signified by hair, must be concealed.[11]

By taking on an erotic function female hair similarly takes on an impure function. The Hasidic female body is considered at times to be impure, thus it is not too far of a leap to suggest that hair at times may be considered to be impure or unclean as well. As is evident in the following passage hair can be seen as a hindrance to ritual purity:

> I cover my hair in the way that Satmar Chassidic women always have: I shaved my head the morning after my wedding, and I shave it again every month before I go the *mikvah*...
>
> Once you're married, you just can't show your hair, so it's easier to shave it. Then you know nothing will show.
>
> It was a decision that the rabbis made, so all women do the same thing. And it makes it easier when you go the *mikvah*; if you have no hair, then none of it will rise to the top when you go

under the water. If one hair floats out of the water, then it is not a kosher dunking...[12]

Thus, in the Satmar Hasidic tradition, the shaving of women's heads is the only natural course to take, as this will ensure ritual purity.

Similar to most rituals in Hasidic Judaism one can find a myth that acts as a basis for hair covering. This is found in *Bamidbar* (Numbers 5:11-20). The first instance of a woman's hair being covered appears with the ordeal of the *sotah*, or suspected adulteress:

> God spoke to Moses saying, "Speak to the Children of Israel and say to them: This is what any man should do if his wife shall go astray and lay with another man carnally, whether it is hidden by seclusion, with no witness against her, and she was not raped, or a spirit of jealously passed over the husbands, though she was not defiled: the man shall bring his wife to the priest, along with an offering for her... it is a meal-offering of jealousies, a meal-offering of remembrance, a reminder of iniquity. The priest shall bring her before God... And the priest shall stand the woman before God and *parah* [to uncover or let down hair] the woman's head... and in the hand of the priest shall be bitter waters that cause a curse. The priest shall make her swear and when she drinks the waters, if she is innocent, she will be untouched by the curse..." (Bamidbar 5:11-20 Margollin Torah)

In Hasidic women's rituals, myth is used as the legitimating factor for ritual action. The "myth of impurity", which can be found in the Hebrew Bible, the Babylonian and Jerusalem Talmuds, and the *Midrash* is used as the grounds to authenticate women's ritual activity as it is played out in the binary classification of purity/impurity. However, just as myth is used as a legitimating factor for this ritual activity, this ritualised action daily reinforces the myth.

This ritualised action can be seen in the film through the *mikvah* ritual. The Torah states that a woman becomes *tumah* (ritually impure) during her menstrual period. As seen in Leviticus, the scriptural advice is to abstain from sexual relations during the period of *niddah* (impurity). *Tumah*, ritual impurity, and *taharah*, ritual purity, are spiritual conceptions. Women enter the state of *niddah* according to orthodox sources when, "any woman — even if she is pregnant, nursing, or past menopause- discovers a discharge of blood which originated from her uterus".[13] A woman is to be knowledgeable of these laws so that she is able to detect the possibility of her becoming *niddah*. While a woman is *niddah* she does not have any contact with her husband. This period is marked by psychological and physical separation that is concluded and sanctified by the *mikvah*. The ritual of *mikvah* is central to *Kadosh*. Women's experience as gendered beings is performed in this ritual. By partaking in this ritual, women adhere to the gendered discourses, which shape their lives.

It is evident in *Kadosh* that the female body is presented as source for defilement, impurity, and profanity: it is necessary but problematic from the outset. This is perhaps best represented by the presentation of the *mikvah* ritual and as well the separate beds that married women and men sleep in. This signification of women as source of defilement is legitimized by mythic narrative and is ritually enacted in the daily lives of Hasidic women. The separation of husbands (the male) and wives (the female) at specific times and in specific places speaks to the gender ideology of Hasidism as presented in this film. Interestingly the Hasidic gender ideology is not made apparent to the viewer. Rather, Hasidic cultural attitudes and beliefs are represented through the use of gender ideology and gendered separated spheres in this film. Thus, through Gitai's portrayals of Hasidic life the viewer is being shown and told that the female and feminine are conceptualised as impure, profane and sexual in Hasidism. The women in these films come to signify subordinated beings to the viewer. And, women and men are separated only on the basis of the binary impure/pure. Although, women have the ability to move to either side of the binary they are considered primarily impure (however this can change when women take part in the ritual of *mikvah*). This is depicted in *Kadosh* when Rivka and Meir and Malka and Yosef each avoid sleeping together in the same marital bed for fear of contamination and in addition the separation of women and men in the synagogue by way of the *mechitzah* (partition).

In addition to this, the director also raises the issue of modesty within this film. A Hasidic woman is expected to be modest and not call attention to herself at *all* times. The female body is represented in two ways. Firstly, the character of Rivka, adheres to "traditional" female dress, she is always shown in a full length skirt, a long sleeved shirt which covers the collarbone and elbows, and in addition she is usually shown wearing a head scarf except in the bedroom scenes in the movie. Thus, she comes to represent the traditional Hasidic modest woman. Secondly, the character Malka represents the perceived challenge to traditional ways of life, Malka wears makeup and she is often shown asserting her independence. Furthermore, the portrayal of women wearing traditional Hasidic dress signifies the resistance to outside challenges that the Hasidic community argues comes from the secular world. Dress, rituals, and "proper" female behaviour are used as a means of communicating to the non-Hasidic world, what Gitai conceives of the Hasidic world.

Gender and gender ideology are the primary means in which Hasidism is engaged within this film. The use and depiction of the certain modest roles, behaviours, dress, and hair becomes a means in the film for signifying Hasidic culture. The category of gender is used to tell us (the viewers) something of what non-Hasidic culture at large believes takes place in Hasidic communities. Therefore, this is not a true portrayal of Hasidism. Rather, the director plays upon and represents what non-Jewish or non-Hasidic culture at large understands about certain religious/cultural groups. Thus, female characters are shown primarily in their relation to their subordinated body and being. The body is the means in this film to represent a cultural view on Hasidism.

Griselda Pollock's "What's Wrong with Images of Women?" (1977) addresses the stereotypical images of women in media or film. Pollock makes use of Saussurian linguistics and argues that women should be recognised as *signifier* over and above being recognised as *signified*. What this suggests is the idea that "images of women" merely *reflect* meanings, which originate elsewhere (directors of film, or the social body). Pollock's approach views representations as a product of an ongoing process of "selecting and presenting, of structuring and shaping, and most importantly of *making things mean*".[14] Although it may seem that film simply reflects reality, Pollock's influence on film theory has directed attention to that fact that film, like any written text is composed of textual segments, a linked series of shots which form units of meaning. These units of meaning are produced and structured by socio-cultural codes. This implies, then, that film does more than reflect reality. Rather, it constructs without acknowledging the socio-cultural codes and therefore it mystifies the existence of such codes. This is apparent in *Kadosh* as the film uses gender to construct an image of Hasidic society as "fundamentalist". Gitai takes the assumptions of non-Hasidic society's view of Hasidic women and runs with this view throughout his film without acknowledging that this view of "fundamentalist" Hasidic society is grounded is sociological ideology.

Using Griselda Pollock's argument one understands that the portrayal of the female body in film is merely a product of selection; of presenting and selecting, structuring and shaping a specific idea or image in order to give significance to the "sign" woman. In this film, the director structures and shapes the "sign" of woman as "other". She is "other" based on her impurity and the sexual connotations that surround her body. Throughout most of the world, women play this designated role of "other" in socio-cultural contexts that are defined by men. In this way the female body comes to represent all that is undesirable or threatening in human existence: sexuality, emotion, pollution, sin and mortality.[15]

The portrayal of women within this film depicts women as under the mantle of their husband's power. As noted previously, women in *Kadosh* follow the modesty codes of Hasidism and wear the appropriate head coverings. As seen through the work of Carole Delaney, one understands how covering the hair/head is symbolic of covering the genitals. In covering, a woman's sexuality is bound. Since covering of the hair/head only takes place when a woman marries, this ritual act signifies the binding of woman's sexuality to her husband.

Conclusion

As sub-genres of belief systems, the discourses of myth and ritual provide analytic categories for exploring the construction of society. Within a Hasidic perspective it has become clear that ritual is dependent upon myth in order to be legitimated (at least in the case with *mikvah* and with hair coverings), and that together the discourses of myth and ritual have upheld and structured an operative gender ideology in Hasidic communities. In this way myth uses ritual and ritual in turn uses myth in order to be legitimated. The myth of impurity in Hasidism is amenable to notions of the female body as a source of defilement. This myth, as delineated in practice, has limited Hasidic women's participation in religious life. As noted previously, women have been barred from sacred space because they are considered impure.

In looking at ritual and gender as performance on the cinematic screen, I have attempted to demonstrate the relationship between myth, ritual, gender, and power. Discourse of mythic narrative is directly related to ritual performances in Hasidic culture. The discourses of myth and ritual, which further legitimates the discourse of gender, emerge from within a masculine hegemony operative within Hasidic ideologies. Narrative discourses such as myth work in a very powerful way, as they make no room for how women might consider their own bodies.

Women's daily lives in Hasidic culture are ritualistic. Through the representation of women in *Kadosh*, the ritualistic lives of Hasidic women are brought to the forefront in cinematic performances and this film speaks to women's ritual actions and savvy. The rituals depicted in this film highlights women as daughters, mothers, wives, and furthermore sexual beings. In addition, women are signed in this film as impure and the property of their husbands. The portrayal of women within this film depicts women as under the mantle of their husband's power.

In watching this film the viewer is taken out of his/her ordinary reality and is allowed a glimpse into the lives of Hasidic women as depicted by film. The marginalised experience of Hasidic women and their "foreign" traditions and rituals provide a stage upon which scripted performances elicit interest and attention in the viewer. Historically mainstream (malestream) scholarship has focussed attention on Hasidic men and their rituals; as such Hasidic women's rituals have often been ignored. Until recently with growing awareness in Jewish feminist circles, the topic of Hasidic women has been relatively untouched. In some measure Hasidic women's ritual lives are still not discussed within a scholarly approach. Furthermore, the discussion of Hasidic women in film is something that has been untouched. Gendered-cultural analysis of ritual discourse in film is needed. It is my hope that this chapter contributes to this discussion and shows how gender plays an active role in ritualised Hasidic life and how gender has becomes a means for understanding Hasidic life as represented in film.

Chapter Seven
Semen, Semolina and Salt Water: The Erotic Jewess in Sandra Goldbacher's *The Governess*
Judith Lewin

By focusing on Sandra Goldbacher's 1998 film *The Governess* this chapter will examine Jewish women, Jewish passing, Jewish otherness, Jewish exoticism, Jewish sexual desire and the desire for Jews in mid- nineteenth century Britain. Analysis of this film will give us insight into what those attitudes were and are, how and why they may have changed, and how and why they may have remained the same.

The Governess did not show up on a lot of people's radar. As British director Goldbacher's first feature, a period piece based on an original screenplay rather than an adaptation of a classic Victorian novel, the independent film played in art-house cinemas in larger cities and used neither established Hollywood cash cows nor members of the BBC/Merchant-Ivory coterie; what is more, with Minnie Driver as lead and with its Brontëesque title, the film was murkily marketed as an historical romance/chick-flick while failing to target overtly one of its major potential audiences: Jews. Since 1998, only a handful of articles appearing in film journals and film books have primarily focussed on *The Governess*. Although each of these critiques has offered a very useful perspective for understanding the film, each fails to ask what I feel are crucial questions about it.

The Governess tells the story of a crypto-Jewess and her sexual and professional rebellion. Rosina da Silva, a Sephardic Jewess living a comfortable life in East London, suddenly loses her father to murder. Rather than marry in order to gain financial support for the family, Rosina goes to work as a young girl's governess. In order to do so, she must adopt the name and Protestant identity of "Mary Blackchurch", and travel to the Isle of Skye to serve the daughter of the Cavendish family. As governess, she really takes on a role of *bonne à tout-faire*; in helping to establish the technology of photography, she begins an affair with the photographer-scientist, her charge's married father. The two come into conflict over control: of the camera, of the action of depicting, of the meaning photography is to take on as a science or an art, and of the power of the gaze and becoming its object. After Rosina subjects her unwitting lover to an improvised nude photo shoot, he bars her from the studio and his presence. Denied her due as an inventor and cast off as a mistress, Rosina "appropriates" the new technology and founds a London photo studio specialising in artistic portraits of "her people".

What critics have failed to note is how each of the three intertwining plots of this film (a story of passing, a *künstlerroman*, and a love story) *hinges* on the fact that the main character is a Jewish woman. As we shall see, a Victorian Jewish woman in a cinematic fiction must choose from paths available to her — a marriage of convenience, a life on the stage, or prostitution — or find a way to create more paths, in this instance by passing as a Christian. The fact of the protagonist being a Jewish woman who, through her disguise, is able to interact with the Christian world beyond her community, allows her also to develop as an artist — as art (in opposition to science) is attributed to (and denied) both women and Jews. The fact of the Jewish heroine's ambiguous position of disguise (passing as a Christian but truly being a Jewish woman), alongside the traditionally liminal class position of the governess, allows for her love story to flourish and for her to function as sexual, experimental, active, liberated (fun, radical, modern, and anachronistic) yet ultimately rules out any conventionally satisfying resolution to her story. According to Antje Ascheid, "Rosina's rather anachronistically liberated way of Jewishness... helps the narrative to free her from the conventions of gentile Victoriana that stress sexual repression and the inability to express erotic desire directly".[1] Whereas Ascheid argues that historical romance films generally feature storylines in which displaced twentieth-century male and female protagonists try to escape the entrapment of Victorian Gothic space (and achieve sexual fulfilment in so doing), I would like to add the distinction that the Jewish female figure is already doubly displaced (geographically and temporally) and therefore offers a special case that eludes romantic union.

I offer in the following a close reading of Goldbacher's film with the object of unearthing the many and varied Jewish associations layered in it that participate in making the choices about sex and Jewishness relevant and revelatory, if not even necessary to its interpretation.

La Rachel and Prostitution

The opening sound of the film is the recitation of the Jewish credo, the *shema*, and the opening image is that of the Jewish prayer shawl, the *tallit,* overlaid with the super-title "The Governess, a film by Sandra Goldbacher". The credits pass atop images of anonymous Jewish men, seen from the back and above. With the shot of Rosina (Minnie Driver) and the fact that the first words of the film are a sexual banter between Rosina and her sister above the intonation of prayers, we realise that the point of view is intimately connected to this woman and that not only is she Jewish, but also unorthodox, rebellious, and sexual. As Jackie Byars warns: "Point of view is power and... control of point of view by a female character constitutes sexual aggression" which is then punished.[2]

The scene proceeds with two further markings both of the historical context and of Rosina as a sexualised Jewess. Exiting the synagogue alone and in exotic, presumably Sephardic regalia (including a black fez), she passes in front of an advertisement for the "first appearance of Rachel La Grande Tragedienne — Jewess and Jewel of Paris" just as she is accosted by some prostitutes as a "Jew girl" and offered "lessons" in the form of a bared breast. These so-called lessons would be presumably in acting, associated with the poster Rosina contemplates, but also in sex, since acting would be understood as almost synonymous with prostitution, as will be explained below.

Rosina's ambition to become an actress (or performer) confirms a choice of career associated in the nineteenth century with Jews. Beginning in the late seventeenth century, when the restoration of Charles II in 1660 permitted women for the first time to perform on the stage at the same time as he also continued Cromwell's policy of admitting Jews to settle in England, Jews were prominent in the field of entertainment, contributing playwrights, theatre directors, "conjurers", many players and avid audiences.[3] Jewish women, in particular, delighted London audiences as both singers and actresses. Nevertheless, women actresses and Jewish actors, "who occupied space [in the] public imagination" released anxieties about proper feminine behaviour among nineteenth-century spectators and about the "the power of Jews both as performers and as audience".[4] One *London Chronicle* review from the period reads: "The number of Jews at the Theatres is incredible", leaving open to interpre-

tation whether the reviewer means on the stage or in the audience.[5] In one famous incident, Thomas Dibdin was forced to rewrite his play "after Jewish audiences demonstrated to protest a song in it that portrayed Jewish women as prostitutes".[6] La Rachel (Rachel Félix), the Parisian Jewish tragedienne who toured London for the first time in 1841, notably stirred the emotions of English audiences, of theatre critic G.H. Lewes, and stirred the discomfort of London visitor Charlotte Brontë. In her letters home, Brontë writes: "I have seen Rachel — her acting was something apart from any other acting it has come in my way to witness — her soul was in it — and a strange soul she has... [sold] I fear — to Beelzebub [the Devil]". In subsequent letters she calls Rachel a "fiend", a "demon", a "snake", "not a woman", "a glimpse of hell", a "strange being" and "the — [sic]".[7] Brontë channelled her inflammatory impression of the actress's power into the character Vashti, who sets even Lucy Snowe aflame in *Villette*. Many years later, Lewes' companion, George Eliot, transposed her positive and negative feelings toward the Jewish actress onto her young, Jewish chamber singer, Mirah Lapidoth, and her jaded, maternally-defective opera singer, the Al Charisi in *Daniel Deronda*. Sarah Bernhardt, the British, late nineteenth-century scandalously sexual diva, though baptised a Catholic at an early age, changed her name from Rosine to the stage name Sarah to underscore her Jewish heritage. Bernhardt was world-famous and became identified with roles such as the consumptive prostitute Marguerite in *La Dame aux Camélias* (*La Traviata* in opera houses), which she performed over three thousand times. The poster of Rachel and Rosina's name clearly allude to these famous, scandalous, lascivious, nineteenth-century Jewish actresses.

Rosina almost simultaneously encounters London prostitutes, another Jewish trope. In fact, the distinctions between actresses, prostitutes and exotic Jewish women were blurry in the eighteenth and nineteenth centuries when the "assumption that actresses were prostitutes understood the female on the stage as on display and thus sexually available".[8] The idea that "the woman who nightly demonstrated passion must herself be passionate" explains the elision between actresses and prostitutes, but why was there so close an association with Jewish women?[9] One obvious explanation is that Jewish quarters and criminal quarters such as in London's East End were found side by side — and Goldbacher's film demonstrates this when Rosina leaves the synagogue and is immediately accosted by prostitutes. But as Jeannette Jakubowski explains, on a deeper level the desires and fear of Christian patriarchal culture shape the image of Jewish women, who embody sexual sin — serving as the erring Jewish Eve to the chaste Christian Mary.[10] (Eve may also be transposed into heroic-sexual, Old Testament heroines, as we shall see below, or into Mary Magdalene, the reformed prostitute.) The secularised nineteenth century still retains the anti-Semitic association between Jewish women and sexually aggressive, money-hungry prostitutes. The fact that Rosina flaps open her shawl to flash her own chest (covered, however, since she is on her way home from synagogue) in answer to them underscores her worldliness.

Rosina's cosmopolitan portrayal and sexual availability, quite absent from other traditional governess tales, derives particularly from the conventional Jewess figure of fiction. This is the Jewess figure as overwhelmingly sensual and carnal, prominent not only in Shakespeare's Jessica, but also in Balzac, Maupassant, and the

Goncourts. Slurs against the Jewess intensified during the nineteenth century as she was increasingly perceived as threateningly invisible, that is unmarked, due to assimilation. Although Rosina's initial appearance in Sephardic garb counters this argument of invisibility, her ability to pass (or act) as "Mary Blackchurch" later on resonates with the nineteenth-century anxiety about Jewish women. The "eroticised Jewess" becomes an emblem of the "dangers of assimilation", especially in the form of the actress, for "acting is fundamentally reliant upon masquerade, thus ideally suited to the chameleon-like nature of the modern Jewess".[11] The dialogue between Rosina and her sister recounting her experience with the prostitutes goes like this:

> **Rosina:** I don't see why I shouldn't go on the stage. Aunt Sofka is an actress.
> **Sister:** And she never married. [*Pause*] What else did the prostitute say?
> **Rosina:** [*Imitates voice*] "Wanna make five shillings, Jew-girl?"
> S: [*Laughs*] Do they enjoy it, do you think?
> **Rosina:** What? [*Slowly and dramatically*] Drinking semen?
> **Sister:** [*giggles and grimaces*]. You know Gentiles eat a dessert that looks like semen. It's called semolina. I've seen it.
> **Rosina:** Yes, but you haven't seen semen…
> **Sister:** No! [*gags*]
> **Rosina:** No. I would like to see it [*takes a sip of water*] but not to drink it. [*Pause*] I kissed Benjamin.
> **Sister:** But you're not married!
> **Rosina:** Actresses care not for such convention.
> **Sister:** What was it like? [*No reply*] Well, you don't look any different.

A conversation such as this is really quite unusual; it certainly would never have appeared in a nineteenth-century novel. It may strike some as anachronistic whereas others might react by thinking that finally we get a glimpse of "what was really going on behind closed doors" in Victorian times. The da Silva family already contains one actress, Aunt Sofka, who "never married". Her single status begs the question: does this mean that she is a lesbian, like Sarah Bernhardt, or that her profession excluded the possibility of marriage, as it will for Rosina? In response to the reprimand that she should not have kissed her intended, Benjamin, before marriage, Rosina replies, "Actresses care not for such convention". This dialogue, including the reference to semolina/semen foreshadows the turns that Rosina's story will take. For Rosina and her sister, "drinking semen" (and eating its semolina equivalent) is something only prostitutes and gentiles do. For them, within the Sephardic Jewish enclave, there is no association between prostitutes and Jews. Semen itself becomes an emblem of mature sexuality and is viewed as a curiosity — gentile and *trayf* — Rosina would like to observe but not commit to ("I would like to see it but not to drink it"). Semolina returns with dramatic irony as the first dessert she is served and unwittingly eats at the Cavendishes.

Seeking Fixation
Rosina's creative solution to her suddenly bereft financial status is to advertise under the name "Mary Blackchurch" for a position as a governess. She travels to the Isle of Skye to take up residence in the Cavendish household and quickly makes herself indispensable to the master as an assistant to his experiments in scientific photography and his pursuit of the fixative process. Rosina's secret practice of Judaism, in the form of a nostalgic Seder in her father's *tallit*, offers the sought-after solution to fixation: sodium chloride, in this case found in the traditional Seder salt water. In this way, photography's progress seems to depend on Rosina's Judaism and the fact that she cannot sustain the charade of passing in private.

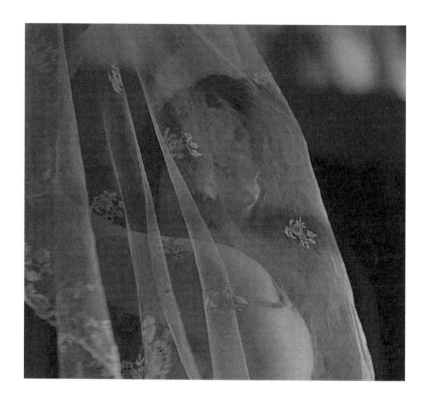

Rosina's crypto-Judaism may become the key to invention, but her transgressive Jewish sexuality becomes the reason for her exile. Twin photo sessions form the centrepiece of the film. Sex between Rosina and Charles is initiated when Rosina says, "I dreamt of a beautiful picture we could make of Salomé". She then proceeds to take off her outer clothing. Cavendish looks at her prone body and says, "Your eyes are so huge. They devour me". "Then do not look at me", she replies, covering herself with a white veil and adding, as if to reveal who she really is amid the double masquerade, "I have heard it said that the ancient Hebrews used to express love for each other entirely covered". Seemingly obeying the injunction not to undress, Cavendish fumbles with his fly, quickly penetrates her (to which she gasps, presumably to reinforce the idea that she was a virgin), and just as quickly he collapses at her side. Her first words to him afterward are: "Do I look different? [My sister and I used to say we'd look different afterwards".]

The veil, according to Mary Ann Doane "incarnates contradictory desires — the desire to bring [a woman] closer and the desire to distance her".[12] Like the veil that they use between them, the sex between these two characters emblematises a problematics of passing: Rosina reveals her desire to convert her first lover into an "ancient Hebrew" yet does so while "acting" as Salomé, another ancient Hebrew, not herself; when she thinks of herself as profoundly changed and absolutely naked, having lost her virginity, she finds that the change is invisible or only visible to those who wish to "look".

In the first of twin photo sessions, when Rosina/Mary invites Cavendish to take portraits of her (before they proceed to have un-shown sex — "We have Salomé to complete first", she says) instead of photographing still-life objects, she says, "I want to know how you see me". Yet even in its phrasing the invitation shows the pair's unconventional relative power positions on either side of the camera: "I want to know" and "me" envelop in Rosina's subjectivity Cavendish's ostensibly autonomous act of seeing. In this way, the spectator perceives the storyteller constructing just how "you" are to see "me". What is more, Rosina suggests in this first photo portrait session that she appear allegorically — in other words, not as herself, but as exotic Jewish sexual projections of how, in fact, she wishes her photographer-lover to envision her (or how she envisions herself). Her poses include portraits as Queen Esther, who notoriously passed as a Persian until it became time to save the Jews, and as Salomé, a frequent figure for the seductive *femme fatale* (at times conflated with the more heroic Judith, who seduces and decapitates Holofernes in order, again, to save her people). As Aron Rodrigue points out: "'The story of Salomé does not come from a Jewish text... [it] is part of a heavily Christian tradition. She's hardly a positive figure, and it seems quite unlikely that a Jewish woman would choose to identify with the young girl who offs the head of John the Baptist'".[13] Why then these particular allegories? Esther and Judith/Salomé, aside from being messages about Rosina's Jewishness — ignored by Cavendish, but loud and clear to the film's spectators — are also figures for female sexual threat. Rosina, ironically perhaps, proposes these figures, ostensibly stressing the artistic value of photography while encoding a message that supports conventional fictional stereotypes of Jewish women as sexually available, aggressive, and potentially

96

dangerous. Yet, contrary to Aviva Kempner's triumphal cry in the title of her film review, "Finally: Jewish Women Have Sex on the Screen", virtually all of the sex in this film is implied and unseen.[14]

A second photo session occurs while Cavendish is sleeping, post-coitally rapt yet vulnerable, and without his knowledge Rosina undresses him and poses him as a classic reclining nude. Rosina's appropriation of the gaze of the camera, and objectification of Cavendish as a male nude, reveals explicitly her potential threat as rival, competitor and usurper. Indeed, the sequence suggests an inversion frequently seen in relation to the Jewish woman: the convention of the effeminate male Jew who becomes inverted into the masculine Jewess. Indeed, Sarah Bernhardt has been viewed in that respect.[15] Rosina slips into the position of the one who looks from what she thinks is an egalitarian, loving, collaborative partnership. After Cavendish exacts retribution by banishing her from the studio and publicly denying her contribution to the discovery of fixation, she steals the power position outright by appropriating the technology of the camera — her new weapon — and leaving behind the indelibly "fixed" evidence of the affair in the form of the nude photograph that she deposits on the wife's lap. When she appears to disrupt the family dinner and brandish the photo-revenge, she undergoes a "visual transformation", by going back to her Jewish clothing, which had previously been hidden. The change in clothes is an emblem of gender transformation, the Jewish woman reveals herself to be a powerful Jewess.

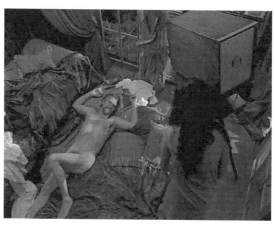

97

Cholera strikes London

Upon returning to London, Rosina discovers that a cholera epidemic has stricken the Jewish quarter and her mother has died. One interpretation of the epidemic that kills Rosina's mother is to read it as "justice", or divine punishment for Rosina's aberrant sexual behaviour, even if that self-same behaviour affords her the independence to go into business for herself and support her remaining family. We may think of this interpretation, if we accept it, either as a tip of the hat to fictional morality codes (endorsing a rather puritanical morality), or perhaps as an allegory for plague of the fin-de-siècle, AIDS. Either of these interpretations, however, is fraught with implications for Jews. Do Jews have a separate sexual moral code or are they to be held to the Christian code of denial of the body? Do Jews have a special susceptibility to AIDS, like other "diseases" thought typical of Jews in the nineteenth century: neuroses, hysteria, homosexuality, hyper-sexuality, bad feet and male menstruation? Rosina's mother dies under "mysterious" circumstances (cholera) just as the Rosina's father died at the beginning of the film, also under a cloud of mystery. At his funeral, his wife laments confusedly, "Murder? Debts? We do not get murdered in our family. I told him not to go out...". The combined mystery of a murdered, debt-ridden father who goes out at night suggests taint as well. Was he visiting prostitutes? Maintaining a mistress? In nineteenth-century terms, a tainted father and mother produce a tainted, syphilitic child. Syphilis, as Sander Gilman has written, had been associated with the Jews since its first appearance in Europe in the fifteenth century.

> The literature on syphilis in the nineteenth century contains a substantial discussion of the special relationship of the Jews to the transmission and meaning of syphilis.... The need to "see" and "label" the Jews at a time when Jews were becoming more and more "invisible"... made the association with socially stigmatising diseases which bore specific visible "signs and symptoms" especially appropriate.[16]

Therefore, illness and even murder take on a sexual valence; Rosina's orphaned status comes to suggest her potential sexual threat: her pathological inheritance invisible, what is visible is only her beauty as "a sign of her danger to all human beings".[17] It is interesting to note that upon her return to London, Rosina is trans-formed into a professional — a "sterile" intellectual — and completely divorced from the sexual escapades she partook in up north.[18]

Apart from seeing cholera, like syphilis, as a disease of the Jews, the disease itself encodes a "Jewish" message. The disease resulted in an "ugly, nasty, and repulsive death [in which i]ndividuals often lost consciousness and it was sometimes difficult to determine whether the individual had actually expired".[19] Thus, communities forbade burial sooner than twenty-four hours after death, explicitly contravening the Jewish law prescribing burial in twenty-four hours. (Of course, this death, unknown to Rosina and viewers, remains unseen.) *Cholerae vibrio* also has a specific relation to the film's symbolism of the salt water, associated with the Passover Seder. The disease invades and subsists in water sources. Once ingested, the bacteria "produce a toxin which inhibits the absorption of water and salts".[20] Thus, the cholera epidemic not only punishes Rosina by depriving her of her mother, it does so symbolically by depriving the mother of the very salt water (or Jewishness) that her daughter had used to further her career and start her affair with a Christian man. Cholera's association with sin, degeneracy and foreignness taints Rosina's return and the establishment of her independence.

Conclusion

In the end Rosina chooses theft (is it the equivalent of her lover's theft of the credit for her discovery?), independence, and creativity, and most impressively, she chooses to claim her subjectivity by switching sides of the camera. The professional photography studio resolution opens up the possibility of a new text, one that rejects both the conventional endings of Governess tales (marriage) and those of Jewess tales (conversion, sacrificial death or exile). Goldbacher's final scene depicts Rosina composing her own self-portrait while she speaks in voice-over — in much the same mode as Jane Eyre's final announcement, "Reader, I married him" — ironically of her satisfaction in solitude. However, the plot ultimately confirms the conventional exile of the Jewess character (as in, for example, Rebecca's exile at the end of *Ivanhoe*). In this way, it no longer innovates but rather returns to a formulaic plot structure. Yet, unlike plots that expunge the Jewish characters from the narrative in order to reach a positive resolution for the (Christian) main focus, Goldbacher's story allows for the spectators to follow the Jewess into her (albeit celibate) "exile" and share it with her, retreating from the Christian Gothic space of the Cavendish family (where she was, in a sense, "passing" in exile) and turning the exile into a homecoming — to the East End, to the city, to the family, and to portraits of Rosina's people, the Jews. This homecoming allows Rosina to return to herself — to her name, her shop, her clothing, her choices. Perhaps we should call it conventional with a newly focussed conclusion.

As we have seen, Goldbacher adds to the choices of marriage, acting or prostitution a fourth choice for the Jewish woman of passing (and passion) — at least for a time — and finally one of professional achievement. The idea of passing/passion certainly reflects nineteenth-century fears about Jewish women, as do the resonant symbols of this film: La Rachel, prostitutes, salt water, Biblical tableaux, and cholera. Yet, what one thought was a film recreating a lost Victorian moment of active female independence and contribution to the genesis of photography (without which, movies would not exist), turns out to be a fraught, self-authorising move, where Goldbacher not only imagines a model progenitor but she also tangles with the problem of confirming or revising constructions of the nineteenth-century Jewish woman. Without Rosina's (read Goldbacher's) Jewishness, the science/ art of photography would have remained a passionless Christian dilettante's ephemeral practice at best, or so the film would suggest.

Chapter Eight
Perverts and Purists:
The Idea of Jewish Sexual Difference in Britain 1900-1945
Gavin Schaffer

Understanding the sexual construction of Jews in the British imagination is no simple matter. Images of Jewish sexual difference seem to have been frequently unstable, contested and even contradictory. In one of the most revealing analyses of modern British understandings of Jewishness, Bryan Cheyette has argued that nineteenth and twentieth century constructions of Jews show a remarkable degree of fluidity and inconsistency: "The radical emptiness and lack of a fixed meaning in the constructions of 'semitic' difference... results in 'the Jew' being made to occupy an incommensurable number of subject positions which traverse a range of contradictory discourses".[1] Constructions of Jewish sexuality indeed seem to fit this pattern of discourse analysis. With remarkable inconsistency, Jews have been labelled at different moments as sexually pure and sexually immoral, as corrupted and as hygienic, as predatory and as clannish.[2] Conflicting sexual discourses have managed to operate in the same period contexts, and none could be described as ever having become dominant in Jewish representations.

This chapter will explore some of the common themes in Jewish sexual discourse in an attempt to gauge whether any kind of over-arching pattern is discernible in the ostensibly contradictory ways in which Jews have been sexually imagined. It will focus on two prominent and conflicting images of Jewish sex: the Jew as sexually diseased and corrupt and the Jew as the bastion of sexual health. It will also probe attitudes towards Jewish and non-Jewish sexual mixing in recognition that the issue of sexual assimilation was throughout a thorny one in Jewish/non-Jewish relations in Britain. Finally, the chapter will consider what sexual images may tell us about wider perceptions of Jews in modern Britain.

In his ground breaking study of the subject, Michel Foucault presented sexuality as an "especially dense transfer point for relations of power".[3] Foucault argued that sexual discourse (or "sexology") had been focussed by European men onto "peripheral sexualities", enabling them to cement their social control by constructing themselves as normal in opposition to rival social groups.[4] Foucault observed that this historical tendency deflected attention away from men's sexual fears, neuroses and habits by transferring attention onto the sexuality of less powerful sections of the population. Foucault cited women, children, the mentally ill and criminals in this context, but some scholars have argued that racial minorities have been similarly utilised. Hoch has contended in this context: "In the sixteenth and seventeenth centuries, the attribution of lust to Africans went hand in hand with the development of a pronounced economic interest in treating them like animals (in particular with the institution of slavery)".[5] As historians (most significantly gender historians) have engaged with Foucault's ideas, the argument that racial sexual difference has played a key role in shaping host-minority relations in the twentieth century has come increasingly to the fore. Scholars have emphasised that time and again, minority communities have been constructed as sexually unlike their indigenous equivalents, often as deviant and immoral. Most obviously, the idea of Black sexual difference has played a prominent role in shaping the reception and absorption of Afro-Caribbean immigrants in Britain. Black communities have repeatedly been victims of allegations of sexual immorality and perversion and Black men in particular have often been constructed as supersexual predators, whose presence is a threat to the safety and purity of British women. This idea has, at extreme moments, played a substantial role in fuelling anti-Black rioting, notably in 1919 and 1958.

The history of Black sexual demonisation has been quite well covered, even if historians have sometimes underplayed the sexual motivations for racial violence in Britain, arguing that these issues masked more entrenched inter-racial employment and housing conflicts. However, sexual tensions between hosts and non-Black immigrants and minorities have received far less historical attention. It is with this dearth of scholarship in mind that this chapter sets out to explore British sexual perceptions of Jews in the first half of the twentieth century, and specifically to consider the extent to which perceptions of Jewish sexual difference impacted on host-immigrant relations.

The Jew as an Example of Sexual Health

Constructions of sexual difference did not always entail a negative reading of immigrant/minority sexual behaviour. In Britain, many commentators and scholars believed that the breeding habits of Jews provided a lesson for the rest of society. Up until the 1930s, the idea that human populations could be assessed as races, and that these races differed in their physical and mental characteristics, was prominent in British science and society. Indeed, I have argued recently that although contested, these beliefs continued to be influential long after this period.[6] In this atmosphere, the question of how to improve and protect the stock of the British race abounded, and Jews were often seen as providing a lesson.

Many scholars contended that Jews had been highly successful in preserving their racial qualities; most significantly, by refusing to mix sexually with non-Jews. The analysis of doctor and eugenicist Robert Rentoul provides a good example of this kind of thinking. In his tellingly titled study, *Race Culture or Race Suicide?* Rentoul described Judaism as "a religion of health" and presented Jewish sexual habits as a lesson in eugenics:

> No race has been so scrupulously particular as has the Hebrew in prohibiting the inter marriage of those of their own race with the Gentiles. And with what result? That this race has for 5,000 years retained all their racial features, racial qualities, and racial ambitions — all keen and supreme, although they have lived amongst all kinds of nationalities.[7]

Rentoul was a marginal figure in many ways but his analysis of Jewish sexual practice was common currency amongst racial theorists. The influential American bacteriologist and eugenicist Thurman Rice famously argued that the survival of the Jewish race was partly explained by the fact that "Jews have not mixed blood with other races as much as have other peoples". Rice was clear about what he thought that this behaviour had done for Jews. "Although scattered to the four winds the Jews remain Jews; races rise and fall but Israel is immortal".[8] Similar analyses were carried out by British writer Anthony M. Ludovici and doctor and eugenicist Parkes Weber.[9]

In Britain, these views were similarly prominent amongst scholars of Jews and race. The geneticist Redcliffe Salaman argued that the Jewish racial type, having survived for so long, needed preservation and guarding. To Salaman's mind, Jewish breeding with non-Jews threatened a unique racial heritage. Salaman believed that Jewish characteristics were "recessive" and as such that inter-racial mixing could lead to the destruction of Jewishness, which would be swamped in mixed race offspring by other "dominant" racial strains.[10] The Jew, he recorded, "will not be assimilated but being recessive he will simply be swallowed". In this way, Salaman argued that allowing non-racial Jews (converts) into the community was the equivalent of "letting in a thief in the dark"; such was their threat to the racial stock of Jewishness.[11] In contrast, the social scientist Joseph Jacobs proffered the opposite argument in earlier research, suggesting that Jewish stock would be dominant in mixed-race offspring.[12] Other scholars did not see Jewish racial qualities as so delicate. The anti-Semitic biologist and botanist Reginald Gates seems to have believed in a racial Jewish ability to absorb and incorporate other racial qualities within a preserved Jewish type. "The Jews have all through their history, since the Maccabees absorbed the Edomites, been absorbing the racial elements among whom they have lived".[13]

Beliefs about the superiority of Jewish breeding habits crept into discussions of Jewish intelligence in the interwar period as some scholars argued that Jewish sexual practice over generations had ensured the superior intellect of the Jewish race. Arthur Hughes, a psychologist who, together with Mary Davies, wrote an influential study of the comparative intelligence of Jewish and non-Jewish children in 1927, asserted that the Jewish superiority which was found in their research was rooted in Jewish mating behaviour.[14] Hughes cited in particular the "tradition for rich Jewish fathers to seek out men rich in learning rather than in goods" as the explanation of superior Jewish intelligence.[15] This argument was also made by Salaman in 1925, who claimed that:

> The old custom of marrying the rich man's daughter to the most promising student of the chevra was one of the most successful and illuminating eugenic experiments ever conceived, and we can never be too grateful to our forbears for thus artificially breeding an aristocracy of brains.[16]

A corresponding belief was also prominent that the sexual etiquette of Jews, prescribed by law and ritual, had served to ensure healthy breeding. Rice argued that "sex hygiene began with the Jews" and many of his British contemporaries concurred.[17] For example, Joseph Jacobs cited perceived benefits to the Jewish "regulation of the connubial relations" as outlined in Leviticus, proscribing sexual congress during menstruation.[18] Similarly, Rentoul presented Jewish sexual practice as wholesome and socially conscious, arguing that it was entirely driven towards breeding success. Jewish men and women, he argued, "did not live for themselves, but that theirs was the duty to the nation in the matter of begetting healthy children for the nation or the state".[19]

These beliefs about Jewish racial good practice often merged with corresponding beliefs about the Jewish family, which was presented as offering a superior environment for child rearing. In this way, Jewish breeding was championed for its attention to the importance of both "nature" and "nurture". The author Sidney Dark, in his study of contemporary British Jews, argued: "Here in England, the Jew is distinguished by his devotion to family. He has a far acuter sense of family obligation than the average Englishman, and a far greater devotion to family life".[20] Similarly, Hughes's article on comparative intelligence took into account, within an explanation of Jewish precocity, the "acknowledged care which Jewish mothers bestow on their children".[21] As the interwar period continued, studies which explained difference in terms of environment became more common. In a survey of the literature of the comparative psychology of Jews and non-Jews, Rumyaneck argued that it was Jewish family life which made the key difference in shaping Jewish success:

> The home conditions of an English or Jewish coalman or caretaker would be worlds apart. The stimulus and encouragement to study and the sobriety of the wage-earner, which are found in the lowest of Jewish homes and which are part of the Jewish tradition, are not found as frequently in similarly situated English homes.[22]

In this confusing and often confused terrain of racial and environmental explanations of Jewishness, Jews were frequently portrayed as superior to indigenous Britons in their sexual and familial habits. However, whilst Semitic discourses were sometimes positively prejudicial about Jewish sex, negative images of Jews were also commonplace. Far from the painting a picture of perfect Jewish family life, these images presented Jews as sexually corrupt and immoral: as perverts, pimps and predators.

The Jew as a Sexual Deviant

Many writers constructed the Jew, and especially the foreign immigrant male Jew, as a sexual predator, who posed a specific threat to British women. Unlike Black men who were repeatedly painted as animalistic, super sexual primitives, portrayals of the Jewish predator were, in keeping with wider Jewish representations, tied to the idea of the Jew as a psychologically powerful sly manipulator. Here, Jewish interests in women stemmed not from a natural impulse (as theorists often argued that it did with Black men) but from a more calculated awareness of an opportunity to corrupt, gain and defile. Some analysts of anti-Semitism have highlighted this tendency of linking perceptions of Jewish sex to wider Semitic discourses. Cheyette, for example, has argued that sexual deviance was a long standing aspect of Semitic discourse in Britain. Sander Gilman has cited the tendency of considering Jews to have a "sexualised" relationship with capital, whilst Memmi has highlighted the importance of circumcision within perceptions of Jewish sexual deviance and promiscuity.[23] However, alongside specifically Jewish racial sexual images, Jews were sometimes also sexually demonised as essentially Black, only with added powers of manipulation and deviousness.

Novelist and eugenicist Austin Freeman outlined mixed perceptions of a Jewish/Black sexual threat in a 1921 book, where he argued that Jews controlled the businesses of "procuration and 'White slave' traffic". Jews, Freeman argued, were totally lacking in any form of sexual morality. "Of the younger women an appreciable portion were prostitutes and made no secret of the fact", he recorded.[24] This thinking was conditioned by Freeman's notion that Jewish deviance was essentially similar to the behaviour of Black people. Jews, similar to the "far inferior" Negro race, were "animal like in habits [behaving] like a monkey might do".[25] Freeman was not alone in seeing Jews as Black in this way. This was in fact a tendency which repeatedly featured within strains of British thinking and literature.

Where this Jewish/Black linkage occurred, it enabled the demonisation of Jewish sexual habits conducive with anti-Black sexual discourse, only with added psychological menace. A good example of this construction of Jews can be seen in the writing of the anti-

Semitic agitator Joseph Banister. Banister's work stands out as one of the most vicious examples of modern British anti-Semitism and it would be a mistake to present his ideas as representative of wider currents of opinion. However, it is interesting that in his attacks on Jewry he saw fit, as Freeman would do later, to construct Jews as "Negroid tribesmen", as well as ascribing to them the more common allegation of control of the sex industry.[26] In his book, *England under the Jews*, Banister outlined his belief that Jews both controlled an international sex trade and delighted in the corporal corruption of Christian girls. To Banister, the Jewish sexual threat was both physical (because Jews were Black) but also manipulative and conspiratorial, essentially Jewish.

> The introduction of foreign women for immoral purposes is carried on, as is the white slave traffic everywhere, chiefly, if not entirely, by Jews... No Jew is more of a hero among his fellow tribesmen than the one who can boast of having accomplished the ruin of some friendless, unprotected Christian girl.[27]

Contrasting Images and the Question of Assimilation

It has been argued here that images of sexual impropriety mingled freely with ideas of Jewish sexual healthiness creating a seemingly unstable image of Jewish sexuality in Britain. The most obvious manifestation of this uncertainty about Jews and Jewish sex can be seen in contrasting thinking about whether or not it was desirable for Jews to assimilate with non-Jews in their British home.

Conditioned by ideas of Jewish intelligence, some late nineteenth and earlier twentieth century writers based their antipathy towards Jews around what they perceived as the Jewish refusal to assimilate. George Bernard Shaw argued in *The Revolutionist's Handbook* (1903), that Jewish refusal to mix in with the indigenous population was a major obstacle to the development of the "racial superman". The child of such a union, Shaw argued, "might be very superior to both his parents; but it is not likely that the Jewess would find the squire an interesting companion".[28] Eugenicist and politician Arnold White also based his hostility to Jews on the perceived Jewish refusal to blend with the societies in which they lived.

> No race or fragment of a race can be deemed English when their diet is foreign, their origin, oriental, when their ties with alien

107

co-religionists in other lands are closer than with Britons, and when, for successive generations, they have proudly declined to inter marry with the people of their adopted country.[29]

Historian Anthony Goldwin-Smith concurred that anti-Semitism was the fault of the Jews themselves for "refusing to mingle with humanity".[30]

However, other scholars and writers were not so keen for Jews to blend into the racial stream of the British nation. In one notorious comparative study of the potential of immigrant Jewish children, written by biometrician and mathematician Karl Pearson with Margaret Moul before the First World War but not published until 1925, a strong case was made against allowing Jewish immigrants to assimilate with their British neighbours. According to Moul and Pearson's findings, there was no evidence that the immigrant Jews would add anything positive to British racial stock and clear indications that they may damage it. Their research, taken from an examination of children at the Jews' Free School in Spitalfields, held that in categories of physical health, such as proneness to heart disease and eye quality, the Jewish immigrant children did not match up to their British peers. To Moul and Pearson, this inferiority was racial, not environmental, so that the implication was clear. "The welfare of our own country is bound up with the mainte-nance and improvement of its stock, and our researches do not indicate that this will follow the unrestricted admission of either Jewish or any other type of immigrant." Yet, in a display of the flexibility of Semitic discourse, Moul and Pearson also advised against Jewish immigration on the grounds that Jews never allowed themselves to be "absorbed". A refusal to assimi-late was, to the authors' minds, such a serious issue that it "might very reasonably be made a criterion of the fitness of a race for immigration into a settled country". Constructing Jews as immigrants who would resist sexual integration, Moul and Pearson argued that Jewish immigration needed to be halted: "...for men with no special ability — above all for such men as religion, social habits, or language keep as a caste apart, there should be no place".[31]

Here, therefore, in one report, it is possible to see the contra-dictions and incoherence of readings of Jewish sexual practice in this period. Just as Jews could be labelled as an example of sexual health and as terrible perverts and corruptors, so both the racial threat of sexual mixing with Jews and Jewish refusal to assimilate could be held up by Moul and Pearson as reasons to prevent further Jewish immigration into Britain.

Conclusion

In this terrain of conflicting images of Jewish sex, it is difficult to present any image or stereotype as dominant or definitive. At some levels, the inherent contradictions in Semitic discourse prevent any such analysis. Nonetheless, it is possible to some extent to loosely tie together these British sexual imaginings about Jews. For one thing, all the images have in common the idea that Jews were sexually different. The significance of this seemingly minor point should not be lost. In a period when the established British Jewish community was trying to fight off formal and informal discrimination, in the face of unprecedented numbers of Jewish immigrants arriving from Eastern Europe, many Britons were unready to perceive their new Jewish neighbours as similar to them. For better or worse they tended to see Jews as different, essentially "alien" in their practices and urges.

Thus, nearly all the sexual labelling of Jews discussed in this chapter owed something to perhaps the most persistent strain of Semitic discourse in this period; the idea that Jews were clannish, an alien nation living aloof within a nation, bonded to their own loyalties and rules. Either Jews were trying to undermine British racial stock by diluting it, or they were perpetuating their inherent differences by refusing to assimilate. Their sexual purity ensured their separation; their predatory and perverse natures indicated their distain for their non-Jewish neighbours. Amid the contradictions, Jews were consistently "sexualised", so that perceptions of Jewish sexual difference became an obstacle to Jewish assimilation in British society.

Chapter Nine
Polymorphous and Perverse:
Sex in Contemporary
British Jewish Novels
Peter Lawson

Introduction

Sex is prodigious in contemporary British Jewish novels. In this essay, I want to consider four novelists on this topic: Linda Grant, Howard Jacobson, Adam Thirlwell and Naomi Alderman.

As we shall see, Linda Grant tends to reaffirm gender stereotypes of tough, even macho, men and dominated, dependent women in order to reach a post-feminist reassertion of "femininity". By having her female protagonists make love with future and past members of the Israeli army — in *When I Lived in Modern Times* (2000) and *Still Here* (2002) respectively — Grant suggests a romantic allocation of gender roles which has traditionally been dismissed by feminist writers.

By contrast, Howard Jacobson tends to dismiss romance while exploring sexual excess in novels such as *Who's Sorry Now?* (2002) and *Kalooki Nights* (2006). Jacobson constructs a version of Jewish desire through outrageous writing which sometimes straddles the fuzzy line between pornography and eroticism. This is, perhaps, most shockingly evident in the S/M scenes of *Kalooki Nights* which take place in the Nazi death camp of Buchenwald.

Finally, I want to argue that a younger generation of Anglo-Jewish authors has successfully challenged a gendered opposition between heterosexual romance and polymorphous perversity. In *Politics* (2003) Adam Thirlwell has produced a post-romantic novel which both incorporates and parodies pornography. More recently, Naomi Alderman's *Disobedience* (2006) has depicted lesbian romance in an Orthodox Jewish milieu. Its queer scenarios suggest that polymorphously perverse sex and sexuality can complement Judaism and romance.

Linda Grant

Linda Grant is the author of three novels (*The Cast Iron Shore* [1996], *When I Lived in Modern Times* [2000] and *Still Here* [2002]) and three non-fiction works (*Sexing the Millennium*

[1993], *Remind Me Who I Am, Again* [1998] and *The People on the Street: A Writer's View of Israel* [2006]). All three novels feature Jewish protagonists, with the latter two tackling Jewish experiences in Europe, America and Israel. Of the three non-fiction works, *Remind Me Who I Am, Again* concerns retrieval of Jewish family memories while *The People on the Street: A Writer's View of Israel* surveys Israeli society through diasporic eyes. Like *The Cast Iron Shore*, *Sexing the Millennium* has an explicitly Jewish narrator but deals with a not explicitly Jewish subject.

What, then, is the relationship between the narrator of *Sexing the Millennium* and her ostensible subject matter? Firstly, it is autobiographical:

> The book you are reading is a personal story... I am a product of the sexual revolution. I grew up in Liverpool, my parents the newly middle-class children of working-class Jewish immigrants. Judaism, with its emphasis on justice and the redemptive work of social action, framed my moral world.

This autobiographical element leads Grant to note that sexual liberation in the twentieth century owes much to Jews. Alma Birk, for example, was instrumental in founding the landmark Sixties magazine *Nova*. Grant stresses that Birk's "upbringing, in a newly affluent Jewish family, had hammered into her the need for education in order to achieve economic stability and social advancement, underlined by the traditional Jewish respect for learning". Furthermore Freud, Herbert Marcuse and Wilhelm Reich merit places in Grant's cast of Jewish sexual revolutionaries. All were refugees from Nazi Germany. Grant also mentions the "Yippie Jerry Rubin's book *Do It!*, published in 1969" which links sexual "Puritanism" with "imperialism". In Rubin's worldview, repression is a version of Protestantism and sexual freedom of Jewishness.[1]

There is a tension at the heart of Grant's polemic in *Sexing the Millennium*. For while the narrator extols such libidinous liberation, she is also wary of the Sirens who call out for "polymorphously perverse" behaviour.[2] Such behaviour, as Freud defined it in *Three Areas on the Theory of Sexuality* (1905), appertains to the "infantile" stage of sexual development.[3] In Grant's understanding of Judaic imperatives, it implies an abdication of "the redemptive work of social action" and moral

111

engagement with politics and power. Grant judges "S/M" to be both "polymorphously perverse" and "an expression of the powerlessness of radical politics...with the failure of a generation to take charge of its own future". So, sexual experimentation becomes infantile in a book which claims to champion just that. In a purported study of the body's passions, Grant concludes that "sex is just the ghost of freedom". The corporeal is vapourised, only to become the "ghost" of Judaism's messianic hope for "Utopia". Instead of sex, *Sexing the Millennium* ends on a romantic note as it invokes the heart: "Perhaps sex is just the ghost of freedom but, until we have Utopia, it can speak eloquently of what the heart desires".[4]

Indeed, there is a strong strain of romance running through *Sexing the Millennium*. It accords well with the romance discernable in *When I Lived in Modern Times* and *Still Here*. Grant supports the notion of fundamental gender differences. This is why she can share her "hunch" that "women are attracted to power, men to youth and beauty". Further, she can discuss the relationship between pornography and the "Harlequin Romances and Mills and Boon bodice-rippers" in terms of gender. Whereas women are concerned with emotional questions such as "why is it that when I try to get close to you, you act like I'm trying to take something away from you?", men want to know things like "how important is penis size?"[5] Grant's women are creatures of sensibility, attracted to male power; whereas Grant's men are somatic presences drawn to "youth and beauty" and concerned with "penis size".

Significantly, this line of gender separation leads Grant to suspect a feminism which advocates "sensible" rather than sexy women. If women are essentially different from men, they should celebrate this difference in "fashion", cosmetics, "stilettos" and everything else that dowdy feminists reject.[6] Consequently, *When I Lived in Modern Times* and *Still Here* prioritise gender differences, romance and the paraphernalia of female performativity rather than simply somatic sex.

When I Lived in Modern Times won the Orange Prize for Fiction in 2000. It concerns the last years of the British imperial presence in Palestine, and the foundation of the State of Israel. The novel presents Zionism as an anti-colonial struggle, a fight for national self-determination in the face of oppressive British imperialism. It also offers a new type of Jewish man: "He's a very simple man, I

112

thought. He's like a Bauhaus building, straightforward". Strangely enough, this new type of Jew is also a stereotype. He is a soldier who militarily and sexually occupies "territory".[7] For the novel's protagonist, Evelyn Sert, he epitomises the sexiness of Zionism.

Appropriately, the soldier's name is Johnny. He is gendered through military behaviour and role models: "I always wanted to be a soldier", he tells Evelyn. "All my childhood heroes were Jewish warriors — King David, Spartacus, Ben Hur. I never loved the guys like Moses, the wise guys, the sages, the prophets. No, I read my Bible to see who in those olden days went to war for us Jews". War is "a man's business and if women get hurt that's a tragedy because they've managed to stumble into something that has nothing to do with them". Still, Evelyn does help Johnny in her female way to get some information: women too are "ideally placed to play our role". Unsurprisingly, Mills and Boon romance blossoms:

"Evelyn," he whispered. "Don't worry, I won't let any harm come to you."

"Yes, but who's going to protect you*?"*

"Don't worry about me. I'm a man. I protect myself. That's the order of things."

Just before I fell asleep, I [Evelyn] thought of Mrs Linz and pitied her, the new woman who had no need of any of this.[177]

Poor Mrs Linz is the doctrinaire feminist who sleeps alone, cuddling up to nothing but her bitterness. She is to be "pitied". Evelyn, by contrast, is sexually satisfied and safe in the arms of a Jewish soldier.

Still Here reproduces romance in a similar pattern. Here again, an Anglo-Jewish woman (Alix Rebick) meets a foreign Jew (Joseph Shields from America) and experiences sex with military associations (Joseph is a former Israeli soldier). Just as Joseph learned to "defend the Jews" in the Yom Kippur War, so he powerfully protects Alix. Though Alix considers herself a feminist, she also understands that "in the early stages of a relationship it is men who must be in control". She may "hate the passivity",[8] but she nonetheless accepts its rightful place in the mating game. Interestingly, romance and feminism are not presented as opposites in Grant's fiction and non-fiction.

Howard Jacobson

Howard Jacobson is the author of nine novels and four works of non-fiction, among which are *Roots Schmoots: Journeys Among*

Jews (1993), *Who's Sorry Now?* (2002) and *Kalooki Nights* (2006). Generally, his fictional protagonists are uncomfortable with romance; and this is explicitly associated with their Jewishness.

In *Who's Sorry Now?*, Marvin Kreitman is "a serial faller-in-love, a sentimental maker of goo-goo eyes". However, "because he was dark and shiny, with a complexion as polished as the carapace of a beetle, people took him to be a hunter and a carnivore. He was the victim of his appearance".[9] Kreitman would like to be romantic, but he is a "victim" and this disables him. It is left to his best friend, Charlie Merriweather, to have everything denied Marvin: a happy marriage, WASP Englishness, stability and self-love. Marvin embraces the opposites: an unhappy marriage, Jewishness, instability and self-hatred.

In relation to sex, however, Marvin seems to come up trumps, while his best friend is left feeling frustrated. Marvin explains to Charlie: "your marriage is fucking killing you. And I'll tell you which part of it is killing you — the nice-sex part. Fantasy, Charlie. Sex isn't nice". Since *Who's Sorry Now?* is very much about binary oppositions, it comes as no great surprise when Marvin and Charlie agree to swap wives and, in the process, sex lives. Yet despite this comic and clunky plot device, Marvin remains a victim of his desires. Sex for him is "sorrow, pain, talk — 'Tell me, tell me' — excrucation, vehemence, violence even". Embracing Charlie's frumpy wife, Marvin becomes besotted by the Great British power she symbolises: her "imperious heels" set him thinking of the Royal Family and "Camilla Parker Bowles". Like a colonised subject of the Empire, this Anglo-Jew is led through sexual fantasy "into painless but permanent captivity, her hand the collar and her arm the chain".[10] He is masochistically disempowered.

Kreitman is aware of his sexual submissiveness. The hilarious epilogue, or "Finale", features him in the dungeon of a dominatrix. Yet he also fights sexual victimisation through misogynistic and homophobic humour. For example, his intellectual and artistic daughter Cressida is derided for writing on "the iconography of 'black' in popular porno" while her "first show...looked to him like a whore's bedroom". Pornography and prostitution are Cressida's natural elements here. Her mother, Hazel, is similarly described as a "harlot-wife".[11]

Gays come off no better. Fearing "exclusion" from English culture, Kreitman is quick to displace his fears onto the figure of a gay courier, Nyman, and then onto gays in general. "I fear him [Nyman] as I fear clowns or madmen. They negate everything. They negate me, anyway", Marvin tells Charlie, before adding: "When everything else has been destroyed, two things will be left in control of the planet — cockroaches and camp".[12] If these homophobic words were applied to Jews, this novel would be anti-Semitic. Arguably, the unpleasant depiction of Kreitman is itself anti-Semitic.

Since Kreitman treats women as whores, he only respects other heterosexual men. However, because he feels "in sexual competition with everybody" he has "no male friends. It's a choice you make: either you go chasing women or you have friends". So, Kreitman is in thrall to his libidinous imagination ("His dick waited on his imagination"); and this imagination is sexually obsessional like pornography. Solipsistically, Kreitman deals with failed romance and its onanistic substitute:

> obsessional repetitiveness, on and on, page after page, hunting for
> that ideally disgusting image, the one that would give you every-
> thing, the one where the stranger's outlandish pose finally met,
> in every specific, all the prerequisites of your own deranged
> desires... the miracle of revealed porn.

Kreitman hates himself for being a failed romantic — a "victim of his appearance" in England — and for falling prey to all that England seems to allow him: estrangement and submission, sex and consumerism, "porno in a green leather Harrods magazine rack".[13]

Jacobson's most recent novel, *Kalooki Nights*, won the *Jewish Quarterly* Wingate Literary Prize for Fiction in 2007. Although it features the romance between an Orthodox Anglo-Jew and the daughter of a German immigrant, its focus on sex and sexuality is confined, for the most part, to the fantasy of a Nazi/Jewish relationship in a concentration camp. The narrator, Max Glickman, imagines an S/M bonding between the wife of the commandant of Buchenwald, Lisa Koch, and a Jewish prisoner, Mendel. He claims to conjure this fantasy because of exposure to the Holocaust and the consequent warping of his sexual predilections:

> Sex, surely, once we've put the animal state behind us, is an aber-
> ration, and therefore, for it to be sex at all, must thrive on

115

imbalance and reversal, on usurpation of the decencies, on disregard for what is usually owing. As civilised beings we cannot do without respect; as sexual beings we cannot do without the opposite. All of which might not tell you anything except that *The Scourge of the Swastika* fell into my hands too early.

The Scourge of the Swastika, we are reminded near the start of the novel, was Lord Russell of Liverpool's 1954 delineation of the Nazi death camps. It has shaped Max's sexuality. To be aroused, he now needs the "opposite" of "respect". Together with S/M scenes from Buchenwald, the reader is taken through Max's marriages to English women with German-sounding names: "Zoë, Chloë, Björk, Märike, Alÿs, and Kätchen". Comedically reflecting on this preference, Max remarks: "Good thing I never met Der Führer at an impressionable age". He knows full well that he is suffering from sexually-exciting "*Masochismus*":

> No doubt we both [Max and Chloë] had problems in the area of what popular psychologists call self-worth. We corroborated each other's damaged self-esteem. We stayed together for the time we did because, Jew to Gentile, Gentile to Jew, we were a confirmatory insult to each other.[14]

Max chooses wives who do not respect Jews because exposure to the Holocaust has made such disrespect sexually stimulating.

Needless to say, S/M fantasies around Nazis are not original. One has only to think, for example, of Liliana Cavani's popular mainstream movie *Il Portiere di Notte* (*The Night Porter*, 1974), starring Charlotte Rampling as a former concentration camp inmate, and Dirk Bogarde as an SS officer, and their resumption of an S/M relationship after the war. Jacobson adduces far more hardcore pornographic movies such as "*Love Camp 7 — All the youthful beauty of Europe enslaved for the pleasure of the Third Reich*" and "*Ilsa: She-Wolf of the SS*" to illustrate that Glickman is certainly not the only pervert on the Nazi block.[15]

Back in Buchenwald, Ilse is busy tormenting and stimulating Mendel. She is also treating him as "a Jew". Meanwhile, Glickman as narrator explains that "as a Jew, of course, I don't hear in the word *Jew* what the Gentile hears. And when I do hear it for myself I become what is known as a self-hating Jew". This leads the reader to surmise that "self-hating" — *within the confines of pornographic fantasy* — sexually delights

116

Glickman. This caveat is fundamental. Social self-hatred is strongly deplored in *Kalooki Nights*, together with the anti-Semitism of Gentiles. Max tells his Jewish friend Errol that all English women are anti-Semites: "They can't help it. They drink it in with their mother's milk". The result, as the closing sentence of the novel makes clear, is damaged lives. Beyond sexual fantasy, "it's your lives that are ruined" by the Holocaust and its aftermath.[16]

Adam Thirlwell

Adam Thirlwell's debut novel, *Politics*, appeared to critical acclaim in 2003 and Thirlwell was duly hailed by *Granta* magazine as one of the twenty "Best of Young British Novelists". According to the British Council Arts website, "*Politics* is a gently humourous and inventive novel about love, relationships, sex and romance".[17] This is broadly right: the novel combines "sex and romance" with aplomb. By foregrounding pornography and its intimate manifestations within a romantic relationship, *Politics* fuses what Grant and Jacobson had torn asunder. *Politics* presents gender politics for a younger generation, apparently less divided in its perspectives on romance and pornography.

From the novel's first sentence — "As Moshe tried, gently, to tighten the pink fluffy handcuffs surrounding his girlfriend's wrists, he noticed a tiny frown"– the reader is plunged into a world of kinky eroticism. With postmodern playfulness, Thirlwell later announces: "the Marquis de Sade was not an expert in kinkiness. He was too theoretical. When it comes to kinkiness in prose, I am a better writer than the Marquis de Sade".[18] This is a double-joke, firstly because of its novitiate chutzpah and secondly since Thirlwell's approach to kinkiness is itself, if not theoretical, at least highly cerebral. This author wants to explicate sex and its polymorphously perverse games.

Note too the Jewish name, Moshe, and the playfulness with which it is explained to a British readership:

> Moshe's name is difficult. It is a very Jewish name... Perhaps you do not know how this name should be pronounced. Possibly, you have not had a Jewish upbringing. Well, I will tell you. Moshe is pronounced 'Moisha'. That is how you pronounce it. You see? I don't want this to be private at all.

117

Just as Jewishness is not a "private" matter in Thirlwell's political *Weltanschauung*, so romance is eased away from its Mills and Boon connotations of hermetic coupledom. Jews and sex are presented as properly public subjects. "Romances", the narrator explains, "are complicated". To hammer home the point, he introduces a *ménage à trois* and counsels that "there is no need to romanticise the love triangle".[19] This does not entail the jettisoning of romance, but rather its contextualization in eroticism and the body politic.

Nor do the repetitive descriptions of Moshe's sex life with Nana and Anjali extol a version of pornography. On the contrary, their very repetitiveness dulls the reader's mind. As the narrator remarks: "I know what you are thinking. You are thinking that you have had quite enough of their sex life. You want something else entirely". He is right. Like pornography, imaginative writing about sex becomes tiresome. Thirlwell parodies pornography by stressing its ultimate tediousness. The narrator is striving to move beyond both romance and pornography. He states: "I hate pornography, I hate its magic realism". Anjali is similarly "bored" by it.[20]

Thirlwell is writing about sex for political reasons. He invokes the Surrealists who "thought that talking honestly about sex was a necessary beginning to the creation of a just and perfect society. They thought it was the first political step". Further, sex is conceived as anti-Nazi and therefore feasibly philo-Semitic. Sex for Moshe is "the triumph of the underdog". While fucking, he tells Nana about the Nazi occupation of France because "Moshe was scared of the Nazis". Thus, Moshe's *ménage à trois* represents liberation on three related fronts: romantic, pornographic and Jewish. It is, we are told, "not just a sexual thing. It is not just a pre-Nazi decadent thing". It is political freedom on a minor, and therefore emotionally major, "domestic" stage.[21]

"Nationality is a romance", and "like romance, nationality does not exist". One good reason for critiquing romance in *Politics* is simultaneously to critique nationalism. Both offer delusional and destructive closure. Linda Grant's *When I Lived in Modern Times* is an extended love letter to Israel *as well as* a romantic novel. This, as they say, is no coincidence. By contrast, *Politics* has its focus on whoever does not "worry about his nation". This is not to suggest that Thirlwell's novel is anti-British or anti-Zionist. Rather, *Politics* is concerned with "diaspora", or those people who are "living abroad". Israel is recognised as the "personal homeland" of many Jews, but Nana remains interested in "one adorable Jew in particular". Her notion of romance respects nationhood but does not ally itself with nationalism. This is romance tempered by a deep scepticism of romanticised nationalism. It is from this sceptical perspective that we can begin to understand references to the national romances of totalitarian Nazism, Stalinism and Maoism which pepper the text of *Politics*.[22]

Naomi Alderman

Naomi Alderman's debut novel *Disobedience* was awarded the Orange Award for New Writers in 2006. It was a landmark in British Jewish fiction, being the first lesbian novel to be set in London's Orthodox Jewish milieu. Like *Politics*, it features a love triangle — though not quite a *ménage à trois* — and challenges social orthodoxies through sexual desire.

Disobedience juxtaposes the strict order of ritualised Orthodox life in Hendon, North London, with *"desires"*. As Ronit, the British Jew who has returned from years in New York, walks "through Golders Green, passing by the rows of Jewish stores", she thinks about "how God, belief in God, in this God, has done *violence* to these people. Has warped them and bent them so that they can't even acknowledge any longer that they have *desires*, let alone learn how to act on them". To be sure, such "repression" is not presented as wholly Jewish. Rather, it is imagined as a sort of unholy alliance between the British "stiff upper lip" and "the Jewish fear of being noticed". The British Jewish Orthodox community which Alderman depicts is characterised by "reticence" as much because it is British as Jewish: "These British Jews were British — they shuffled awkwardly, looked at their feet and drank tea".[23]

Ronit's resumption of a lesbian affair with Rabbi Dovid Kuperman's wife, Esti, shatters this Anglo-Jewish silence and highlights what has been rendered culturally "invisible". Lesbian love dares to speak its name when Esti announces to assembled Orthodox dignitaries that she has "desired that which is forbidden to me", and adds for good measure: "I continue to desire it". Significantly, Alderman sees similarities in being gay and Jewish:

> You don't choose it, that's the first thing. If you are, you are. There's nothing you can do to change it... The second thing is that both those states — gayness, Jewishness — are invisible.

Which makes it interesting. Because while you don't have a choice about what you *are*, you have a choice about what you show. You always have a choice about whether you "out" yourself.

Sexual and ethnic frankness are related in so far as they may be repressed or expressed. The latter is the course of Alderman's novel and its lesbian protagonists. When Dovid takes up his role as religious leader of the Orthodox community, with Esti as his publicly lesbian wife, romance and polymorphous perversity finally find a fictional place within mainstream Judaism.[24]

Conclusion

This essay has surveyed some sexual concerns of contemporary British Jewish novelists. Although such concerns are related to ethnicity, it should be stressed that they are by no means restricted to Jewish novelists. Ian McEwan, Pat Barker and Alan Hollinghurst are among a host of British novelists focusing on sex and sexuality today.[25] Nor is it a new development. Simon Blumenfeld in *Jewboy* (1935), Bernice Rubens in *Madame Sousatzka* (1962) and Clive Sinclair in his collection of short-stories *Hearts of Gold* (1980) represent some of the lineage of British Jewish fiction featuring sex. Further, much remains to be explored on this subject in contemporary British Jewish drama and poetry. The playwright Patrick Marber and poet Joanne Limburg, for instance, are fascinating in this regard. My essay offers only a fragment of what deserves to be studied in wider generic, ethnic and national contexts.

Chapter Ten
"Barbie's Jewish roots":
Jewish Women's Bodies and Feminist Art
Lisa E. Bloom

Introduction

This chapter examines some of the possibilities and problems currently haunting the subject of Jewish participation in the making and the history of feminist art in the United States and the United Kingdom and the explicit role gender, the body, and sexuality plays in these concerns. Sander Gilman's work on *Difference and Pathology* (1985) and the *Jew's Body* (1991) is critical here since he argues that abject sex is used historically to mark Jewishness as "other". He charts this history in his analysis of the sexualization of nineteenth-century urban prostitutes in Europe examining how Jewish women were marked as both lower class and sexually abject. Gilman's work on tracing the history of anti-Semitic discourses that associated Jewish identity with disease, a pathological sexuality, and non-middle-class status is provocative and has not been adequately explored in relation to women and feminist art to understand how the renegotiation of Jewish feminist artists also entailed an examination of issues of their class and sexuality.

Sexuality is understood to encompass how people experience and express themselves as sexual beings. As Michel Foucault wrote in *The History of Sexuality, Vol. 1: The Will to Knowledge* (1976), the concept of what activities and sensations are "sexual" is historically (as well as regionally and culturally) determined, and it is therefore part of a changing "discourse". He goes on to explain that the construction of sexual meanings is an instrument by which social institutions (religion, the educational system, psychiatry) control and shape human relationships.

Following Foucault, this chapter discusses the way artists raise questions about the regulation of Jewish women's, and, in some cases, gay men's bodies and sexualities through both historical anti-Semitic discourses, as outlined by Gilman, as well as more recent ones, and the visual strategies they employ to articulate Jewish self-consciousness and engage with aesthetic questions. Jewishness in the context of this chapter stands for a cultural identity rather than a strictly defined religious one, and for a shifting set of historically diverse experiences rather than a unified and monolithic notion of Jewishness. This piece will also draw on research completed in my book, *Jewish Identities in American Feminist Art: Ghosts of Ethnicity* (2006), that examines the unacknowledged but powerful roles of assimilation and Jewish identity in US Jewish feminist art, but will take further some of its insights in relation to the new context established by this anthology. The artists' whose art work I will discuss include Rhonda Lieberman (USA), Deobrah Kass (USA), Rachel Garfield (UK) and Ruth Novaczek (UK).

Until the 1990s, public discussions of Jewishness and sexual identities in the New York art world were very rare given how the arts at that time were dominated by a white, heterosexual male power structure. Given the power of the anti-Semitic discourses which Gilman writes about and which underscore the idea that Jewishness was seen as an undesirable pathology, the anxiety about making Jewishness visible was felt widely among secular Jewish-Americans particularly in the second half of the twentieth century following the Shoah, and continues to create a generational fault line among Jewish artists and critics of both genders. To expose the erasure of Jews and their sexuality in the art world in 1991 and the artists' own participation in that, artists Rhonda Lieberman and Cary Leibowitz put together a landmark exhibition titled *Fear of a Jewish Planet: Let my People Show!* at Four Walls Gallery in Brooklyn, New York. This was followed in 1996 by a major exhibition and catalogue curated by Norman Kleeblatt appropriately titled *Too Jewish?: Challenging Traditional Identities,* presented at the Jewish Museum in New York. Part of what made both exhibitions so important was that it touched on the issue of how Jews historically were trying to pass as non-Jews not only in the art world but also for each other, at a time that the AIDS pandemic and the culture wars were dividing art communities in the United States around the issue of homosexuality. Some Jewish artists were out in the art world if they were homosexuals or lesbians but somehow it wasn't acceptable for them to be out also as Jews.

Rhonda Lieberman and Deborah Kass: Popular Culture as a Therapeutic Ally

Rhonda Lieberman, a New York artist and essayist who had her work exhibited in the *Too Jewish* exhibition in 1996, scripts herself very much in terms of her suburban Jewish-American identity. The Jewish values set forth in her parents' home were intensely secular and liberal but, as she puts it, "It was okay to be a 'person of the book' as long as you made a good living!" When she entered the doctoral programme at Yale, she deviated from familial expectations since a career as an academic was not considered lucrative enough. What is significant about the artwork and writing of Lieberman, is the way her work consciously keeps the tension of what she refers to as the "conflicted space" alive, and how she refers to it as an integral part of her "Jewish experience". This tension is then presented visually in her provocatively titled *Chanel Hanukkah* from 1991, which she did for the *Fake Chanel* show with gay artist Cary Leibowitz.

In this work, the artists teamed up to take on the constructed image of Jewish women and gay men as the embodiments of a vulgar and un-erotic Jewish materialistic identity and to parody this stereotype by using overt Jewish content as well as designer products as part of their strategy. Using a fake Chanel bag, they fashioned a Hanukkah *menorah* from it using nine designer lipsticks as substitutes for candlesticks. The force of the work comes

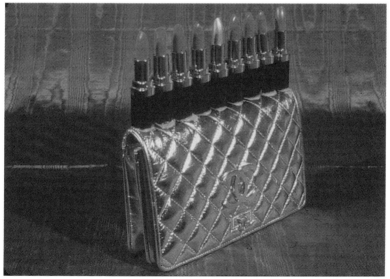

Rhonda Lieberman and Cary Leibowitz, Chanel Hanukkah, mixed media, 1991. Courtesy of the artist.

from its subversion of the sacredness of the Jewish holiday by eroticising the *menorah* through material consumer objects that are associated with fashion rather than religion. In addition, there is a tension between critical distance and humour in the work. The artists express how they are caught between self-identifying as secular Jews and feeling entrapped by derogatory stereotypes of secular Jews as materialistic. Indeed, in this artwork Lieberman and Liebowitz are trying to open up another space of Jewishness outside of the religion from which they can throw stereotypes of being "conspicuous consumers" back at the audience, at the same time, they express a more ironic Jewish identity through this kind of public gesture.

Such is also the case with her *Jewish Barbie* series a humorous lament over a frustrated Jewish princess who has "body image issues" and undergoes a "healing journey" to repair her sense of self. Ran in "Glamor Wounds", the provocative column that launched her career at *Art Forum*, her satirical narrative details the life of Jewish Barbie a creation spawned from the story that Barbie was invented by a Jewish woman, Ruth Handler, and was named after her daughter Barbara. Dissatisfied with the depressing "real" story of Barbie, Lieberman writes her a new origin story:

> ...born, in 1959, in a parallel universe an *Other*. Barbie emerged with all the qualities *repressed* from the Barbie we have come to know in our one reality system; for example: Barbie — blond, Jewish Barbie — brunette or frosted; Barbie — no thighs, Jewish Barbie — thighs; Barbie — mute, Jewish Barbie — whines incessantly about perceived injustices. Jewish Barbie is not evil, merely *repressed*; the conscious system we call "reality" can't recall where it has stored her information.[1]

Fascinated by the idea of "Barbie's Jewish roots", Lieberman tells a satirical narrative about this "other" Barbie, though traumatised by birth she eventually succeeds to become "a beaconness of Jewish glamor in a world hostile to multitalented strong women".[2] The piece conveys a wry and ironical story about the set of choices that propelled Jewish Barbie to come to terms with her psychological and physical alienation from a materialistic, normalised Barbie, using tongue in cheek humour to mock any simple notion of "liberation" in her attempts to repair her psyche/sense of self from what is after all a plastic

*Rhonda Lieberman, Portrait of Rhonda Lieberman, photo credit: Dana
Byerly, 1995. Courtesy of the artist.*

character. After all, Jewish Barbie, like Barbie herself, is a plastic character.

Deborah Kass is an appropriation artist who, along with
Lieberman, was a key participant in the Jewish Museum's *Too*

Rhonda Lieberman, Barbie Chocolate Bar (in Hebrew), photo credit: Dana Byerly, 1995. Courtesy of the artist.

Jewish show. Kass shares with Lieberman a certain sensibility about Jewishness, but she extends it to critique some of the assumptions implicit in the cool Pop Art aesthetic of the 1960s and its legacy, particularly in terms of Andy Warhol's work. Warhol made art about commodity culture that brought together actresses that were sex symbols such as Marilyn Monroe and Liz Taylor, as well as politician's wives such as Jackie Kennedy, as cultural icons. He would start with an iconic and glamorous photographic image and then print multiple versions of it in a colourful grid. Kass questions the very context of Warhol's work. She asks: for whom are these images iconic and for whom are

126

they not? Though Warhol did a whole series of Jewish intellectuals and celebrities as well as other portraits of Jewish collectors, Kass also questions why Warhol left out equally iconic female stars from his period that did not conform to his notion of American feminine beauty and erotic sex appeal.

Kass imitates the format of Warhol's celebrity portraits to make us see what most artists and critics have failed to notice about his work: that he excluded from his 1960s cosmopolitan Hollywood register the one major female star whom he frequently cites in his diaries as the embodiment of bad taste, in Warhol's words, "a nouvelle riche" — Barbra Streisand. Given Warhol's own modest background and subsequent rise to fame, his comment makes one wonder why he was so particularly troubled by Streisand's similar shift in social class, and why he saw her as incapable of being seen as unglamorous, Kass's rendition of Barbra in her ironically titled, *The Jewish Jackie Series* is not only is meant to point out Warhol's refusal to engage with Barbra in his work, but also pays homage to Barbra Streisand, a cultural figure that had a particular resonance for Kass (as well as for

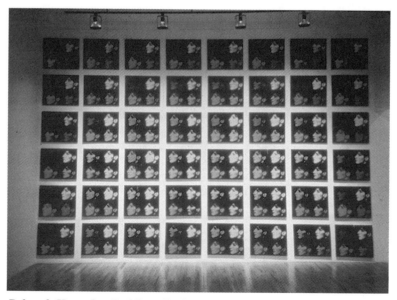

Deborah Kass, detail of Four Barbras, 48 Times, *from* The Jewish Jackie Series, *silkscreen ink and acrylic on canvas, 1992. Courtesy of the artist.*

127

Lieberman) growing up as a Jewish girl on Long Island: "She [Barbra] was really in touch with her difference as an attribute. It was fantastic. For me it was as if she was saying: I'm me; I'm not changing my nose; I am not changing my name; I'm not changing my ethnicity. I know how glamorous that can be".[3]

What appealed to Kass was the way Barbra unapologetically flaunted her sexuality and her Jewishness together and that made her a new kind of star that she could relate to. For Kass, the combination of Barbra's looks and her own understanding of her appearance, talent and brains — created a new kind of cultural and erotic power. Because Kass identifies with Barbra as iconic of Jewish glamour, someone who publicly presented herself in a way that shifted the norms of female beauty and sexuality during the period when Kass was growing up — her "appropriation" is an ironic commentary on her relation, as an artist, to the legacy of Pop Art and Warhol as it relates to Jewishness and

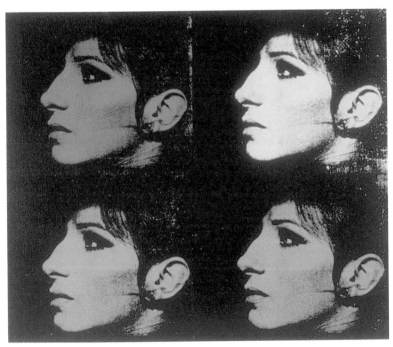

Deborah Kass, Four Barbras, from The Jewish Jackie Series, silkscreen ink and acrylic on canvas, 1992. Courtesy of the artist.

128

dominant norms of acceptable femininity, social class, and ways of behaving publicly that express desire and sexuality.

Issues of Subjectivity and Sexuality in Britain: Rachel Garfield and Ruth Novaczek

It was also in the 1990s that British Jewish women artists felt more confident in dealing with their Jewishness in a more direct way. The landmark 1996 show in Britain *Rubies and Rebels: Jewish Female Identity in Contemporary British Art* was exhibited at the Barbican Centre in London and at the University of Leeds. It was also the subject of a conference and influential special issue of the journal *Issues in Architecture Art and Design* entitled "Gender, Religion, and Ethnicity: Jewish Women in the Visual Arts" (1998). Comparing the British exhibit to the American one: *Too Jewish*, Monica Bohm-Duchen, the curator wrote:

> The absence of humour, evident in the work of many Jewish writers in this country, was duly noted, both by us, the curators, in the course of our researches, and by others. How much this has to do with the visual arts in general lending themselves less readily to an exploration of the comic aspects of life, and how much to a lack of the brazen, ironic and confident self-mockery characteristic of contemporary American Jewish artists (and by implication, American Jewry as a whole) — must remain open to question.[4]

Norman Kleeblatt, the curator of *Too Jewish*, reminded a British audience that *Too Jewish* was influenced not just by the confidence of American Jews but the influence of a series of exhibits in New York that focussed on identity issues, including exhibits such as "Extended Sensibilities" that focussed on gay issues in the arts at the height of the AIDS pandemic and the culture wars in the United States. For Bohm-Duchen, "in the present cultural climate (itself of course the product of a very different history), an exhibition such as the [*Too Jewish* exhibition] would be unthinkable in Britain",[5] citing the most critical review of her own show, which she claims uncomfortably reminded her of the anti-Semitic and anti-American response to the Kitaj retrospective at the Tate in 1994.

Rachel Garfield, one of the artists in the *Rubies and Rebels* exhibition, is one of the few artists in Britain to foreground her Jewishness in her work and has written at length about Jewish artists such as herself and Ruth Novaczek and others, who acknowledge their identity as Jews in their art making. Throughout Rachel Garfield's writing and art practice, the fabric of Jewish identity has been interwoven with the complex formations of anti-Semitic discourses and how they form Jewish subjectivity in contemporary Britain. In *Unmade up* (2002) Garfield records the reactions she received when interviewing Jews about their feelings towards dating other Jews. Her artwork is a large video installation featuring a series of self-portraits of the artist where Garfield moves between presentations of her private and public self. In part of the tape's loop that is continuous, Garfield appears as the cultural critic using headphones as she listens to the responses of her interviewees. However, her self-presentation is not static as she also functions as a transfer point of sorts for the Jewish women that are being referenced by her male subjects. In this sense, she is both subject and object of the gaze, looking at various moments pensive and other moments sexually available.

The comments taken from the twelve people she interviewed for this project range from the stereotypical to the ridiculous and many of the comments often contradict each other. Jewish women are criticised by the Jewish men interviewed for their conventional notions of identity and narrow bourgeois middle-

Rachel Garfield, Still from Unmade Up, 2002.
Courtesy of the artist.

Rachel Garfield, Still from Unmade Up, 2002.
Courtesy of the artist.

class values. Jewish women are seen as "middle-class girls that don't like to take risks", but another voice claims that they are "unstable but become transformed when they became married". Another explains that he "put a ring on her finger and she turned into the exorcist". For most of the men Jewish women were "too Jewish" in the wrong way: retrograde, narrow, rule-ridden and authoritarian and many of the men, as well as the women, who were interviewed, were eager to place as much distance as possible between themselves and the Jewish community by marrying a British man or woman.

It is significant that Garfield deliberately refuses to present herself in a visually appealing way and the jarring self-portraits are a deliberate part of Garfield's critical style. Her self-portraits are too close to the camera and her pose is deliberately one of exaggeration. Thus, these anti-aesthetic self-portraits with their physical excess is meant to deliberately fall outside the traditional concepts of acceptable middle-class British female beauty and sexuality and which are referenced as desirable by the Jewish men in the tape. Her work is also deliberately meant as a critique of the documentary form and her tape refuses to speak about Jewish women on their behalf through a first-person testimonial in which she presents herself as the "authentic subject", or illuminates their "truth" from a safe distance. In this way, the viewer is not given the satisfaction of hearing from a first person narrative a heart-felt account regarding an experience derived from anti-Semitic hate speech. Indeed, we never get a direct reaction from Garfield regarding what she thinks of what is spoken — thus she avoids presenting herself as a victim, but at the same time she sets up a tension between the viewer and viewed that can't be easily resolved since her work refuses to make claims about safe notions of community and ethnic insiderism.

Throughout the tape, Garfield creates a subject — the British Jewish woman — that seems to be crushed under the weight of the anti-Semitic discourses of Jewish men directed towards Jewish women within the community. The desired Jewish woman's sexuality as discussed by the men seems to conform more to the one-reality system of the British version of Ruth Handler's Barbie than Rhonda Lieberman's more enlightened version of *Jewish Barbie*. Garfield's work evokes questions regarding the alienation and marginality experienced by Jewish women and the racial dis-identification that might emerge from such discourses in its interest in the distinction between the visible and invisible other fundamental to the position of Jews in the contemporary West. In this respect, Garfield's work deliberately recalls that of the light-skinned African-American performance artist, Adrian Piper, whose performance work draws on the indeterminacy of race and raises questions about what it means for someone like herself to pass as white in the New York art world of the 1970s and 1980s where being a darker skinned black could have destroyed her hopes for a career as an artist.[6] Garfield is also interested in what it means for Jews to go public with their Jewishness in the British art world, but she programmes dissonances — between the shifting self-portraits of herself and the voiceovers to create another kind of uncertainty, revealing the way that Jews specifically — both men and women — can also feel unsafe and distrustful about each other within the Jewish community itself, an issue also raised by the work exhibited in the *Too Jewish* exhibition.

Like Garfield's work, Ruth Novaczek's *Rootless Cosmopolitans* (1990), as well as some of her later work, also deals critically with issues of Jewish subjectivity in Britain, and she is one of the first artists in Britain to interrogate issues of Jewish identity along such lines. However, the style of the two women is completely different. Novaczek has a more cinematic sensibility than Garfield — her work borrows more from art house cinema and includes influences Wong Kar Wai, Derek Jarman and Jean-Luc Godard. Garfield's work by contrast borrows more from art world conventions of New York feminist performance art from the 1970s and the rewriting of that history by feminist art historians and cultural critics such as Amelia Jones and Judith Butler, as well as important critical writing on race, post-colonialism and nation coming out of Britain by writers such as Stuart Hall, Paul Gilroy and others. Both women play with humour in their work, but fantasy plays a more important part in Novaczek's work. What draws these two women together is their focus on Jewish women directly as subjects and a multicultural perspective situated in response to the prevailing narratives of difference in the visual arts in Britain. This preoccupation comes through in some of their shared visual strategies that one can see in their work by the way both artists self-consciously shift the ways Jews might look in their work by positioning their Jewish subjects amongst and in relation to other cultures, as evidenced in Garfield's *So You Think You Can Tell* (2000) and Novaczek's *Rootless Cosmopolitans*.

Characteristic of Novaczek's style is the way that humour and fantasy comes through in the energy Novaczek puts into her film's sound track, as dialogue and music often carries equal weight in her work with the visuals. The images and voices of women in Novaczek's work are often seductive, fragmentary, and haunting; her soundtrack can at times be poetic as informed by the Beat poets or direct and funny as influenced by Jewish comedians as when she introduces her main character, Lily Klein, in *Rootless Cosmopolitans*: "Take Lily Klein, a real Princess. She didn't have real estate, she didn't have media control. She drank".

"Growing up in Americana" is the umbrella theme for a series of short films that Novaczek made between 1998 and 2005 during a period that she spent in New York. Most of these films are quite short — at around five minutes each — and are striking for the rawness of their soundtrack that combines American popular music, fractured voices from the media and her own gravelly seductive voice. References to the United States repeatedly turn up in her soundtracks throughout her work, as in her use of American voiceovers and urban US landscapes, as in *Series 2* from 1999 in which the humour is the most parodic and her imagery the most irreverent among all her tapes. In this tape she delights in the "too Jewish" kitschy humour of US public culture — the jokes of Jackie Mason and Barbra Streisand.

The restlessness of her films and soundtrack from this group of films is evident in the following sequence of visual found footage and verbal non-sequiturs found in *Series 2*. Garfield, an astute critic of Novaczek's work also gives weight to this film, and the description of this particular sequence is highlighted in Garfield's own writing on Novaczek's.[7] Novaczek's *Series 2* starts with a degraded image of the Statue of Liberty, with a voice-over of the US comedian Jackie Mason "you know you look Jewish, you *dreck*, you look Jewish, you'll be lucky if you don't get hit by a truck *shticks*". Mason continues, "they don't mind if you sound Jewish but look Jewish forget it!" From Mason, Novaczek jumps to the somewhat hysterical voice of Streisand that repeats a number of times a phrase from the film *The Way We Were* "I'm also taking a course in laughing and I'm studying Protestant cookery" with alternate images of a white-bread sandwich cut in half, hen quarters, an image of Woody Allen about to eat a chicken leg, a can of *tcholent*, and a Mexican cowboy on a horse with a guitar strapped to him.

In Novaczek's chaotic imagery of fast-cut images of food and other found imagery of a degraded urban landscape clearly identified as from New York, the energy of the tape makes New York City appear as a promised land where British Jewish women can align their interests with a community that shares a similar diasporic sensibility, a level of comfort with a gritty and sometimes scary urban landscape combined with a sense of kitschy Jewish-American humour. Thus, New York is envisioned as a space that enables the viewer the experience of cinematic pleasure and identification, whereas in much of her later work the scenes often shift from London, to New York, to Italy, to the Middle East and it is often difficult to tell where it is being filmed to underscore her point that her body of work is about being uprooted and the tapes are also about conjuring a feminist Jewish community out of diaspora.

A powerful female sexuality and energy seeps out of her film in the way her urban landscapes are eroticised and through the sensuousness of the images and soundtrack, and in this respect she transforms imagery and sound that might be ordinarily

134

Ruth Novaczek, Still from Sense, 2005. (Growing up in Americana trilogy, 2002-2005). Courtesy of the artist.

Ruth Novaczek, Still from Series 2, 2000. (Growing up in Americana trilogy, 2002-2005). Courtesy of the artist.

associated with a more masculinist tradition of avant-garde art cinema and pop music into something more feminist and transgressive. Using this unexpected visual and verbal vocabulary, her films manage to convey that Jewish women's desires are no longer limited to the narrow patriarchal world with its conventional heterosexual and national boundaries. At the same time there remains a poignantly sad overlay to most of her films of the long shadow cast by British culture's erasure of Jewish difference and Jewish women's sexuality. This otherwise unacknowledged "ghost" contributes to the haunting and restless style of most her films.

Conclusion

I want to conclude with an image from one of Kass' new paintings titled ironically "Oh God I Need This Show" (2007) which draws its aesthetics from an American modernist painter Barnett Newman, heavily influenced by the aesthetic positions of Clement Greenberg, and derives its incongruous text from the first song in the 1970s play "A Chorus Line", the first Broadway play in the United States ever to feature a character who was out as a homosexual. Thus, in a single gesture, Kass reiterates the ongoing problems and difficulties that remain for women artists in negotiating their Jewishness and sexuality within a tradition

Deborah Kass, Oh God I Need This Show, oil on canvas, 2007. Courtesy of the artist.

of aesthetic practices that remains hostile to bringing together the complex and disparate influences and traditions that matter most to these artists. Indeed, for feminist visual cultural critics like myself writing in a post-identity moment where questions of difference signal divisiveness rather than ways to think through tensions and disagreements, the problem of how to conceptualise US and British Jewish feminist artists as visual producers remains unresolved and hard to write about. By complicating notions around Jewish feminist art and identities and sexualities, the artists' work that I have discussed trouble a pervasive reticence on the topic in both the United States and the United Kingdom even at a moment of a revived interest in feminist art.

Chapter Eleven
Ira Stigman's "Jewish Salami":
Sex and Self-Hatred in the Work of Henry Roth
Alan Gibbs

[H]e was only a Jew because he *had* to be a Jew; he hated being a Jew; he didn't want to be one, saw no virtue in being one.[1]

In a review of *A Diving Rock on the Hudson*, the second volume of Henry Roth's *Mercy of a Rude Stream* series, Mary Gordon criticises the way in which this autobiographical novel reveals that the protagonist and his sister are conducting an incestuous adolescent sexual relationship. Chief amongst Gordon's concerns are that Roth's sister was still alive when the book was published, a fact which apparently did not trouble Roth. More tellingly, perhaps, Gordon is uncomfortable about the "tenuous web" constructed by Roth, "connecting his writing, his sin, and his Jewishness".[2] Gordon finds herself unable to account for the range of connections Roth makes in the first two novels of the series between writing, sex, guilt, and Jewishness. When Roth addresses the latter, for example, Gordon discerns a "veil... over his eyes, vital connections aren't made, vital admissions are glossed over."[3] The following essay contends that with the publication of two subsequent novels in the series, the various connections Roth makes become stronger, more meaningful, and less tenuous. Taken as a whole, the published series of four volumes provides a rich insight into the sexual guilt which blighted Roth's life, and warped both his feelings about his Jewishness and his ability to write.

Mention of Roth's writing career is germane, since he is known as much for the sixty-year hiatus in his writing career as for what he produced. Roth's writing career stalled at the age of 28, following the publication of *Call It Sleep*. Until the 1994 publication of his second novel, *A Star Shines Over Mt. Morris Park* — the first volume of the *Mercy* series — he published only a scattering of short stories. Roth's blighted efforts to write are clearly connected to the links he perceives between his Jewishness and feelings of sexual guilt.

Roth was born in Tysmenitz, Galitzia, in 1906, but he and his mother joined his father in New York a year-and-a-half later. They lived in Brownsville, Brooklyn, then Manhattan's Lower East Side, before moving to a mainly gentile area of East Harlem in 1914. Roth described the homogenously Jewish Lower East Side as a "very secure enclave",[4] but amongst the Italians and Irish of Harlem he claims to have "felt outnumbered and defeated from the start",[5] retreating into the home and growing "fat with the lack of activity."[6] Roth's Jewish identity, which had begun to flourish in the Lower East Side, was severely challenged by the move to Harlem, and in later years he was prone to suggest this as one reason for his stalled writing career. Removed from the Lower East Side, Roth claims to have felt isolated from Jewish culture, a source of inspiration in writing *Call It Sleep*. Significantly, *Mercy of a Rude Stream* begins precisely at the point where the family has moved from lower Manhattan to Harlem, and with Ira's consequent lament: "If it had only happened a few years later… if only he could have had, could have lived a few more years on the Lower East Side".[7] It is tempting, given the revelations contained in the *Mercy* series, to dismiss the effects on Roth of the childhood move to Harlem as a smoke-screen, concealing the true explanation: Roth's residual and persistent guilt regarding his adolescent sexual acts. This would be erroneous, however, and as the following suggests, Roth's feelings of being removed from his Jewish roots are in fact problematically bound up with his troubled sexuality.

Roth's was a tough childhood, enduring the attentions of a domineering and unstable father whilst growing up in an area often hostile to Jews. It also included a harsh introduction to sexuality. At the age of nine or ten, Roth was abducted and sexually abused by an adult male, an incident that appears to have played obsessively on the older Roth's mind. Around two years later, when Roth was aged twelve and his younger sister Rose was ten, their alleged incestuous sexual experimentation began. And in 1924, when Roth would have been aged eighteen, he apparently began also to have sex with his younger cousin Sylvia, then only eleven. These acts of incest and the associated guilt, only revealed around seventy years later in Roth's *Mercy* series, are a second reason adduced by Roth for his failure to continue his career as a novelist after *Call It Sleep*. Roth not only felt so fractured as an individual by these experiences that he was unable to write, but

139

continuing the semi-autobiographical narrative of *Call It Sleep* beyond the childhood years would have forced him to confront the issue of incest before he was ready to do so.

Roth's life during his early twenties comprised an uneasy admixture of Jewish and gentile worlds. Whilst a student at City College New York, Roth continued to live at home, but experienced continued and increasing alienation from his Jewish background. This was partly caused by new possibilities emerging before him. Roth had become friends with fellow student, Lester Winter, a middle-class Jew whom Roth had initially taken for a gentile, so awed was he by Winter's accomplishments and refinement. By their sophomore year, Winter was conducting an affair with Eda Lou Walton, an NYU instructor more than ten years his (and Roth's) senior. Walton, a specialist in modernist poetry, was initially enamoured of Winter's writing accomplishments, before his dilettantism became apparent and she transferred her affections to Roth and his genuine artistic potential. Over the following few years, including the period during which he wrote *Call It Sleep*, Walton fulfilled for Roth a role that encompassed muse, lover, and maternal figure.

The influence of both Winter and Walton on Roth was profound, not least in introducing Roth to the works of T. S. Eliot and Joyce, whilst on a wider level presenting him with the hitherto unsuspected vibrancy of American gentile culture. Roth himself characterised this period of his life as a shuttling between two worlds, the Jewish and the gentile, a process which became increasingly difficult to accomplish without experiencing qualms. Hana Wirth-Nesher observes that this "boundary crossing, as the character moves out of his Jewish domestic world into an American public space", becomes a crucial theme of the *Mercy* series.[8] As he is introduced to the gentile, patrician milieu of Edith (Walton's textual surrogate in the *Mercy* series), Ira experiences the first pangs of discomfort, eventually feeling equally out of place in both worlds. Wirth-Nesher's description of this period of Ira's (and, by implication, Roth's) life is telling, since it encompasses transgressions perpetrated both within and without the Jewish home: "The crossing of boundaries becomes Ira Stigman's, and the dramatised aging narrator's, obsession. Whether he remains within the fold, where he crosses sexual boundaries, or whether he leaves the fold and crosses ethnic and cultural boundaries, he is always guilt-ridden".[9] As we shall see, the guilt experienced by Roth due to his sexual behaviour at home becomes increasingly linked to that emerging from his uneasy straddling of Jewish and gentile domains.

For the purposes of the following argument, it is important to recognise that virtually all Roth's output as a writer is based in autobiography. Although insistently presented as a novel, the disguise for the semi-autobiographical *Mercy* series is gossamer-thin. Its protagonist, Ira Stigman, has much the same family tree as his creator (Roth didn't even change the names of his parents). Both Ira and Roth went through similar sexual initiations, attended the same educational institutions, and published the same literary works, whilst the old, narrating, Ira suffers appalling pain from rheumatoid arthritis, in identical fashion to the elderly Roth. In many ways the four published volumes of the *Mercy* series represent only the tip of a substantial iceberg; another manuscript — still unpublished — of around two thousand pages continues Ira Stigman's story into the late-1930s. In the retrospective light of the *Mercy* series, even *Call It Sleep* can be seen to comprise considerably more autobiographical material than critics had previously appreciated.

That Ira of the *Mercy* series is clearly a sexual surrogate for Roth is not even belied by their different names; "Ira Stigman" represents a highly appropriate moniker for the protagonist. "Ira" may be separated as "I, ra", and as the elderly narrator explains in volume one of the series, "Ra" is Hebrew for evil, "anything bad, the whole spectrum of bad".[10] Stigman clearly suggests "man of stigma", and so from the outset the protagonist of the *Mercy* series is saddled with name that evokes tangible guilt, a "mark of evil". Ira's name therefore provides a stark indication of the way in which Roth viewed his adolescent self from the perspective of old age, blighted with a mark of Cain. Ira's stigma emerges in diverse, complex and interdependent ways throughout the series.

For example, towards the end of *A Diving Rock on the Hudson*, volume two of the *Mercy* series, the nineteen-year-old Ira is invited to a picnic with Larry (the textual version of Lester Winter), Edith, and the latter's flatmate, Iola. Ira asks his mother to prepare sandwiches of "fine Jewish salami, thickly sliced, to be sandwiched between fresh *bulkies*".[11] On his way to meet the others, however, Ira grows uneasy about the overpowering smell of the sandwiches:

141

Redolence of salami, garlic redolence... The more he sniffed the paper bag, the more worried he became, the more the contents assaulted and alarmed his nostrils. Jewish immigrant boor, he was certain to be judged, slum, Jewish boor. He had blatantly violated the most elementary rules of etiquette: no one but a gross numskull, an ignorant chump, would outrage the delicate palates of two such well-bred ladies by offering them food that reeked of garlic to high heaven.[12]

Ira here conflates the signifier of the salami's garlic aroma into a sign of both his Jewishness (especially in comparison to the two gentile women) and his proletarian background. For Ira, this sign denotes the stigma, the "reek", of his own boorishness and ignorance when compared to the decorous bourgeois set with which he is enamoured.

Shame and Jewishness are here conflated, then, but the coda to this episode also introduces the element of sex and its associated guilt. Appalled at what they suddenly represent for him, Ira discards the sandwiches on the way to the picnic, only to be "roundly... reproved by the others... By Iola in particular. She was terribly fond of Jewish salami... it was so pungent and substantial".[13] Ira and his Jewish salami are attractively exotic, rather than boorish, to these "well-bred ladies". Iola is posited as a potential sexual partner for Ira, albeit one he finds himself unable to pursue, given his continued clandestine relationships with his sister and cousin. Nevertheless, the crude pun on Ira's "Jewish salami" helps to construct a clear link between two sources of Ira's sense of shame: his Jewishness and his sexual behaviour.

This complex nexus of associations — Jewishness, guilt, and sex — is construed in opposition to a mainstream (i.e. gentile) American life that Ira incessantly romanticises. Despite his behaviour on the trip, for example, Ira reflects on the picnic as a "traditional, innocent, untroubled diversion... a day in the company of two cultivated women".[14] Earlier on in the same volume, Ira similarly notes "the imponderable gulf that separated him from everything he beheld — and was enchanted by — that separated him, the immigrant, from the American-born, the Jew from the gentile".[15] Thus "enchanted" by the American hegemony, Ira naively perceives "nothing to flaw the wholeness of the kind they were who lived in those well-kept homes beneath the trees where he walked. And worst of all, he was sure, he was sure, no secret canker had already begun to mar the contented wholesomeness they seemed to possess".[16] In opposition to this almost comically idealised conception of middle-class gentile America, Ira problematically aligns the "secret canker" of his sexual behaviour with his Jewishness.

That this is a problematic — and therefore unstable — opposition is suggested through the character of Larry. Ira is initially incredulous that someone so tastefully dressed could be Jewish: "you just felt it, even if you didn't know what good taste was, refinement...had to be gentile".[17] This disbelief that his urbane and handsome friend is Jewish actually points to the invalidity of assumptions Ira has made about his own ethnicity. Larry's difference from Ira's conception of Jewishness is constantly emphasised. In contrast to Ira's sordid sexual awakening, for instance, Larry relates how he lost his virginity on a cruise, "an initiation so beautiful... on a night in which wave crests glistened under a waning moon, and soft sea breezes caressed cheeks and stroking hands, so beautiful, it seemed to Ira, that it was as if Larry had been with a fairy princess".[18] Again, the purple prose underlines the extent to which Ira absurdly idealises and romanticises gentile life, or any kind of lifestyle which contrasts with the sordidness he links inexplicably to his Jewishness.

His thoughts on Edith similarly underline Ira's inability to associate sexuality with the "enchanted" gentiles. Although the fourth volume culminates in Ira finally sleeping with Edith, for a protracted period he is unable to reconcile her gentile status with sexual appetite: "Jesus Christ. Edith pulling up her knees, drawers off, pussy out, bare-ass. He couldn't. He couldn't think of her that way. Delicate, refined, Ph.D., professor of English literature, a professor".[19] Ira frequently experiences crippling shame when in Edith's company, the result of a number of converging factors: his self-perceived plebeian boorishness, his Jewishness, and his covert sexuality. These come together most clearly when it seems as if Ira will be forced to introduce his cousin Stella to Edith, when he fears (erroneously, it transpires) that he has made the former pregnant. Significantly, Ira's shame here is associated less with revealing to Edith his sexual encounters, than with his belief that Edith will disapprove of his choice of Stella: "the ignominy of taking her to Edith's — of exhibiting her before Edith! Oh, Jesus, that simpering wad o' lascivious lard. *Oy.* One glance at her and Edith would be appalled at the fake he was".[20] Ira's major fear is that in perceiving his attraction for Stella, Edith will see through his intellectual and artistic pretensions that she has done so much to nurture.

One final association remains to be observed: a textual motif that Roth employs apparently to conflate the various forms and sources of shame already discussed. At one point in *Requiem for Harlem*, Ira returns home from meeting Edith and discussing Stella's apparent pregnancy. He finds his father alone, in agitated mood, and the reader learns much later that this follows an episode where Ira's mother discovers her husband sexually abusing Stella. Ira's first visual impression on returning is of his father with "the Yiddish newspaper spread open wide in front of him on the green oilcloth of the kitchen table".[21] In another brief incidence, during the "Jewish salami" excursion Ira notes Iola's green hat, closely followed by an observation regarding the boat's "leaving a creamy wake in the green water".[22] These cases point to an extraordinarily persistent usage of colour codification running through the *Mercy* series, as Roth uses green to denote anything that draws together his associations of guilt, sex, and Jewishness.

Stella, for example, is described as possessing "shallow blue-green eyes", and is often depicted wearing a green cloche and/or coat.[23] Iola, similarly wears, "almost invariably, a green costume or green accessory... green dress, green earrings, green pendants".[24] The dominance of green here not only underscores her possibilities as a sexual partner for Ira, but also provokes suggestive connotations of sexual trauma in the following paragraph, which relates an episode after her mother died and Iola's father, "either in fury or sexual furor, chased his daughter with an ax over the fields".[25] The incestuous theme of this memory is not lost on a narrator with the preoccupations of Ira. In the scheme of associative cues constructed by Roth, Iola, like Stella, becomes indissolubly linked with the colour green.

Laurie Vickroy argues that in using visual images in fictional texts, "writers create... effects with repeated words, phrases, or motifs that are narratively dissociative but affectively overdetermined".[26] According to Vickroy, these images can lock the trauma victim into certain connections: "Victims become obsessed with any associations that can be linked to the trauma, even if they exist within different contexts".[27] Roth indeed appears to be traumatised by his past, and both he and Ira are haunted by certain visual associations which recall traumatic events from the past.

The *Mercy* series is suffused with shorthand motifs such as these, usually close to the intersection in Roth's consciousness between sex, guilt, and Jewishness. The most pervasive of these motifs is the continual recurrence of the colour green. This is especially prominent in the Stigmans' flat, wherein the colour of three particular objects is constantly repeated: the green bathtub, the green oilcloth on the table on which the family eats and on which Ira and Minnie sometimes do their homework, and the green walls of the kitchen and dining room. The first and last of these are particularly associated with Ira's sexual behaviour. As both Roth's unpublished short piece "In 17F" and the unpublished manuscripts continuing the *Mercy* series confirm, the bathtub is the place in which the young Ira and Minnie conduct their first sexual experiments (and the earlier manuscript confirms the autobiographical basis of this episode). As for the green, blistered walls of the dining room, these appear to dance and billow before Ira's eyes when he first experiences sexual ecstasy with Minnie. For example, when Ira and Minnie have one of their first sessions of full sexual intercourse, after she stands up from the "homework table, green-oilcloth-covered", Ira perceives that,

> the green-painted, blistery kitchen walls did a jig, a veritable jig — still *she* didn't notice anything, he everything: the walls dimpled, the walls jigged, they rippled to and fro as the little brass nipple loosed the tongue-plunk of the lock, close sesame, magic-charm plunk that freed the walls from being walls, changed them to shimmering, rich green drapes.[28]

Green thus links together in Roth's mind first sexual experimentation, first (guilty) experience of sexual ecstasy, and first experience of sexual intercourse. This initial lengthier description enables later references to be made in a codified shorthand. When Ira later refers to the way in which "the green, blistery walls trembled as if they were stammering with joy", for example, the reader by now recognises that this necessarily indicates another sexual episode.[29]

The green motif effectively links various sources of Ira's shame: not only sex, but also theft. In *A Diving Rock* Ira is summoned to the office of his school's assistant principal for stealing

145

fountain pens and notices the "the green underside" of his blotter holder as he is being expelled. As he leaves the school in disgrace, Ira notices a patch of melting snow "crouching under the green benches".[30] Besides theft and illicit sex, Ira's Jewishness remains — more problematically — at the core of his feelings of guilt. This, too, is associated, albeit more loosely, with green, as in the first two examples cited above. Ira's awkwardness with Iola — the individual character most closely related to green, through her clothing — stems in large part from his cowed Jewish self-consciousness in the presence of "well-bred ladies". When first introduced to Edith, for example, being Jewish and shamefully awkward are depicted as interdependent, as Ira notes his own, "fumbling, his disquiet, his crudities... his Jewishness that he was so conscious of, his ingratiating, silly grin".[31]

In this way, the incest theme of the series also functions as a metaphor for Jewish experience; more than once Ira ruminates on the similarity between his sexual acts and the inward-looking Jewish diaspora community: "Funny the kind of gags that came to mind: *it was all in the family*. And when (Ira's Aunt) Mamie told him they were going to form a Veljisher Family Circle, he laughed outright".[32] Again, this situation is contrasted with gentile America, as when Ira compares its "free and lusty" air — as represented by his occasional outdoor pursuits with gentile friends — with the suffocating location of his forbidden acts with Minnie, "the Jewish atmosphere of the cold-water flat on 119th Street in East Harlem".[33] Whilst Ira's Jewishness is here posited as a site from which his "abominations" flow, this frequent designation of the acts *as* abominations makes it equally clear that they are actually inimical to Judaic law. As Stacy S. Mulder has observed, this absolutely forbids three categories of actions: "eating forbidden foods, seeking mediums, and engaging in prohibited sexual liaisons."[34] Ira not only commits the first of these, in the P & T storehouse in volume one of the series, but more significantly expressly violates the last in his relations with Minnie.

The links between Roth's guilt regarding his adolescent sexual behaviour and his Jewishness are clearer than is suggested by Gordon. Specifically, one must consider the dual-level narration that structures the series, comprising both the tale of young Ira and that of the elderly narrator reflecting on his autobiographical project. Roth initially experimented with drafts that excluded

146

mention of a sister but found this produced intolerable difficulties and denied him the redemption he sought through confession. Admitting the sister and the incest to the narrative, however, forced Roth into changes: earlier typescript drafts largely omit the older narrator looking back over his narrative. Similarly, these early drafts omitting Minnie are autodiegetic, whereas later and final drafts, wherein she appears, are heterodiegetic. A consequence of introducing the incest material into his work was that Roth found himself needing to address these difficult episodes obliquely, using a decentred set of narrators, and producing a more metafictional, self-conscious narrative rather than straightforward autobiography. As a result, the reader of the *Mercy* series is faced with two versions of Ira: one in his adolescence and early twenties, who is in the process of rejecting his Jewish background, and the other in his eighties, who has re-embraced it.

Gordon's failure to pinpoint the connections Roth makes between sex, guilt, and Jewishness perhaps lies in the conflicting and sometimes paradoxical attitudes towards Judaism produced by the separate versions of Ira. In his early life, as copiously illustrated in the *Mercy* series, Roth constructed numerous connections between Jewishness, sexual depravity, and its associated shame. Jonathan Rosen suggests that Roth at this time, "was filled with shame and self-loathing, wounded by a childhood of abuse and a young adulthood that was, in his mind, degenerate. He identified Judaism with weakness and cowardice and sought to purge it from his life."[35] Crucially, however, this perspective is rejected by the older Roth (and Ira), who have achieved a measure of redemption (and the ability to write again) through a celebration of Israel and a return to Judaism.

Gordon correctly notes that Roth "says that he began to be able to write again after Israel's victory over its Arab enemies in the 1967 war", but, she claims, "The connection is never made explicitly".[36] Perhaps we can now make this connection explicit: as a result of Israel's victory, Roth no longer associated Jewishness with "weakness and cowardice". However problematic this celebration of the 1967 war, the point is that it enabled Roth to distance himself sufficiently from the perspectives of his youth in order to write about them. Now perceiving Jewishness as a source of strength rather than weakness, the older Roth could separate himself from his now despised, earlier self. Ironically,

147

Roth's idealisation of Israel — as Steven Kellman rightly suggests, "he sentimentalised the nation" — precisely echoes the romantic view of gentile culture espoused by the younger Ira in the *Mercy* series.[37]

Finally, the different perspectives on Jewishness of the old and young Ira should be noted. Whilst the young Ira sees Jewishness as a source both of weakness and of his depravity, the acts are described by the elderly Ira in ways that demonstrate how they actually violate the most sacred tenets of Judaism. Crucially, these episodes are narrated by the old man, but not fully comprehended by his purblind younger self. Mulder's observation, raised above, that engaging in prohibited sexual liaisons specifically violates Judaic law should alert us to the fact that the adolescent Ira is acting in ways quite contrary to his culture. Similarly, some of the instances of incest specifically underline the taboo nature of Ira's behaviour.

In volume two, for example, Roth writes how sex with Minnie generally takes place upon their parents' bed, but describes how Ira would place "a newspaper, *Der Tag*, under Minnie" when she has her period. The fact that the Yiddish newspaper is comprised of sacred characters from the Hebrew alphabet underscores the extremity with which Ira's acts specifically contravene Judaic law. Similarly, the first time Ira has sex with Stella is when they slip away from a mutual new cousin's *bris*, to their uncle's cellar. After a brief, furious coupling, Ira sends Stella back upstairs, whilst he loiters for a moment, "quietly smearing ejaculate underfoot, as Jews smeared phlegm underfoot in synagogue, as the *mohel* had mashed the infant's foreskin underfoot after stamping on it".[38] This grotesque parody of the *bris* again demonstrates how, regardless of the young Ira's understanding of Jewishness, the elderly narrator clearly understands that his younger self was acting in ways forbidden by Judaic law.

Roth's shifting attitude towards his Jewishness is a complex knot to untangle, not least because the contrasting perspectives of the old and young Ira are not always as easy to separate as the above might suggest. Nevertheless, Roth seems to be aiming to demonstrate that he previously connected sexual depravity with Jewishness, but now appreciates both that he was mistaken, and that his adolescent sexual activity was actually contrary to Jewish culture. Crucially, this sheds some light on that most persistently fascinating question about Roth's career: how did he return to novel writing after an absence of sixty years? And here, the connection between Jewishness and sex is pivotal. Only once Roth re-embraces Judaism through his celebration of Israel's strength, as demonstrated in the 1967 war, is he able to write again. It is at this point that Roth no longer associates Jewishness with weakness, and with the same kind of shame that emerges from the guilt of his sexual behaviour. Having achieved a mature perspective on Jewishness, that contrasts with that of his adolescent self, he now felt sufficient distance to be able to write about that younger self, and plead "Mercy" for this new "Rude Stream" of narrative.

Chapter Twelve
"It's Both Hot and Incredibly Innocent": A Century of Sex on the American Jewish Stage
Ben Furnish

Introduction

Professional Jewish theatre is not much more than a century old. Until modernity challenged "the unquestioned legitimacy of a divinely instituted order", the rabbis held aloof from theatre because of its potential for transgressing laws of sexual modesty: women would play roles in front of male audience members, or else men would perform women's parts, and either practice would be legally problematic.[1] But once a professional Jewish theatre appeared, it became, as Joel Berkowitz and Jeremy Dauber note, "one of the most dynamic and popular forms of Jewish expression in the modern world".[2] Perhaps the rabbis were prescient in deploring theatre on the grounds of sexual modesty, because the Jewish theatre, in Yiddish and later in English in the United States, seriously confronted issues of sex and sexuality in a way that ultimately affected larger discourses about these issues outside the theatre and even far outside the Jewish world. One of the great enterprises of professional Jewish theatre in the past century has been to wrestle with issues of sex and sexuality in a larger framework of the individual's relation to family, community, and nation and the notion of civil rights. One feature that is prominent among serious artists in Jewish theatre is their search for moral understanding and the examination of the psychology of sexual desire. Consequently, their plays have included Jews who are prostitutes, gay men and lesbians, women who seek their own voice in that story, Holocaust witnesses, people with AIDS, heterosexual men and women (including women who might eschew marriage but choose motherhood — or not), non-Jews who become part of the family story — and the unfolding, modern Jewish moral universe within which the conflicts of their lives occur.

Far from reflecting prurience or the kind of hyper-sexuality projected onto Jews by anti-Semites, Jewish drama's moral concern with sexuality in a Jewish cultural context can be understood in light of such massive social dislocations as modernity itself,

150

immigration to America, the Holocaust in Europe, the abandonment of one language (Yiddish) for another (English in the United States, Hebrew in Israel), and more recently, a level of success and social acceptance of Jews in the United States that is unprecedented in Jewish history. That success is accompanied by new anxiety about group survival, including a birth rate well below replacement level and the uncertainties raised by a rising intermarriage rate. These social dislocations coincide, on the wider contemporary American scene, with the changes brought by feminism and the backlash against it, civil rights for racial and ethnic groups and for gays and lesbians (including the controversy over legalised gay marriage), the AIDS epidemic, and the economic and demographic changes wrought by globalisation, a declining birth rate, rising immigration, and an increasingly polarised political landscape.

Sex in the Yiddish Theatre

Director and playwright Avrom Goldfadn is considered to be the father of the Yiddish theatre. One of his key themes was Jewish prostitution which, by the late nineteenth century, was becoming a concern among the Jews in Russia. In fact, as Joel Berkowitz observes, two of Goldfadn's heroines are nearly trapped into sexual slavery. Mirele in *Di kishufmakherin* (*The Witch*, 1879) is tricked into abduction by the eponymous witch of the play, Bobe Yakhne (interestingly, this role is traditionally played by a male actor.) Mirele is transported to Constantinople but saved by her suitor. The Bobe Yakhne character combines an evocation of the superstitious *shtetl* past through her beguiling (even if by her own admission thoroughly fabricated) magic with her very contemporary criminal activity. In *Meshiekhs tsaytn?!* (*The Messianic Age?!*, 1891), a Jewish banker, Shteynharts, unwittingly sells his daughter Lise into prostitution. She is sent to Buenos Aires, another crime capital, but fortunately the ship founders before arriving and she is rescued.

Likewise, playwright Perets Hirschbein's *Miriam*, which he wrote in Hebrew in 1905 and translated into Yiddish the following year, features an orphan girl who finds herself seduced, impregnated, and abandoned. The fourth act of the play is set in the brothel where she ends up, though not at a time when she and two girls with her are working. Hirschbein is interested in Miriam as a character, including her psychological reality and the sociological context for her descent, rather than in any lurid depiction of prostitution per se. Indeed, Miriam retains a kind of heroic innocence as demonstrated by her continued conviction that: "There are still good people in this world", which she says early in the play but repeats at the end, in spite of the misfortunes that have befallen her. Hirschbein's moral view does not seek to condemn Miriam so much as understand her and the circumstances that caused her series of misfortunes.

In 1907, American Yiddish dramatist David Pinski authored *Yankl der shmid*, a drama about a blacksmith who becomes infatuated with his neighbour's wife, Tamara. Both Yankl and Tamara appear bored with their own spouses. During the course of the play, Pinski explores the psychological motivations of adulterous temptation — like Hirschbein with *Miriam*, Pinski's observation is not judgmental against the characters or prurient, though the end of the play does see Yankl and Tamara each return to their respective spouses. This would prove to be Pinski's most frequently produced play, and a film version was made in 1938, directed by Edgar G. Ulmer.

Pinski would go on to explore adulterous attraction in other works. In *Gabri un di froyen* (1908), protagonist Gabri is tempted to stray from his marriage, but the strength of his wife's love motivates his return to her. Gabri's son eventually becomes involved with the woman who had caught Gabri's eye. The play *Professor Brenner* (1918) explored the psychology of an older man attracted to a much younger woman. *Nina Mardens libes* (1920) features a female protagonist who is drawn to a number of men in addition to her husband, though each seems only to take advantage of her. Pinski's *Miryam fun Magdala* (*Mary Magdalene*, 1920) would deal with the former prostitute's human love for Jesus. But perhaps most interesting are Pinski's five short plays based on the life of King David (*Kenig Dovid un zayn vayber/King David and His Wives*, 1920) depicted the biblical David's attraction for various of his wives at various times in his life. Pinski's David was at once familiar to Jewish audiences as the biblical figure, but he was also every bit a fallible human being in the throes of desire. Pinski shows the evolution, or devolution, of David's wandering passion at various stages from youth ("Mikhal") to old age ("Abishag"). What is more, Pinski uses the conflicts inherent in each wife's situation to create a three-dimensional character, though the Bible conveys little actual information about each wife.

But what is today the Yiddish theatre's best remembered depiction of sexuality probably remains Sholem Asch's *Got fun nekome* (*God of Vengeance*), due to its considerable production history in other languages. The play premiered in 1907 in German at Max Reinhardt's Kammerspiele Teater in Berlin. Despite the play's European success (seldom were Yiddish plays performed in other languages), its New York Yiddish premiere later that year caused an outcry due to the play's brothel setting and a lesbian encounter. The play's 1923 Broadway performance in English was shut down by police as obscene.

Got fun nekome features Yankl, who operates a brothel in his basement, yet seeks to raise his daughter Rivkele as a chaste maiden who will enter into a respectable marriage in their home upstairs. He even brings a Torah scroll into the house, almost as though it were a kind of talisman to protect his daughter from sin. Critics picked up on the play's theme of a character's efforts to transcend and expiate the sins of his life by raising a virtuous daughter, and the perils and contradictions of doing so above a sinful foundation (as symbolised by the brothel in the basement). While Rivkele is being kissed and caressed by the prostitute Manke, she is talking to her mother Sore (herself a former prostitute trying to live down her past) about the respectable marriage Rivkele will one day enter. The scene is a powerful and ironic clash between Yankl and Sore's dream for their daughter and the reality. But many American audience members (both for the 1907 Yiddish production, as historian Nina Warnke has shown, and for the 1923 production in English) could see only obscenity in the very fact of Asch's choice of subject matter.[3] Never mind that Asch's play is really about Yankl's doomed efforts to transcend his own wrongdoing by bequeathing some kind of respectability to his daughter without abandoning his own dubious livelihood.

On a literal level, audience members could rationally perceive prostitution and adultery as genuine concerns. Jewish prostitution in Russia and the United States was a definite reality in the late nineteenth century as many Jewish women faced desperation, if not outright abduction.[4] Anxiety about adultery would have been topical for many audience members. The weakening of traditional religious authority together with the tide of Jewish immigration to the United States beginning in the late nineteenth century devastated many marriages. Many husbands

153

abandoned their wives, as documented by the Jewish daily *Forward*'s gallery of missing husbands. Many husbands and wives acculturated to American life at different paces and became strangers to each other. The stress on marriages was emblematic of larger stresses that immigrant Jews faced in learning a new language, redefining or abandoning their religious practices, learning new livelihoods, and dreaming of a more stable future for their children.

From the 1920s until the 1960s, issues of Jewishness and sexuality were muted on stage for a variety of reasons. Especially for plays produced before the end of World War II, "it was more common for Jews to write *out* of their American Jewish experience than *about* it", as Ellen Schiff writes.[5] Fewer new plays were produced on the Yiddish stage from the 1930s onward, as American immigration restriction legislation almost eliminated the movement of new Yiddish speakers to the United States from the early 1920s until after World War II. It took a few decades before the intersection between Jewishness and sexuality would become prominent on the English-language American stage.[6] Andrea Most illustrates how the American Jews who were central to the creation of the commercial English-language Broadway musical used this medium as a creative kind of re-enactment of their own efforts at self-reinvention through assimilation into American society. Almost none of the characters in the plays she discusses are explicitly Jewish, however.[7] Theatres in the wider American stage in the late nineteenth and early twentieth century increasingly strove to maintain a respectable image in regard to their depiction of sexuality in order to attract women as well as men as audience members and to avoid legal indecency charges. American theatres and music halls were often the locus for prostitution and drink, and the legitimate professional stage had achieved a certain hard-won respectability by the early 1900s that was also kept in line by the threat of indecency litigation. Vaudeville was more sexually charged though skilfully marketed as wholesome by its (largely non-Jewish) producers, but it was disappearing by the 1930s.

Sex on the American Jewish Stage

Later in the twentieth century, Yiddish declined to be replaced by Jewish drama in English. But the first classic iteration of this, also conspicuously lacked sex as a central concern. *Fiddler on the*

Roof, a 1964 Broadway musical and 1971 film, was adapted from stories by Yiddish writer Sholem Aleichem. As Alisa Solomon writes, it might now be seen as the archetypal modern Jewish family romance.[8] The play is about a Jewish dairyman in Russia near the turn of the last century and while sexuality per se is not an explicit subject, romantic love is the force that breaks protagonist father Tevye's heart as three of his daughters takes a modern approach to contracting her own marriage instead of letting him and the matchmaker choose for her. The first is between Tseitel and Motl, a poor tailor — they are in love and ask Tevye's permission to marry. The second is between Hodel and Perchik, a radical. They are in love and ask for Tevye's blessing. The last of these marriages is between daughter Chava and Fyedka, a non-Jewish Ukrainian peasant. They are in love, but Tevye does not bless their union. The stage Tevye, like Sholem Aleichem's original, also rejected Chava's intermarriage. However, reflecting the mid- to late-1960s concern about the Jewish future of their children, the stage ending left some hope that he would still at least acknowledge her existence.

Many of the subsequent social dislocations to unfold as the 1960s progressed into the 1970s which involved sexuality and civil rights more directly were acted out upon the American stage. They included the feminist and gay and lesbian movements as well as a less repressive environment for heterosexual behaviour as well. One major landmark was the success of Harvey Fierstein's *Torch Song Trilogy*, produced on Broadway in 1981 after off-Broadway productions. Fierstein went beyond merely depicting gay characters on the Broadway stage (an honour that might go to Asch) but broke ground as essentially a gay Jewish family romance with a happy ending. In fact, some critics found fault with Fierstein's imitation of the norms of the heterosexual family.[9] One of the play's most famous scenes is a comic enactment of an unsatisfying, anonymous sexual encounter that protagonist Arnold has in the backroom of a bar. The stage is dark except for Arnold's face, and Fierstein defuses with humour what might have been a shockingly explicit scene even for Broadway in the early 1980s: anal sex in which the stranger penetrates Arnold. His facial expressions register his reactions. Ultimately, the scene underscores and motivates Arnold's subsequent refusal to settle for less than a loving, committed adult relationship.

In the 1979 play *Bent*, playwright Martin Sherman stages a frank love scene between two men on stage. But this scene was entirely verbal, spoken by two concentration camp prisoners to each other while they were under a guard's watch and unable to have actual, physical contact. *Bent* generated controversy as the first major work to call attention to the Nazis' persecution of homosexuals. Although by some measures, the play might not fit within this study's parameters since the characters are not Jewish, the protagonist Max does pretend to be a Jew and eventually is able to trade up his pink triangle for a yellow star in a concentration camp. Some critics have criticised Sherman, a gay Jewish playwright, from trivialising the Holocaust's memory by depicting the Nazi treatment of homosexuals as worse than their treatment of Jews. Although in *Torch Song*, Fierstein makes clear parallels between Jewish and gay suffering by mentioning Arnold's tears in watching an American Nazi march on television and in having Arnold's lover Alan murdered in a hate crime, Sherman goes further by trying to redress the virtual silence that had prevailed in Holocaust historical narratives about Nazi persecution of homosexuals. Taken together, these plays established parallels between Jewish and gay oppression, and those parallels would recur in a number of plays that would follow. Even more than legitimating gay and lesbian claims to minority status by linking their concerns with those of a long-recognised minority group such as the Jews, the gay-Jewish analogy also created a means through which heterosexual Jews (and by extension, other heterosexual audience members) could identify with or at least comprehend their concerns. Even *Bent* contains a love story that ultimately redeems Max even as it seals his doom. Max, in the play's early scenes was able to divorce sex from morality altogether; a nude blond youth whom Max does not even remember bringing home emerges from his bedroom in the first act — the youth turns out to be a member of the Nazi S.A. But Max eventually discovers within his own sexuality a moral imperative to finally claim his identity even at the cost of his life.

Playwright Larry Kramer would draw clear parallels between the Holocaust and the AIDS crisis in his 1985 play *The Normal Heart*. For Kramer, the silence and indifference with which those in power ignored the AIDS epidemic and its largely gay men casualties directly parallels the world's indifference to the Holocaust's mass murder of Jews. Yet amid Kramer's urgent call to action for research and prevention efforts against AIDS, a love story unfolds between gay activist Ned Weeks and reporter Felix Turner, whose relationship unfolds amid a historical backdrop of death and fear. Ironically, Ned had been calling on gay men to abstain from sex until the cause of AIDS is determined — then he enters a relationship with Felix. Even as Ned seeks to rally support to fight the epidemic, Felix learns he has the disease. On Felix's deathbed, the two men have a symbolic marriage ceremony. Some critics found fault with what they saw as Kramer's reactionary stance against promiscuity and in favour of conventional romantic relationships. But the play, as one of the first major cultural responses to AIDS, created a space within which to speak of AIDS not merely as a venereal disease, or as some divine retribution for sexual sin, but as a legitimate civil-rights issue.

William Finn and James Lapine's musical *Falsettos* (1993, with parts previously produced in 1981 and 1990) brought gay, Jewish, and AIDS issues together around the American Jewish family romance event par excellence: a bar mitzvah. In New York, producers promoted *Falsettos* as a family show. Goldfadn himself might have loved *Falsettos*, combining as it does music, contemporised Jewish folk motifs (the kosher caterer and her doctor spouse who live next door are lesbians), a tragic love story, and occasion for unfettered sentiment. The stage directions for the one scene sexually suggestive scene, with Marvin singing while Whizzer sleeps next to him in bed, indicate, "It's both hot and incredibly innocent".[10] The lachrymose ending has young Jason deciding to celebrate his bar mitzvah ceremony in the hospital of his father's lover, who is dying of AIDS instead of before two hundred temple guests. Jason, who is heterosexual, nonetheless understands a moral necessity to claim Whizzer as family.

Tony Kushner's Pulitzer Prize-winning *Angels in America* represents a culmination of the major themes in the late twentieth-century works mentioned above. As Peter F. Cohn writes, *Angels*, like *The Normal Heart*, interweaves a political storyline about AIDS with a love story.[11] Like Fierstein, Sherman, Kramer, and Finn, Kushner deals explicitly with the intersection of gay and Jewish issues. Like *Fiddler* and *Bent*, Angels draws upon history — the late Ethel Rosenberg visits, from the hereafter, the hospital room of Roy Cohn, the right-wing Jewish lawyer who had sought the death penalty for her in the 1950s as a Soviet spy.

Cohn, a closeted but very sexually active gay man, is dying of AIDS. The play opens with a Jewish funeral conducted by an elderly old-world rabbi for the grandmother of Louis, a gay man who leaves his WASP lover Prior, who is ill with AIDS. Louis becomes sexually and romantically involved with Joe Pitt, a young conservative Mormon who works for Roy Cohn. In part two, *Perestroika*, Louis seduces Joe; later, the nude couple in bed are visited by the spirit of Joe's wife Harper. Louis struggles, and never quite succeeds, in constructing a coherent moral basis for his actions. Instead, he experiences guilt over such actions as abandoning his lover Prior at the very time Prior learns he has AIDS, and over sleeping with and then falling in love with a right-wing, Mormon acolyte of the loathsome Roy Cohn. Implicit within the plays of Fierstein, Kramer, Sherman, Finn, and Kushner (as well as Judy Gold, discussed below) are the parallels between Jewish and gay identities. "The model I used in coming out was everything I knew about the Jewish experience in the twentieth century", Kushner said in an interview. Although, as Eve Kosofsky Sedgwick notes, the gay/Jewish analogy is imperfect, for each of these playwrights, gay and Jewish identities evoke similar concerns related to minority status, civil rights, and self-acceptance.[12]

In contrast, Wendy Wasserstein's first three plays are comedies that depict characters from the 1960s through the 1980s who witness and participate in the women's movement. In a field as male-dominated as playwriting, the very fact of a woman's success was notable, though some feminist critics expressed disappointment with what they saw as her dismissive portrayal of the women's movement. Wasserstein's protagonists Holly Kaplan (*Uncommon Women*, 1977), Janie Blumberg (*Isn't It Romantic*, 1983), and Heidi Holland (*The Heidi Chronicles*, 1989) all seek to build lives for themselves that live up to their liberal-feminist-inspired ideals. Holly enters Mount Holyoke College just as it abandons its finishing-school trappings. Six years after graduation, she reunites with a group of her women friends and admits, "For the past six years, I have been afraid to see any of you. Mostly because I haven't made any specific choices. My parents used to call me three times a week at 7am to ask me, 'Are you thin? Are you married to a root-canal man? Are *you* a root-canal man?'" The vague sense of failure to live up to great expectations haunts Janie and Heidi as well. Janie is a recent

158

college graduate just breaking into television, and Heidi is an art historian whose specialty is previously ignored women artists from the past. The ethics by which Wasserstein's three female protagonists measure themselves includes the following standards: women should support each other emotionally as friends; seek their own potential as individuals according to their own interests and abilities; they should not conspire to steal each other's boyfriends and husbands; and in which they would rather live alone than settle for a marriage or even a sexual relationship that will diminish their sense of self-worth. Janie ends her relationship with a Jewish doctor (who is almost a walking stereotype of the ideal, marriageable Jewish man, but who rents an apartment for them without letting her see it first), saying, "I guess to a man I love I want to feel not just that I can talk, but that you'll listen". Scoop Rosenbaum decides not to marry Heidi because they want the same things in life: "Self-fulfillment, self-determination, self-exaggeration". He tells her, "You'd be competing with me". But when years later he returns to her, saying, "Maybe we should try again", she sends him back to his wife. Heidi then holds up the daughter she has adopted as a single mother and proclaims her a heroine for the twenty-first century.[13]

Neil Simon's coming of age trilogy *Brighton Beach Memoirs* (1984), *Biloxi Blues* (1986) and *Broadway Bound* (1987) form an autobiographically inspired, coming-of-age cycle. In *Biloxi Blues*, protagonist Eugene Jerome enters the army during World War II and loses his innocence. Yet that loss of innocence is as relevant to the 1980s when it was written as it is as a nostalgic, historical period piece. Eugene loses his virginity (one of his goals when he joined the army) in a brothel and decides he never wants to pay for sex again. He temporarily loses his heart to an Irish Catholic girl in a chaste infatuation. But he loses his innocence as a Jew when confronted with anti-Semitism, homophobia, and what he sees as his own failure of will to stand up to wrongdoing. Arnold Epstein, one of Eugene's fellow soldiers, not only endures anti-Semitic abuse from some of the soldiers, but when Eugene speculates in his journal if Arnold is homosexual, other soldiers read it and assumes it must be true. Eugene is doubly disappointed in himself for his failure to defend Epstein earlier and what he sees as a betrayal of him now. At another point in the play, a soldier is arrested in front of the other soldiers for committing a homosexual act, and Eugene must struggle between his

159

own discomfort with homosexuality and his compassion for the soldier, who faces prison.

The third play in Simon's autobiographical trilogy, *Broadway Bound*, depicts Eugene after returning to New York City from the army and as he strives to launch a career writing television comedy. In this play, the Jewish family romance eschews a happy ending. Although Eugene achieves career success as a comedy writer and falls in love himself, he sees his father abandon his mother after years of philandering and the home in which he grew up disintegrate. In what is perhaps the play's most poignant scene, Eugene's mother reminisces about a favourite memory from her youth, when she was attractive and once danced with a celebrity. On an impulse, Eugene asks her to dance, and for a moment, she imaginatively returns to her youth. Eugene realises he is a stand-in for his now-absent father.

Comedian Judy Gold's *25 Questions for a Jewish Mother* (2006) brings together just about all of the modern Jewish-American concerns — about Jewish life, sexuality, and the nature of motherhood itself — into one show. The mothers discuss gay and lesbian marriage and family, feminism, and AIDS, along with the nature of Jewish identity itself. Gold spent six years with co-author Kate Moira Ryan interviewing over fifty Jewish mothers from the full range of Jewish denominational and secular commitments. Gold, a lesbian Jewish mother of two, also includes anecdotes from her somewhat conflicted relationship with her own traditional-minded mother.

Conclusion

At least a century ago, the Yiddish stage began to help Jews to comprehend the complexities of sexual desire in the modern world. More recently the Jewish-American theatre has done the same for Jews and other audience members. Historically, *Torch Song Trilogy* not only opened Broadway for openly, affirmatively gay drama, but it depicted a gay Jew forming a family many years before gay marriage would become a national controversy. *Bent* revived the virtually forgotten memory of Nazi persecution of homosexuals during the Holocaust. *The Normal Heart* won national attention to the AIDS epidemic in part by comparing the widespread indifference to AIDS to the prevailing indifference to the Holocaust during the 1930s and 1940s, and it opened the door for many other plays about AIDS. *Angels in America* wove gay,

Jewish, and larger American themes into one of the late twentieth-century's most celebrated plays. Wendy Wasserstein's first three plays explored the challenges of finding love and family for women who refuse to settle for men who don't respect them. Neil Simon's alter ego Eugene Jerome came of age by witnessing anti-Semitism and homophobia, learned he did not want sex without intimacy, and embarked on his first serious love affair while watching his parents' marriage disintegrate. And *25 Questions for a Jewish Mother* sums up how the family in the Jewish family romance has changed in the last century, and how it hasn't. Taken together, this body of work takes a moral view of sexuality that affirms (even as it may redefine) family, commitment, and Jewish identity in the face of modernity and the upheavals of the past century. Jewish American dramatists after *Fiddler on the Roof* find a freedom to depict openly Jewish themes and subjects in much the same way as American dramatists at this time are able to begin depicting themes and subjects of sexuality more openly.

Chapter Thirteen
Vaginal Voyages: Performances of Sexuality and the Jewish Female Body
Roberta Mock

Burl-X Factor: London's East End, 2006

In September 2006, my daughter and I attended The Tournament of Tease Burl-X Factor night at the Bethnal Green Working Men's Club in East London. This was an amateur burlesque competition whose title capitalised on the popular reality-TV talent show, *The X Factor*. The performers — mostly first-timers — playfully stripped on a small stage illuminated by a large pink heart and the winners were a pair of ladies who removed their Victorian costuming while serving each other tea. Among the judges was Marisa Carnesky whom *Time Out* magazine once credited with the invention of "grotesque burlesque": her edgy, political, "high end" performances once included one in which she played Eve, ate an apple, and took off her clothes while it was squashed in her mouth.[1] She was particularly supportive of the evening's odder acts which she attributed to her perspective as a performance artist. It was Carnesky's combination of erotic entertainment, show business, and live art that established her at the forefront of what is currently called feminist neo-burlesque in the UK.

Carnesky knows the East End well; she lives and maintains a studio here. In 2002, she marked her retirement as a stripper by staging her own funeral on its streets in a one-off performance called *Carnesky's Ghost Box*. In showgirl costuming, she lay in a glass casket that was drawn by plumed horses. This was followed by her friends, dressed in black and carrying wreaths, accompanied by a marching band; as the cortege passed the clubs at which she used to work, tokens of her career (such as garters and tassels) were left behind. To the amazement of onlookers, Carnesky's body magically seemed to appear and disappear in the casket. Two years later, she collaborated with the same illusionist, Paul Kieve, to produce *Carnesky's Ghost Train*, a specially constructed fairground ride featuring optical tricks and live performers, all of whom were women. Those who paid to take the ten-minute ride saw these women spin through the air, fall through floors, levitate, and disappear. With every lap of the circuit, the vignettes and tableaux Carnesky presented became both more violent and sexually charged.

In their different ways, both the ghost train and *The Girl from Nowhere* — a solo theatre show set in a fairground that Carnesky made with Kieve in 2003 — presented "a world where the phantasmagorical collides with fragmented stories of broken journeys, shifting borders and disappeared women".[2] In *The Girl from Nowhere*, woven around the story of her own family's exile, Carnesky seemed to rehearse the back stories of the inhabitants of the ghost train. Among them is a girl who is sold into prostitution when she believes she is coming to England to work as a nanny, and a Russian stripper who makes a huge amount of money and buys a loft apartment in London's now trendy East End. By inter-textually considering Carnesky's body of work as a whole, it is possible to see precisely how she "entwines the personal and the political, individual testimony and collective memory".[3] London's East End (which is where the ghost train was first sited before it toured Britain), with its strong historical associations with Jewishness, radical politics, and the commercialisation of sexuality, is Carnesky's ground zero.

Carnesky's Ghost Box was produced by club/performance art promoters Duckie with whom Carnesky also collaborated on *C'est Duckie* (this won an Olivier award for Best Entertainment when it transferred to the City of London's Barbican as *C'est Barbican* in 2004). Although this performance featured a cabaret-style staged opening and finale, it centred upon "bite-sized burlesque" turns that were ordered by audience members from a menu and paid for using "Duckie dollars".[4] Carnesky was one of the performers who, dressed in a flesh-coloured body-stocking to simulate nudity, had also devised *C'est Duckie*. In a show that was saucy, satirical and kitsch, sex itself blinked in and out of sight like Carnesky's body in its glass coffin. It was about looking back to the art of tease. Among the acts Carnesky performed, if it was ordered and paid for, was a detailed account of growing up Jewish.

This wouldn't have surprised audiences in 2004; in fact, by then they might have been disappointed if she hadn't at least mentioned it. Five years earlier she (literally) made her name with her first one-woman show, *Jewess Tattooess*. In this work, Carnesky self-consciously examined her relationship with

Jewishness and the Shoah by juxtaposing the taboos of tattoos, bleeding and menstruation in Judaism with the fact that the Nazis tattooed millions of Jews in concentration camps. *Jewess Tattooess* integrated on-stage (self-)tattooing, nudity, story-telling, gestural choreography, film, and freak show performance staples such as "the bed of nails". It featured Jewish folk tales, such as that of the Golem, which were chosen to echo the back-ground of her great-grandparents who emigrated from Lithuania to England. *Jewess Tattooess* consolidated Carnesky's themes, her self image, and her stagecraft. It was also the first time she used the name Carnesky, reclaiming the Latvian family name that had been anglicised in the 1940s. Prior to this she worked under the name with which she was born.

Marisa Carnesky, Jewess Tattooess. Courtesy of Marisa Carnesky.

As Marisa Carr, she had worked at the Raymond Revue Bar in Soho with the Dragon Ladies. Here she appeared as a triple-breasted stripper-cum-music-hall-entertainer and, in a parody of the Bluebeard story, suggestively fingered an enormous lurid latex tongue in the place of a vagina. As Carr, she performed in London's fetish club, The Torture Garden, and also in Robert Pacitti's infamous 1994 performance piece *Geek*, pulling a string of Union Jacks from her vagina to the tune of "God Save the Queen". But in 1999, with *Jewess Tattooess*, she found her niche and this was neatly signalled by her professional name change: Carnesky, as one critic has noted, is "fortuitously redolent of both carnival and the carnal".[5] In other words, Carnesky began to play with dominant assumptions of what it means to be a Jewish woman and, in doing so, began to situate herself within a long tradition of sex-positive Jewish female performers.

Smut Fest: New York's Lower East Side, 1994

In 1995, the American cable station HBO televised an hour-long documentary filmed the previous year as part of its *Real Sex* series. It focussed on women artists who worked in the sex industry, and culminated in the staging of a "Smut Fest" in New York's Lower East Side. Organised by ex-punk Jennifer Blowdryer since 1988, Smut Fests were originally shows that "featured strippers reading their own poetry, a little before the term sex worker was coined".[6] Quickly embraced by the avant-garde scene, they broadened into more recognizable cabaret events that included bands and performance artists. Early Smut Fest entertainers in the still-dirty, pre-Giuliani, pre-zero tolerance city of New York included Tracy Love ("the 212-970-PEEE girl"), stripper/dominatrix/writer Danielle Willis, and prostitute/porn star/film-maker/photographer/sex educator/performance artist Annie Sprinkle.

It was during a Smut Fest that Sprinkle first performed the sketch for which she became notorious, "A Public Cervix Announcement". The premise is simple: Annie inserts a speculum into her vagina and invites audiences to come on stage and look at her cervix with the aid of torch. She chats amiably to those who choose to do so, with the aim of both demystifying and celebrating female sexual organs. Some spectators take photos or make videos. *Village Voice* critic C. Carr, writing about a 1989 Smut Fest at the Harmony Burlesque Theater in New York, quotes Jennifer Blowdryer as saying: "Take pictures. All kinds of exploitation are welcome". Carr wonders whether it is possible to be exploited if you actually want to be exploited and are drawing attention to the shared mechanisms of exploitation for performer and audience (both of whom seem to be simultaneously profiting from them). Smut Fest punters queued to pose for photos with Sprinkle's large breasts resting on their heads for three dollars.

165

Sprinkle and Blowdryer told Carr that they aimed to "save sex" from the conservative backlash triggered by the AIDS crisis.[7] Thus, like Carnesky's later burlesque work, Smut Fests emerged from a retro-sexual impulse, one that celebrates sexual freedom through reference to earlier, more "simple", erotic contexts like burlesque or even pre-AIDS sex clubs.

By the early 1990s, Blowdryer had moved to San Francisco making this the Smut Fest home city. Regular performance events there were soon supplemented by occasional franchised manifestations worldwide. In 1993, London staged its own Smut Fest, organised by a young Marisa Carr under Blowdryer's guidance. One of its most fondly remembered acts was Tuppy Owens (Britain's leading pro-sex activist and performer at the time), standing on top of a ladder in an angel costume, pissing on a drag queen wrapped in clingfilm below her who was lip-syncing to "Singin' in the Rain".[8] According to Blowdryer, Smut Fests were "no-hidden-meanings entertainment, elevating both perverts and sex workers to a scary level of camp".[9]

For the filming of *Real Sex*, HBO and Blowdryer chose a number of acts from the London Smut Fest and re-mounted them back in the States in a picturesque abandoned synagogue. Guest of honour in the live audience was Annie Sprinkle who was among the artists (along with Blowdryer) that featured prominently in the rest of the documentary but who didn't appear on the Smut Fest stage herself. The symbolism of the specific choice of venue is rarely commented upon, yet seems very significant. Jennifer Blowdryer, Marisa Carr, and Annie Sprinkle are all Jewish women. Secularised Jewishness is made material in a flamboyant historicised landscape, echoing the cultural memory embodied in both the concept of (and many of the individual performances that comprise) the Smut Fest itself as an event.

In the historical moment captured by HBO, the presence of Jewishness verges on spectrality; it remains unconscious and uninterrogated by the majority of spectators and commentators but may productively haunt the meanings made by others. This duality is mirrored ironically in the very title of HBO's offering: what is being presented live at Smut Fest and mediated to home viewers is not "real sex" itself but references to and comments on "real sex". These are understood through the tensions between the "authenticity" of the performers as sex workers and the "artifice" of staged performance itself. What links them both is the eroticised body that engages in performative role-play as a career strategy and means of political agency.

Between 1994 and 1996, Annie Sprinkle established herself as a sex-positive icon in the mainstream media, largely via her four appearances on *Real Sex*. Sprinkle — who describes herself in the author's biography of her illustrated scrapbook, *Post-Porn Modernist: My 25 Years as a Multimedia Whore*, as a "sex artist" — was already well-known across surprising separate and converging communities: connoisseurs of hardcore pornography during and from the 1970s and early 1980s; devotees of fetish magazines and clubs; members and supporters of prostitutes' rights movements; and those who regularly attended, enjoyed, and studied avant-garde performance events. *Real Sex* introduced television audiences worldwide to Sprinkle through segments about her Sluts and Goddesses role-play workshops for women and her live show *Post-Porn Modernist*, as well as through a full-length special programme about the making of her Pleasure Activist Playing Cards.[10]

Each card in this deck features an erotic photo made by Sprinkle. According to the booklet that accompanies them, "pleasure activists" are artists who "employ their bodies as the inspiration and raw material of their work... bringing to their creative acts a sense of joy and a firm conviction that sexuality is perhaps the most valid and important subject of creative work".[11] The deck I own features two Jokers: Sprinkle in a self-portrait taken in her photographic studio with legs akimbo (clearly displaying her labial piercing) and a finger up her nose, indicating that we shouldn't take her all that seriously; and Jennifer Blowdryer (captioned "Smutfest Showperson"), wearing a jester's hat over her long platinum blonde hair, nipples rouged to echo her highly made-up baby-doll pout. Marisa Carr/Carnesky also appears on the six of spades, here called "Marisa Trollop" and captioned "Nice Jewish Girl". She's topless, wearing "vintage" blue bathing costume bottoms with a gold Jewish star embroidered on the front and presenting the equally oversized matching bra top (with a gold star on each cup) to camera. The biographical blurb in the accompanying booklet claims that she fantasises about submitting to sexually sadistic Nazi captors. This is something she strongly denies; when she confronted Sprinkle with her discomfort about this text, Sprinkle apparently apologised with the explanation that she meant it to emphasise

167

Marisa's image as a provocative and "deviant performance artist".[12]

Sprinkle chose her photographic subjects because, "besides being erotically gifted and having beautiful bodies", they represented an "over-looked and under-appreciated faction of the feminist movement". Most of the photographs on the playing cards originally appeared in *ADAM*, a sex magazine in which Sprinkle had produced her own column entitled "The Sprinkle Salon" for the previous decade. Approaching the age of forty when the cards were made, she had recently decided to cancel the column as she entered "a new phase of life".[13] Redolent of 1940s decks of girlie pin-up cards, Annie considered her homage an apt sex-positive retrospective of an earlier period in her own life.

Explicit (Jewish) Bodies in Performance

By the turn of the millennium, Annie Sprinkle had been letting us into her life, and her body, for some time. Her first one-woman show as a "performance artist" in 1990, *Post-Porn Modernist*, incorporated turns like "A Public Cervix Announcement" and her "Bosom Ballet" that she had refined in burlesque, Smut Fests, and experimental performance venues like Franklin Furnace in New York. Even before she shared her cervix with art world audiences, those so inclined could check out the first film she directed, 1982's second largest grossing sex film, *Deep Inside Annie Sprinkle*. Besides experiencing her image via hundreds of porn films, videos, and photo-spreads, we have also had the opportunity to voyage into her vagina on the internet, learn how to orgasm with her self-help videos, and read a lot about what her work may mean in books by academics. The woman about whom C. Carr wrote "to look inside somebody's body is to see too much"[14] is in danger of suffering the overexposure of scholarly canonization.

However, that Annie Sprinkle is a Western *Jewish* woman is something which is consistently overlooked by academic critics. In fact, Sprinkle has much in common with many of the other Jewish women who are now considered the pioneers of women's body-based art: Leslie Labowitz, Rachel Rosenthal, Hannah Wilke and Judy Chicago. It is not a coincidence that, as Geraldine Harris has noted, much of their art has been interpreted in ways that demonstrate opposing ideological positions: either "postmodernly," showing "woman" to be a culturally constructed

168

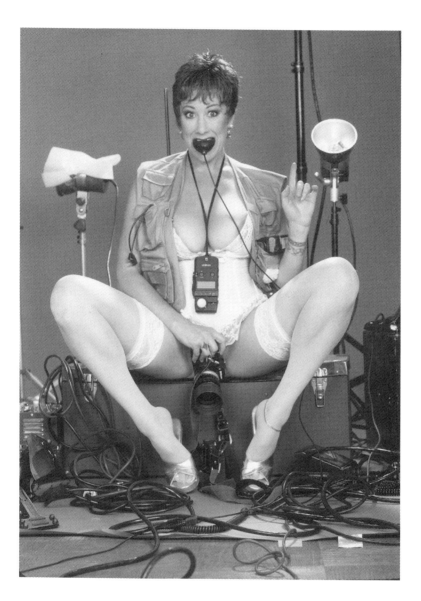

identity category or else as "radical" or "cultural" feminists whose work, according to Jill Dolan, uses autobiography, the often nude body and a privileged concept of women's natural "spiritual" capabilities.[15] I would argue that this very contradiction is the signature of a history of female Jewish performance practice, one which continues unbroken from the classical actress Rachel of the Comedie-Francaise in the 1840s to the present day. Annie Sprinkle and Marisa Carnesky are working in a tradition which inter-textually responds to and exploits the stereotypes of Jewish women that were consolidated in the late nineteenth century and were often conflated with representations of "universal womanhood". Their relationship as artists is a clear example of how this tradition operates and continues.

Annie Sprinkle's work demands to be read inter-textually, across time and media. It is in this way that her Jewishness appears. Occasionally she seems to be playfully leaving a trail of *challah*-crumbs for Jewish detectives to follow. What follows is one example. The box containing Sprinkle's *Pleasure Activist Playing Cards* features a photo of her as the Queen of Hearts (inside the pack, this is actually the image on the Queen of Diamonds); she's wearing strings of pearls and a tiara, puffy emerald green sleeves and matching corset, and is holding a sceptre. Her chest is bare, except for gold nipple tassels with a gold and pearl chain connecting them. Published in her book *Post-Porn Modernist* is a photo clearly taken at the same time. In this picture, the pasteys under her tassels have become giant *mogen davids*, and little Jewish stars are also mounted on the tops of her tiara and sceptre. The caption reads "Portrait of Annie Sprinkle as a Jewish-American Princess" and the credits list the creator of "photo effects."[16] This deliberately constructed self-presentation — part opulent orientalist slut, part fairy mother — in this specific context seems to be offered as a clue to discovering an open secret.

Post-Porn Modernist is meant to be read as an autobiographical scrapbook and we learn in it that one of Annie's grandfathers, Hymie, was a kosher butcher from Poland and the other was an artist who emigrated from Russia.[17] One of the reasons Sprinkle's Jewishness is often missed is because she refers to her upbringing as Unitarian. The Unitarian Universalist Church is one that is pluralist and liberal, respecting Jewish, Christian and humanist teachings. Although it is not mainstream Judaism, it is not entirely antithetical to it and Annie herself feels that she is, and was brought up, Jewish.[18] Unitarian spiritual teachings are based on earth-centred traditions, celebrating the sacred circle of life and living in harmony with the rhythms of nature. Sprinkle's "alternative" or New Age spirituality — evidenced in her

170

Prostitute/Porn Star Turned Sex Guru/Performance Artist

characterization, Anya, the sacred prostitute who represents an aspect of her own sense of self — is actually rooted in *her* concept of Jewishness. It is not located, as Harris suggests, solely in opposition to the Judeo-Christian tradition, at least not as Sprinkle experienced it.[19] Furthermore, staging Jewish womanhood in the

171

tradition that I have established elsewhere has never necessarily meant explicitly naming it in performance.[20]

La Belle Juive

A century earlier at the *fin de siècle*, Sarah Bernhardt came not simply to embody the stereotype of the Jewish woman — *la belle juive*, the Jewess — but practically set its template. This is despite the fact that she never explicitly admitted that she was Jewish and there was no aspect of Jewish practice in her life. *La belle juive* is excessive: "too much", "overexposed". She includes almost every binary opposition in her construction, expressed in terms which always indicate a blurred middle space: hyper-feminine and aggressively masculine; "oriental" and bisexual; she possesses an imaginary phallus (Jewish women were among those accused of having enlarged clitorises); she cunningly "passes" within dominant cultures while remaining estranged; she seems to live "everywhere" and cannot be identified with one "home"; she transcends class distinctions through artifice; she is the innocent (because "primitive" and "natural") whore. It is because of this duality — negotiating actuality and illusion, acting as both an icon and material presence — that a powerful triangle of association was established between performer, prostitute and the Jewess.

The images of embodied self that Annie Sprinkle and Marisa Carnesky present resonate uncannily with those of *la belle juive*. Sprinkle: a prostitute, activist, and artist who has both exploited and dispelled myths of the vagina dentata. And Carnesky: a publicly-funded and award-winning choreographer and performance- maker, who is also a self-created freak of nature, stripper and burlesque artist, the "girl from nowhere", the sideshow hawker selling her own body. Essentially "Jewess" is an erotic label that was (and is) based on a conflation of ambiguous gendered signifiers. She not only expresses the construction of Woman in extremis but is also so much more than feminine that she exhibits masculine traits, and with this added aggression and intellect she can wield power through her cunning and duplicity.

I offer one example here: the story of Salomé, which Sander Gilman identifies as "one of the master narratives" of the stereotype of the Jewish woman at the *fin de siècle*,[21] in which decapitation symbolised the irresistible Jewess's capacity for castration. As Sarah Bernhardt wrote herself, "An actor who per-sonates a character for which he seems to have been born is bound to be a success".[22] It is perhaps for this reason that Bernhardt is so closely associated with Salomé, despite the fact that she never played the role in public. According to Gilman, *La Divine* Sarah was "the embodiment of the sexuality of the Jew".[23] Where Jewish masculinity served as a model of the "other", the Jewish woman was the "other's other". She became the acceptable "taboo", the eroticised and fetishised body of "otherness". In brief, by the 1890s the Jewess came to represent the barely controlled, repressed sex-uality that was presumed to be hidden within *all* women. It is no coincidence that most *fin de siècle* brothels offered a Jewess for hire, for the pleasure of non-Jewish men.

According to Annie Sprinkle, however, she served a very dif-ferent function when she worked in a brothel at the start of career in the sex industry: "I was the token Jewish gal for when Hassidic clients came in. Only the Jewish guys asked for Jewish girls". She also told me that in the 1970s and early 1980s, she knew no other Jewish porn actresses, despite the fact that many if not most of the film-makers and men she performed with (Ron Jeremy, Herschel Savage, Marc Stevens) were Jewish.[24] What has to be remembered is that any signifying representation is contingent and culturally-specific. After a century of aspiring to American middle-class gentility, during which time Jewish women were subjected to Jewish male stereotyping of sexual frigidity, they no longer represented the fetishised erotic. But the tropes of the Jewess remained at the heart of pornocratic femi-ninity just as they did for Jewish femininity, now working with and against the century-old stereotype, both within and without the Jewish community. It could be said that Sprinkle, like Marisa Carnesky later and more explicitly, was responding to layers of stereotyping, excavating and reclaiming the *fin de siècle* Jewess who becomes more complex and subjectified when inter-textually commenting on more recent stereotypes.

The Jewess can only matter (that is, become material and conse-quential) when a Jewish female body intersects with projections of "Woman" and "Jew". For Ann Pellegrini, Bernhardt's ability as an actor is in no way linked to her Jewishness. However, she

seems to represent anti-Semitic constructions of Jewishness as pro-pelling Jewish women into the stereotyped roles of temptress and exotic other. For Bernhardt, the positions of "Jewess" and "actress" are both staged identities. One difference between them is who does the staging. Arguably, Bernhardt reinvents herself on stage and off in response and reaction to being named and identified from without.[25]

Pellegrini's analysis of Bernhardt may serve as a model to indicate the way Jewish women like Sprinkle and Carnesky use stereotypical representation in their careers as performers. When one performs the highly erotic, gendered identity of the Jewess, one is "acting" rather than embodying essentialism.

One of the most common ways this has been achieved is by playfully stripping away in order to make visible the spectacle of masquerade. Erotic expectation has been exploited by many female Jewish performers, supported by displays of nudity or else its simulation or suggestion. Although the nude photos of Bernhardt taken when she was an aspiring young actor were probably a matter of economic necessity, her pose is confident, gazing suggestively at the viewer. Adah Isaacs Menken shocked and delighted international audiences during the 1860s by flashing across the stage on horseback in flesh-coloured tights as Mazeppa (a reference Carnesky cited when she rode naked on horseback through London). Although Menken married a Jewish man and claimed to be Jewish throughout her career, she almost certainly was not. She adopted a Jewish identity at least partly because she recognised the greater "moral latitude" that audiences allowed a Jewish actress like Rachel when the French tragedian toured America.[26]

The star of early Ziegfeld spectacles, Anna Held (who denied her Jewishness vehemently even though she started her career in Yiddish theatre), also made use of this freedom in the 1890s by playing on rumours that she had greeted reporters in her bathtub. Hedy Lamarr gained notoriety for her nude scenes in the film *Ecstasy* in 1933. Xaviera Hollander, a prostitute, madame and adult film star, became notorious as "The Happy Hooker" in the early 1970s. Sprinkle has said that, inspired by Hollander, sex workers like her "began to speak out about...how some of us felt empowered by sex work, grew through it, and sometimes actually enjoyed the sex".[27] In the same year as Sprinkle's *Post-Porn Modernist* premiered, the Jewish comedian and actor Sandra Bernhard was appearing Off-Off

Broadway, gyrating to "Little Red Corvette" in star spangled nipple tassels and g-string.

A slightly different route can be taken charting Jewish female performance practice through the 1960s avant-garde: Anna Halprin's nude improvisatory movement rituals merging the body and the Californian environment. Or Judith Malina in 1968, naked, haranguing the audience of *Paradise Now*, proposing "universal intercourse" as a solution to Middle East conflict ("Fuck the Jews. Fuck the Arabs. Fuck means peace", she shouts from the stage). In Malina's work with the Living Theatre, as in Sprinkle's and Carnesky's, her specific body is meant to be a body of mediation. As Sprinkle has noted, at times she is "worshiped as a goddess" and at others she is hated and her life is threatened: "After all, I am a lot of things people love to hate: a prostitute, a pornographer, a witch, a Jew, an artist, a (full-figured) woman, a bisexual, an avowed masturbator, and perhaps worst of all, a New Yorker".[28] Sprinkle was neither born in New York nor currently lives there; her identification draws attention to a complex conflation. For many non-urban people, living in America or elsewhere, New York signifies decadence and Jewishness.

A (Jewish) Woman Like Me

In her study, *Staging Femininities*, Geraldine Harris is concerned with the way Sprinkle performs the identity category of Woman. Her reflections on this were prompted by a series of questions posed by Elinor Fuchs after she had experienced one of Sprinkle's early performance pieces: "(W)ho is she?" asked a seething Fuchs. "Is she a woman like me?"[29] Annie Sprinkle has always told us quite a lot about the woman she is. As she said, accompanied by an illustrated slide show in *Post-Porn Modernist* (and this has been re-presented on various websites and in her book),

> I was born Ellen Steinberg, but I didn't like "Ellen", so I decided to recreate myself as Annie Sprinkle. Ellen is excruciatingly shy. Annie is an exhibitionist... Ellen wants to get married and have children. Annie wants fame, fortune and a career. After all these years, as hard as it is for me to believe, I've realised that Ellen Steinberg really must be Annie Sprinkle. And the truth is, Annie Sprinkle is still very much Ellen Steinberg.[30]

My spectatorial engagement with Sprinkle's work for well over a decade has produced a recognition that she is very much a woman

175

like me. Annie Sprinkle is Anya the masturbating Goddess is Ellen Steinberg, a nice Jewish suburban girl. Like me. And also like Marisa Carnesky, who cites Jewish screen vamp, Theda Bara, as one of her aesthetic influences. Carnesky creates body spectacles that conjure the diasporic dispossessed. She became the freakish woman who, post-Shoah, chooses to be tattooed as an expression of individuality and an affirmation of mortality. Like me. Sprinkle and Carnesky are continuing a lineage of performing women who reconceptualise a version of Jewish female identity by including foundational positions in its construction and presenting it as a produced material "effect" on, and sometimes in, the body. Chiming with early writing by Judith Butler — who is, perhaps not coincidentally, also Jewish — the gendered identity they are presenting is firmly culturally located, "neither fatally determined nor fully artificial and arbitrary."[31]

In *Jewess Tattooess*, Marisa Carnesky's Whore of Babylon is on vacation: "She's sick and tired of women's sexuality being demonised in traditional cultures, so she's off sunbathing with her friends, Salomé and the Queen of Sheba". In a *Jewish Journal* interview she explained that, "The very sexual, decorated woman is reviled in most cultures, and I was looking for characters that societies have created to guide people away from them".[32] Like many female Jewish performance-makers before her, including Annie Sprinkle, Carnesky knows how to harness the erotic power of taboo to both empower and fascinate.

Chapter Fourteen
Kosher Beefcakes and Kosher Cheesecakes: Jews in Porn — An Overview
Nathan Abrams

Introduction

While pornography may have received comparatively little attention from academics, within the area of Porn Studies itself questions of porn and its relationship to religion and ethnicity constitute an even more glaring knowledge gap. Whereas research has been done on race, class and gender, to date there has been very little scholarly literature addressing the religion and ethnicity of those involved in the adult film industry, or even discussing the representation of religion and ethnicity within porn itself. It is an area which scholars would do well to address. Many of those involved in pornography, on both sides of the camera, belong to faith groups such as Protestantism, Catholicism and Judaism, and the relationship between ethnicity, religion and porn would be a productive area to explore. Indeed, the study of race and ethnicity in porn is woefully underdeveloped and that which has been written has focussed on either black or Asian involvement in porn; where whiteness has been studied, it has been done so only in terms of class.[1] Issues of ethnicity, religion and faith are virtually non-existent. Although Linda Williams noted that "as a cultural form" pornography was "'as diverse as America'", this has not been reflected in academic scholarship.[2] In this essay, I propose to survey what has been written to date on representations of Jews, Jewishness and Judaism in porn. Thus, this article will not so much focus on the *facts* of Jewish involvement in the sex industry, as currently these are hard to ascertain, but rather the *writing* about the subject and the attitudes it reveals. I will use as my evidence online and written material dealing with the subject of Jews in porn. Due to limitations of space, this chapter will be restricted to considering heterosexual, English-language porn in the United States.

Luke Fordism

There is a conspicuous lack of academic and historical research into Jewish involvement in the modern American adult film

177

industry. Presumably, this is due to a number of factors: it is not currently fashionable; it does not fit into the predominant paradigm of current Jewish Studies which has examined almost every other area of Jewish life; the emerging field of Porn Studies has yet to show interest in it; the lack of pornographic material explicitly dealing with Jewishness and/or Judaism beyond a mere handful of examples possibly deriving from a lack of demand for such products; the difficulty of identifying Jews engaged in the industry; and, finally, the fear of an anti-Semitic or anti-Jewish backlash. Consequently, this lacuna has led others to fill the gap. This is particularly evident on the internet where, unfortunately, most of what is posted there is pure speculation, based on gossip, hearsay and industry rumour. The major sources are websites, sexblogs, industry insiders, and ex-industry reporters, in particular, Luke Ford, a self-styled adult industry gossip-monger.

The first thing that we learn from Ford, for example, is the long list of those Jews allegedly involved in the porn industry.

Jews dominate the production and distribution of porn. Leading pornographers with Jewish names include Wesley Emerson, Paul Fishbein, Herbert Feinberg a.k.a. Mickey Fine, Lenny Friedlander, Bobby Hollander, Rubin Gottesman, Fred Hirsch and his children Steve and Marjorie, Paul "Norman" Apstein, Steve Orenstein, Theodore Rothstein, Reuben and David Sturman, Ron Sullivan, Sam and Mitch Weston (Spinelli).

Jews accounted for most of the leading male performers of the 1970s and '80s. Hebrew studs include Buck Adams, Bobby Astyr, R. Bolla (Richard Parnes), Jerry Butler (Paul Siderman), Seymour Butts (Adam Glaser), David Christopher (Bernie Cohen), Steve Drake, Jesse Eastern, Jamie Gillis, Ron Jeremy (Hyatt), Michael Knight, Ashley Moore, David Morris, George Payne, Ed Powers (Mark Arnold), Harry Reems (Herbert Streicher), Dave Ruby, Herschel Savage, Carter Stevens (Mal Whorb), Marc Stevens, Paul Thomas (Phil Tobias), Marc Wallice, Randy West and Jack Wrangler...

Jewish female performers include Avalon, Jenny Baxter (Jenny Wexler), Busty Belle (Tracy Praeger), Chelsea Blake, Tiffany Blake, Bunny Bleu, Lee Carroll (Leslie Barns), Blair Castle/Brooke Fields (Allison Shandibal), Courtney/Natasha/Eden (Natasha Zimmerman), Daphne (Daphne Franks), Barbara Dare (Stacy Mitnick), April Diamond, Jeanna Fine, Alexis Gold, Tern Hall, Heather Hart, Nina Hartley, C. J. Laing (Wendy Miller), Frankie Leigh (Cynthia Hope Geller), Gloria Leonard, Traci Lords (Nora Louise Kuzman), Amber Lynn, Tonisha Mills, Melissa Monet, Susan Nero, Scarlett O. (Catherine Goldberg), Tawny Pearl (Susan Pearlman), Nina Preta,

178

Tracey Prince, Janey Robbins (Robin Lieberman), Alexandra Silk, Susan Sloan, Annie Sprinkle (Ellen Steinberg), Karen Summer (Dana Alper), Zara Whites and Ona Zee (Ona Simms).[3]

Unfortunately, Ford provides no corroborating evidence for any of these names and how he arrived at a definitive conclusion as to their Jewish status. Given that Jewishness is routinely subsumed into whiteness, Jewish ethnicity and/or religious affiliation are largely illegible in the pornographic texts, especially when it is taken into consideration that very few films have contained any overt ethnic or Jewish themes or narratives. Jewish women and men then are literally hidden in pornography (unless they choose to out themselves) as almost everybody changes their names and, given the prevalence of circumcision in America, Jewish men do not even stand out in this respect. When compared to those who, by dint of their skin colour, cannot hide their ethnic and/or racial origins, Jews are much harder to identify.

Aside from some figures who openly discuss their religious/ethnic/cultural identity in published interviews (Jeremy, Butts, Hartley, Pacheco), Ford's laundry list of female and male performers has no clarification as to how it was determined they were Jewish. Were they asked? How? When? Is it rumour? What/who are the sources and how reliable are they? What criteria did he use? One or two Jewish parents? Did he ask them? Did they tell him? This has led to inaccuracies. While many of the names on his list do indeed suggest a Jewish heritage on the part of some of these performers, this is not an exact science. Names as a means to determine origin are a particular complicating factor for if a Jewish male marries a non-Jew, according to Orthodox Jewish law his children are not Jewish although the name would indicate otherwise; conversely, if a Jewish woman married out her children would remain Jewish despite a name which might not. Another problematic factor is the adoption of certain popular American or Americanised surnames. Traci Lords (born Nora Louis Kuzma), for instance, had a Jewish father and non-Jewish mother. Consequently, despite her name, by Orthodox Jewish law (*halacha*) she is not considered to be Jewish (although it should be stated that other forms of Judaism, such as Liberal, operate differing practices). Furthermore, there is no corroborating evidence since many of the performers that Ford mentions did or do not refer publicly to their Jewishness nor did/do they

179

view it as particularly important in the way they either conduct/ed their lives or in motivating their decision to become engaged in the adult industry in the first place.

Support for this thesis does arrive from other industry insiders. Sheldon Ranz, who used to write for industry magazine *Adult Video News* (AVN), stated: "The majority of leading male performers in American pornographic films over the years have been Jews. Not a 'disproportionately high' percentage... but over 50%".[4] Likewise, in a letter to *The Forward* former AVN reviewer Phil Goldmarx pointed out that:

> Both as film character and performer, the "kosher cheesecake" — the proud, curvaceous Jewish woman who delights in consensual, guilt-free and non-reproductive sex — first arose in the predominantly Jewish adult film and video industry. Annie Sprinkle, Nina Hartley, Gloria Leonard, Susan Nero, Melissa Monet, Ona Zee, Traci Lords, Amber Lynn and Alexandra Silk have been among the top pornography stars. During the 1970s and 1980s, 12% of all female pornography performers were Jews, and most of the leading male performers were, in fact, "kosher beefcakes".[5]

I suspect that both Ranz and Goldmarx are using the same sources of information and it is clear that Luke Ford relied heavily on the former for his; however, yet again, it must be asked how they arrived at such definitive figures ("over 50%" and 12% respectively) of the involvement of Jews in porn, particularly when they provide no substantiating evidence to support these claims.

The issue here is that Ford in particular has provided the basic building blocks of the discussion of Jewish involvement in pornography, as many others, especially where the internet is concerned, are content to follow him. Those who allege a Jewish dominance of the adult industry do so largely based on information emanating from Ford's websites which, subsequently, provide the sources for further speculation. Thus, Ford has had a disproportionate influence in shaping the writing about Jews and porn. Beneath or within the topic of the Jewish invasion or domination of porn, therefore, lies the journalistic-gossip of Ford. I confess that, in my original article on this topic, which appeared in the *Jewish Quarterly* in 2004, I was one of these, perhaps naively and uncritically accepting of many of Ford's unconfirmed statements.[6] This is not to say that what Ford says is untrue per se but that until his statements are independently confirmed, then they must be treated with a healthy scepticism. As a measure of this, at least one of Ford's names is inaccurate, namely "Seymour Butts (Adam Glaser)". Not only did Butts begin his adult career in the 1990s but his last name is spelt "Glasser". Some confirmation appears to come from David Hebditch and Nick Anning's 1988 book, *Porn Gold: Inside the Pornography Business*, in which they reported that "some industry insiders claim that porn in the United States is essentially a Jewish business".[7] But yet again they provide little supporting evidence for this assertion. They do point out that, "the 'Debbie' series of porn video titles (e.g. *Debbie Does Dallas*) is considered to be something of an 'in-joke'", a play on the idea that "Debbie is supposed to be most popular name for a Jewish-American Princess" but we are invited to take this journalistic statement at face value.[8]

Positive Jewish Porn

Luke Ford is a prime example of those who support the Jewish involvement in porn. Of course he has to, as a Jew who earns his living as a professional porn gossip-monger, and he can hardly bite the hand that feeds him. Inevitably, this produces an unfortunate myopia and he is perhaps deliberately blind to the realities and negative aspects of the business. The various websites that take his name (www.lukeford.com, www.luke-ford.net, www.lukeisback.com), echoing his book *The History of X*, advance a thesis of Jewish sexual liberalism, which privileges a discourse of Jewish rebelliousness and sexual liberation that, in his opinion, has helped to widen the boundaries of a Puritanical American culture. Jewishness, then, is elaborated here through a familiar narrative pitting "Jewish" sexual liberation and political radicalism versus white American Christian Puritanism.[9]

Ford's information favours those who present a positive, pro-porn narrative and ignores the seedier side of the industry (drugs, AIDS, abuse, exploitation) to push his thesis and is uncritically supportive of his co-religionists who made their living in the industry during the 1970s and 1980s. Ford is very selective in his use of evidence, too, on two counts. First he largely restricts his subjects to those Jews who help to advance his *weltanschauung*; because he's Jewish himself, one suspects that

181

Ford does not want to present Jews as exploitative, seedy merce-
naries, taking advantage of young women. Indeed, some of them
like Ron Jeremy and Bill Margold come across as almost cuddly,
despite the fact that what they did, and Ron still does, for a living
repulses many. Second, Ford sticks to the pre-AIDS "golden age",
when porn was shot on film with comparatively high budgets and
contained narrative plotlines, a period when porn seemed tame,
acceptable almost, as it nearly became mainstream. He tends to
ignore those Jews who do not fit his pro-porn narrative.

What emerges from reading Ford, both online and in his book, is
the notion of the Jewish porn star as the "sexual rebel". During the
so-called "golden age" of porn, the 1970s, if Ford is to be believed,
then there was a deeper psychological and/or political element
beyond the mere financial as to why Jews in particular became
involved in porn, because there was never more than a working
wage to be earned: during his best year as an actor, for example,
Richard Pacheco made about $30,000. But it is not pointed out, dur-
ing that era, that such a sum was above average. For Ford, there was
an element of nonconformity in Jewish X-rated involvement; the
1970s generation of porn stars were in it for the rebellion. Ford
wrote, "they live[d] in a community of rebels" and "Porn is just one
expression of this rebellion against standards, against the disci-
plined life of obedience to Torah that marks a Jew living Judaism".
Ford cites Bill Margold as an example of this for he was someone
who "found a place where I thought I could create and be left alone.
But see, I figured in the X-rated Industry there were no rules.
Apparently there are rules everywhere, and I hate that".[10] Veronica
Hart is drafted in to reinforce the point: "People in pornography are
usually rebels".[11] Martin Blinder is also quoted to support his assertions, "Sex is the one area innately subversive to the rules and
regulations of society, and pornography is the celebration of the subversive side of sex. Pornography revels in all of sex's deliberately
subversive permutations".[12] In this way, then, Ford presents Jewish
participation in porn as a revolt against (often) middle-class parents
who wished their children to be lawyers, doctors and accountants.
Performer Bobby Astyr is quoted as putting it this way, "It's also an
'up yours' to the uncles with the pinky rings who got down on me as
a kid for wanting to be musician".

Ford goes one step further to suggest that Jewish porn stars
were also part of the sexual liberation movement. His description
of Nina Hartley is typical:

True-believing communist and porn star Nina Hartley wants everyone to have a piece — a piece of sex and a piece of the means of production. She descends ideologically from the Marxist Jewish philosopher Herbert Marcuse who prophesied that a socialist utopia would free individuals to achieve sexual satisfaction. Nina descends literally from a line of radical Jews. Her grandfather (a physics professor) and her father (a radio announcer) belonged to the Communist party. Her home celebrated Hanukkah, Christmas, Passover and Easter as holidays rather than holy days.

Likewise, Richard Pacheco is quoted as stating, "Before I got my first part in an adult film, I went down to an audition for an X-rated film with my hair down to my ass, a copy of Wilhelm Reich's *Sexual Revolution* under my arm and yelling about work, love and sex, which were Reich's three principles". Jewish involvement in the X-rated industry is presented as a proverbial middle finger to the entire WASP establishment in America, as a means to get back at feelings of inadequacy caused by anti-Semitism. Astyr is again used to this end when Ford quotes his recollection of having "to run or fight for it in grammar school because I was a Jew. It could very well be that part of my porn career is an 'up yours' to these people". It is noticeable that the phrase "up yours" appears at least twice on Ford's website, and clearly stands as a metonym for Ford's viewpoint.

In this way, for Ford, porn becomes a way of attacking the intolerance of the mainstream culture. As he selectively presents them, some of the porn stars from the golden era viewed themselves as frontline fighters in the spiritual battle between a Christian America and secular humanism. Ford's subjects come across as, in the words of Andrew Ross, "pornographer-intellectuals", individuals who may well have fallen into the industry by accident rather than choice but once they were in it used it to better society and not simply for their own, personal, venal ends. His extensive profile of Nina Hartley certainly helps his case in this respect. His lack of address, in his book at least, of current porn stars such as Seymour Butts, Ariana Jollee, Joanna Angel and Daphne Rosen also works to the same ends, for such individuals are often in it for the money and, if they are to be believed, the enjoyment of sex. The lack of reference to Butts, Jollee and Rosen also pushes the "nice guys and gals of porn" theme that Ford favours so much because they joined the industry after the advent of AIDS.

A similar narrative comes from Daniel Shocket's piece in *Shmate*, itself a reprint of an earlier article published in *Samantha Fox's X-Rated Cinema* (1984). In his interviews with five "top Jewish male porn performers", Shocket, another adult film reviewer, emphasised their niceness, deploying such terms as "dignity", "fairness" and "respect". He first printed the line, which Ford subsequently reprinted (with acknowledgement) on the internet, that "all X-rated actors interviewed bragged about their joy in being anarchic, sexual gadflies to the puritanical beast".[13] It is clear from Ford's writing that *Shmate* was the major source of his information. What is more, while not about the role of Jews in porn per se, Susan Faludi's *Stiffed: The Betrayal of Modern Man* (1999) argues that the first generation of porn actors, "wound up in porn films, partly to make a living and partly out of a vague political urge to rebel, or at least revel in the freedom of the sexual revolution".[14] In support of her thesis, which reinforces that of Ford in the preceding paragraph, she quotes Nina Hartley's derision of the younger generation of female porn performers as "postfeminist princesses": "They are very traditional. They are not sexual revolutionaries".[15]

Negative Responses

If Ford and Ranz present the positive side of Jews in porn, then many anti-Semites are eager to depict its converse. This response is characterised by its privileging of the *dominance* of Jews in porn. Here, they cite articles such as mine which show that Jews were active in the adult film industry on both sides of the camera, both as performers and producers. In terms of the latter category, they draw on the list of names, beginning with the German Jewish erotica dealers in the book trade between 1890 and 1940 and continuing to the present, to argue their case. Such names include Harry Donnefeld, Reuben Sturman, Russ Meyer, Fred Hirsch, Steven Hirsch, Paul Fishbein, Al Goldstein, Seymour Butts, Gloria Leonard, Nina Hartley and Ona Zee (the last four names being performers-cum-producers). In this way, it parallels the same discourses that highlight the Jewish dominance of other areas of American life such as Hollywood and the media in general (the press, publishing and academia). They are not keen to stress the discourse of Jewish rebelliousness and sexual liberation but rather to turn it on its head in order to emphasise alleged Jewish *subversion* of white Christian America. Examples of this can be found at "The 7th Fire" website under the title "Jewish Dominance in the Porn Industry",[16] Focal Point Publications, which bills itself as the "official website" and "Publishers of works of Real History by David Irving and other authors"[17] and the website of David Duke.[18] All of these websites are anti-Semitic in intent. Where Duke is a neo-Nazi, Irving is a convicted Holocaust denier. Their websites are a montage of extracts culled primarily from the print media to prove that Jews are corrupting pure, white Christian society. To that end, they selectively choose their quotations about Jewish involvement in pornography, and other criminal activity with a sexualised content, to back up their spurious assertions. Little is worth quoting here, for they simply recycle what others have written. For example, they unfortunately use my original article to this end, particularly in light of the fact that since it was written by a Jew it provides some sort of legitimacy to their claims.

For this group, the attractiveness of the "Jewish dominance of porn thesis" is due to its updating of the discourses of classic anti-Semitism. As Jonathan Freedman has written, in pre-modern times, the Jewish male seen was seen as "primitive, more fully sexual, impulsive and hyperphallic", as well as "unmanly, weak, effeminate or otherwise outside the norm of properly assertive masculinity".[19] In the anti-Semitic literature of the late nineteenth century, for example, much of which was rooted medieval anti-Jewish polemics, Jewish males were "either seen as debased lechers yearning for Christian girls (preferably virgins) or as men-women". This "cultural contradiction was ameliorated when the two merged into a new character type: the Jewish pervert, a figure who conjoined the will-to-power of the hyperaggressive Jewish male with sexual nonnormativity of the feminised Jewish man".[20]

Outside of the anti-Semitic and racist websites, many such sympathies find their way onto sites that are not designed to disseminate such views. The message board of Ron Jeremy's website is a case in point; the vast majority of posters do not even mention his Jewish identity. However, two posters stand out in this respect and illustrate the sort of thinking that has motivated some of the writing about Jews in porn. Both posters not only identify Jeremy's Jewishness, which in itself is not inherently racist or anti-Semitic, but they also then go on to do so negatively and in classically anti-Semitic terms. "adolf" [sic] writes:

> Ron jeremy you dirty fat JEW.
> You are the embodiment of world JEWRY.
> You're fat, ugly, and fuck everbody.
> Just like all jews.
> Whats your real name Ron?
> Is it Herschel or Schmue or is it Yehudi.[21]

Poster Daniel Bitton takes a similar approach.

> fuck you ron i hope you die of cancer ..i hate you mother fucker jewesh fuck you and fuck all jewesh..mother fucker i hope god will send another one like hetler to fuck you jewesh..mother fuckers..you are all scandela..untill the end of life ..your place will be the hell...it's waiting for you ..bitch..your mother was fucked by german and arabs
> i hope those arabis fuck you jews ,,mother fuckers...you are all hated no boby likes you...fuck you i hope you have aids..as soon as possible..fuck you...i hope you die of sancer...fuck all americans jewesh....fuck jews...scandels...[22]

Little explanation or exegesis here is needed.

Among this group, there is no consideration that Jews in porn do not represent their religious/ethic group. That these performers tend to be secular Jews, having received varying degrees of Jewish education but, by and large, define their Jewish identity in cultural rather than religious terms, is completely overlooked. In fact, the converse is taken to be true: that these Jews precisely are representative of their wider community. That porn is actually dominated by Gentiles is far less interesting to them. That very few porn films have had overtly Jewish themes is never discussed. Jewish performers have either not been willing, or failed, to inject any significant Jewish content into their work. Most likely, this is due to a perception that their audiences would not be interested in such material, as in general, very few porn films have had any overtly ethnic or religious themes. Moreover, since the advent of the "wall-to-wall" and gonzo genres, which privilege sex over plot and hence in which there are no storylines whatsoever, the possibility of Jewish content is even more tenuous. Thus, the Jewishness, which does feature, tends to be either minimal, such as a few Yiddishisms (including Seymour Butts' preference for using the Americanised version of the Yiddish for bottom, viz. *tushy*, in his titles, or *Adam & Eve's House Party 1* (1996), which stars Nina Hartley as "hostess with more than the mostest when she heads up a 'Schtupperware' party" for her girl-friends), or played for laughs, as when Ron Jeremy orgasms to the pulsating beat of Jewish music while wearing a *yarmulke* and *tallit*, and shouting, "Oy, vey! Oy vey!" in his directorial feature *Casting Couch* (1983).

On the other hand, *Deep Throat* does have a character that clearly seems to be based on a Jewish stereotype. In *Debbie Duz Dishes* Nina Hartley plays a sexually insatiable suburban Jewish housewife who enjoys energetic and guilt-free sex with anyone, male and female, who rings the doorbell. It became a commercial success, sold very well, and spawned two sequels. Vivid Video released *The Burning Bush*, which featured "Four Hours of Hot, Jewish Babe Vivid, Sex Action Fiddling on the Roof". *Mitzi's Honor* (1987), a spoof of *Prizzi's Honor* concerned a "kosher capo", a Jewish mobster played by Sol Bloomgarden (Randy West) who cheats on his Jewish wife, Mitzi (Sharon Mitchell), but only with other Jewish women. And *The Three Daughters* was a more serious attempt to chart the career aspirations of the three Clayton sisters who live in upstate New York; a large *mezuzah* is clearly apparent on the doorpost of their house. However, such examples are rare; indeed, it is probable that most spectators of porn do not know that the performers are Jewish in the first place and the market has not shown any sign of capitalising upon the ethnicity of some of its performers as a means of product dif-ferentiation until recently. Yet, none of this is mentioned by those who seek to use porn as another means to attack Jews.

Others who are keen to emphasise that Jews in porn do not represent their communities of origin are Jews who consider Jewish involvement in the adult film industry shameful. On the Jewish website, *Nextbook*, Steve Almond writes: "Should we, as Jews, be proud of our role in this? No."[23] Luke Ford cites Anti-Defamation League National Director Abraham H. Foxman as saying, "Those Jews who enter the pornography industry have done so as individuals pursuing the American dream, not as rep-resentatives of their religious group. Moreover, anti-semites [sic] never seem to take note of the fact that the most prominent pornographers in America are Hugh Hefner and Larry Flynt, neither of whom is the least bit Jewish. Finally, though individual Jews may play a role in pornography, Jewishness does not".[24]

Conclusion

In its *pornographical* survey, this chapter has attempted to open up a new avenue of study which, in general, should be a greater consideration of the role which religion and ethnicity play, as well as their representation, in porn; and, in particular, that of Jewishness, Jews and Judaism. However, the latter, as I have pointed out, presents certain problems and it is the challenge of this topic to begin to write a value-free history of Jews in the adult film industry that parallels and hence is an analogue to that which has been written about Jewish involvement in mainstream Hollywood; one that is emptied of the positive spins that overlook the harmful, as well as the pejorative takes which only serves to emphasise the negative as a further means to attack Jews.

Chapter Fifteen
The Heartbreak Yid: Sex, Intermarriage and the JAP in 1960s and 1970s America
David Weinfeld

In 1974, sixteen-year-old Diana Bletter saw *The Heartbreak Kid* and reacted with intense anger. She voiced her outrage in a letter to the *New York Times*: "Anti-Jewish women jokes", she wrote, like those in *The Heartbreak Kid*, "are brainwashing Jewish men to believe that Jewish women are not good enough for them, and that the ideal wife is a gentile one from North Dakota".[1] American Jewish popular imagery of the 1970s ran rife with representation of intermarriage, or at least, romantic relationships between Jewish men and non-Jewish women. Philip Roth's 1969 novel *Portnoy's Complaint*, followed by a slew of Woody Allen movies, *Play It Again, Sam* (1972), *Sleeper* (1973), *Annie Hall* (1977) and *Manhattan* (1979), all played on the same theme. Simultaneously, the organised Jewish community hotly discussed and debated intermarriage. Yet bizarrely, these two discourses barely intertwined.

What course did these two discussions take and why did they remain separate? Pop culture texts implicitly blamed Jewish women for intermarriage, and frequently described Jewish men fleeing in droves from "Jewish American Princesses" (JAP), to embrace instead non-Jewish women, *"shiksas"*. Jewish communal and intellectual discourse, however, in magazines like *Commentary* and *Moment,* as well as academic journals, did not blame Jewish women, and ignored the "JAP" as a potential explanation for the problem of exogamy. Since these community leaders and academics mostly ignored gender differences in intermarriage, they focussed their discussion much more on religious issues and proposed coping strategies rather than offering explanations or assigning blame.

Materialism with a Jewish Face: The Birth of a Princess
The stereotype of the JAP preceded the rise in intermarriage among Jews in the United States. It began to emerge in the 1950s, as postwar Jewish economic prosperity and suburbanization grew. Despite its age, no uniform image of the JAP has

189

dominated popular culture. The stereotype has undergone considerable transformation in its half century existence, from daughter in the 1950s and 1960s to wife in the 1970s to daughter again in the 1980s, gradually becoming universalised, more American than Jewish.

Despite these fluctuations, the Jewish American Princess stands out as the most negative, stereotypical portrayal of the Jewish woman in popular culture. Spoiled, whiny, materialistic and shallow, the Jewish American Princess dominates her father and then her husband, taking advantage of their money in exchange for the honour of being associated with her. If the Jewish Mother represented everything from the old world that the Jewish male sought to escape, then the JAP represented everything he hated about American culture. The JAP was the catastrophic blend of what is Jewish and American. She possessed none of the charm of her mother. She had her strength and assertiveness but none of her warmth or devotion. As Charlotte Baum, Paula Hyman and Sonya Michel observed in 1977: "the stereotype of the Jewish American Princess is intrinsically critical: it regards her as demanding everything and giving nothing; her assertiveness is viewed as an instrument of emasculation".[2]

America got its first whiff of the JAP in a 1955 episode of *Molly,* a popular television sitcom previously called *The Goldbergs,* which featured an immigrant Jewish family in the Bronx and starred Getrude Berg in the lead role. In this episode, "Rosie's Nose", Rosalie Goldberg, Molly's Americanised daughter, wants to get a nose job. According to David Zurawik in *The Jews of Primetime,* Rosalie may have been "television's first 'Jewish American Princess'".[3] In Zurawik's analysis, "Rosie's advanced consumerist tendencies, as well as her tendency to cry or get extremely upset at the slightest disturbance to the Goldberg's household, go a long way toward defining her in terms of the 'princess' stereotype".[4] She ultimately did not get a nose-job, but the idea that she considers it — ostensibly not just to look prettier but to look less Jewish — is a warning of the dangers of materialism that come through assimilation.

Even more significant among proto-JAP figures, Marjorie Morgenstern, the protagonist of Herman Wouk's 1955 novel *Marjorie Morningstar* and the 1958 film of the same name, further developed the stereotype. Though Marjorie was not a

190

thoroughly unsympathetic character, Wouk established her comfortable upbringing and the requisite self-centeredness that came with it. Her father, once a poor immigrant, ran a successful business and "spent every dollar he earned on the comfort of his family and the improvement of their station in life".[5] The family's upward mobility gave rise to Marjorie's snobbishness. At sixteen, when the family still lived in the Bronx, she dated a simple but well-intentioned fellow named George Drobes, who attracted her mostly because he was four years her senior and had a car. With the words, "then Marjorie moved to Central Park West", Wouk alerted readers not only to George's inadequacy, but also to Marjorie's class-based elitism.

Marjorie aspired to be an actress; "Morningstar" would be her stage name; an indicator of her desire to assimilate and escape her roots. While this ambition did not quite fit the JAP mould, since she sought personal fame, not simply a husband and sugar daddy, in another way, Marjorie displayed the most pernicious aspect of the JAP stereotype: sexual frigidity. She developed this reputation at a young age and held out on her lover Noel Airman for most of their relationship. This unwillingness to engage in sexual intercourse was critical to the demonization of the JAP in the 1970s.

Although other JAP-like figures preceded her, Brenda Patimkin of Philip Roth's 1959 novella *Goodbye, Columbus* best embodied the early stereotype of Jewish American Princess. Beautiful and pampered, she was a far cry from the *yiddishe mamme*. Her expertise at tennis signified her Americanness. Yet this also exemplified her Jewishness. As anthropologist Riv-Ellen Prell noted, the active image of the "Yiddishe Mamme" can be contrasted with the passive, inactive Jewish American Princess. Whereas the Yiddishe Mamme toiled and sacrificed for her children, Jewish American Princesses do not work at all. They "do not sweat".[6] When they do, Prell argued, they produce unproductive sweat: they expend energy on the tennis court, not in the kitchen or in the workforce. In his conversation with Brenda, Neil Klugman, the book's protagonist, learns exactly what kind of girl he was dealing with. While he graduated from the Newark College of Rutgers University, she attended Radcliffe. Brenda did have her nose "fixed" for a thousand dollars.[7] She led a life which "consisted to a large part of cornering the market on fabrics that are soft to the skin". She always relied on mother and maid to do the dishes.[8]

Unlike Marjorie Morgenstern, however, she was not a virgin. The film version of *Goodbye, Columbus* opened in 1969, the same year Roth's *Portnoy's Complaint* was published. The movie's tagline, "Every Father's Daughter is a Virgin" emphasised the sexuality of the young Ali MacGraw, who played Brenda. While this was undoubtedly important to the story, it deviated from the trajectory of the stereotype, which seemed to have taken on a life of its own. Stereotypes and popular imagery are inherently unstable and often contradictory. In the 1970s, the JAP grew up, and carried with it all the worst qualities it had developed in the decades before.

The JAP Wife of the 1970s... and Her *Shiksa* Counterpart
The JAP stereotype that emerged in the 1970s was Brenda Patimkin, now married, but minus the sex-drive. The JAP as wife, as opposed to JAP as daughter, marks an important change. In 1971, *New York* magazine published a cover story, "The Persistence of the Jewish American Princess" by Julie Baumgold,[9] which contained segments from a David Susskind interview with filmmakers David Steinberg and Mel Brooks:

> **David Steinberg**: Well, the [Jewish Princess] is the daughter that's been spoiled and brought up by the parents and they never quite get out of it, and they expect their husbands to cater to them in the same way that their mother and father did.

> **Mel Brooks**: It's codified. If you meet a Jewish girl and shake her hand, that's dinner. You owe her a dinner. If you should take her home after dinner and rub around and kiss in the doorway, right. That's already a small ring, a ruby, something. If, God forbid, anything filthy should happen amongst you, that's marriage and the same grave. You're buried together, screwed into the earth together. They do expect a lot for a little fooling around.[10]

Steinberg and Brooks emphasised the transition from spoiled daughter to spoiled wife — with sex a means to an end, namely, marriage, and after marriage, they opined, the sex ends as well. The stereotype they described is of a manipulative woman, cold, materialistic and selfish, and uninterested in sex.

This image persisted in the 1970s. Journalist Leslie Tonner's 1975 book, *Nothing but the Best: The Luck of the Jewish Princess,* acknowledged the stereotype that JAPs, particularly when married, had no interest in intercourse. She referred to the Woody

Allen joke, in which he asks his ex-wife to have sex with him: "'Over my dead body', she answered. 'Why not?' he replied. 'Isn't that the way we always used to do it?'"[11] This image is fleshed out in folklorist Alan Dundes' 1985 article "The JAP and the JAM in American Jokelore", which examines joke cycles in the 1970s and early 1980s. Here are some classic JAP jokes he records:

> How do you keep a Jewish girl from fucking? Marry her.
> What do you call a JAP's nipple? The tip of the iceberg.
> What's the difference between JAPs and poverty? Poverty sucks.[12]

Dundes argued that the telling of such jokes can be an indication of "genuine ambivalence" about assimilation.[13] Crucial here, however, is the Otherness of the JAP, which distinguishes her from Gentile women. Philip Roth's two early novels, taken together, provide this contrast. Neil Klugman's relationship with JAP Brenda Patimkin failed in *Goodbye, Columbus* (1959). Alexander Portnoy, the public-spirited but sexually depraved protagonist of *Portnoy's Complaint* (1969), showed no interest in Jewish women at all. As I mentioned at the outset, in the 1970s, Woody Allen made several movies harping on the same theme. *Sleeper, Annie Hall, Manhattan* and *Play it Again, Sam,* all featured a Jewish "schlemiel" protagonist, played by Allen, pursuing a *shiksa* lover, played by Diane Keaton.

But perhaps the best example of this scenario was the 1972 film *The Heartbreak Kid* written for the screen by Neil Simon and directed by Elaine May. The movie was based on a 1966 short story by Bruce Jay Friedman called "A Change of Plan", but the film extended the plot and sharpened the imagery so that, according to Jaher, "the chief female character in the movie *The Heartbreak Kid* (1972) is the ultimate *shiksa* courted by a young Jewish status-seeker".[14] The protagonist, New York Jew Lenny Cantrow, meets and marries a young Jewish woman, Lila Kolodny. On their Miami honeymoon, Lenny begins to have second thoughts, which are confirmed when he meets the beautiful, blond *shiksa* Kelly Corcoran, played by Cybil Shepard. Lenny falls madly in love with Kelly and ultimately annuls his marriage and follows his *shiksa* to Minnesota, where he finally convinces her anti-Semitic father to allow them to marry.

Lila does not conform to all the JAP stereotypes. She is not wealthy, but rather crude and vulgar. She refuses to have sex before marriage, but once married she immediately becomes raunchy. Still, she fails to please Lenny sexually, talks incessantly in bed, eats a Milky Way after sex and announces when she has to urinate, much to Lenny's disgust. When she eats, the food goes all over her face. She has a horribly whiny, Jewish voice. In Miami Beach, she refuses to put on sunscreen and gets badly sun-burnt. The whining only gets worse. Kelly, meanwhile, is gorgeous and carefree. Rather than talk all the time, she "loves listening" to Lenny, because he is "so positive about everything", like her father. When Lenny asks her: "Do you always do what your father says?" She responds, "Always". In this way, she is precisely the opposite of a JAP. Though Lenny follows her to Minnesota, he cannot marry her until her anti-Semitic father finally gives in. Kelly is not merely fun and exciting; she is refined, wealthy and sophisticated. She fulfils the fantasy — as described by historian Frederic Cople Jaher — of *shiksa* as saint. She sleeps with Lenny before marriage and satisfies him completely, fulfilling the opposing fantasy of *shiksa* as whore. Because she herself comes from a rich family, she will never be financially dependent on her new husband. She is everything the JAP is not.

In his 1983 article, "The Quest for the The Ultimate Shiksa", Jaher noted the presence of the "'good' *shiksa*" in Jewish-American fiction: "the Christian woman as humble servant". This image "derives from the belief held by many Jewish males that gentile females are less demanding, aggressive, materialistic, and self-centred than females of their own faith". Jaher wrote: "this humble version of the *shiksa* sometimes exists in the consciousness of Jewish-American novelists as the counter symbol of the 'Jewish American Princess'".[15]

Tonner too observed these rival images. "Hundreds upon thousands of Jewish men mix, mingle and even marry the dreaded species of *shiksa* simply because they think *shiksas* are free of all that sexual *mishigoss*. Nice Jewish boys flee the princess en masse in an effort to escape her uptight heritage". She went on: "Hopelessly, helplessly, the princes line up to confess that they cannot rid themselves of the fantasies: Catherine Deneuve, Marilyn Monroe, Swedish airline stewardesses, apple-cheeked Midwestern farm girls. 'The attraction', says one spaced out soul, is definitely sexual, 'the ultimate, fantastic, hallucinatory voyage'".[16] Jaher realised this dichotomy of *shiksa* as saint and *shiksa* as sexual fantasy. The latter is the "sexy *shiksa*, frequently a blue-eyed blonde who offers gratifications withheld, at least until marriage, by proper Jewish girls".[17] Alexander Portnoy, the protagonist of *Portnoy's Complaint,* provided a key example for Jaher. Growing up, Portnoy was a brilliant student, but masturbated compulsively and was extremely sexually maladjusted, supposedly because of his infamous mother's overbearing parenting. As an adult, he was a civil rights lawyer, defending New York downtrodden; at the same, time, he voraciously pursued non-Jewish women to satisfy both his immense sexual appetite and his desire to assimilate and escape his mother. Of Portnoy, Jaher wrote: "the well-behaved achiever should be rewarded with the girl-next-door in an upper-class WASP neighborhood, but the shameful prisoner of lust deserves (and craves) the *shiksa* whore".[18]

Nonetheless, the two images, that of *shiksa* saint and *shiksa* sinner, merged together in the figure of the "The Ultimate Shiksa," who can make a respectable wife and a satisfying lover: "These ultimate *shiksas* represent the exotic outsider in Jewish life. The Jewish men who court them are lured away from their birthright and drawn toward their new nationality. Thus the ultimate *shiksa*... symbolises the plight of the Americanising Jew".[19] The JAP, then, must be contrasted with this *shiksa* image, one which lured Jewish men away from their faith. The JAP, in essence, perverted the American dream. The financially successful husband can never enjoy that success because of the JAP's nagging, spending and frigidity. She reminds him that as a Jew, he will never be able to experience the American dream as fully as a Gentile, unless, of course, he marries the Ultimate Shiksa.

Thus, popular culture representations of intermarriage were highly gendered, reflecting the statistical reality of the time. The Jewish communal and academic discourse on exogamy, however, did not focus on gender. In mostly ignoring gender, Jewish communal leaders and intellectuals were perhaps at first naïve, but ultimately, just as prescient as the novelists who forecast rising intermarriage a generation earlier.

Jewish Communal and Academic Discourse on Intermarriage

In 1964, Marshall Sklare wrote a prescient article in *Commentary* titled "Intermarriage & the Jewish Future". Arguing that the low rate of Jewish intermarriage was misleading, Sklare noted the "well-known fact that considerably more Jewish men intermarry than do Jewish women", indeed, that "seven out of every ten Jews who intermarry are men".[20] Though he did not investigate the matter thoroughly, he did observe that:

> the present state of Jewish endogamy seems to have been grasped more firmly by the novelists than by the sociologists. Even a hasty rundown of the work of such writers as Bernard Malamud, Saul Bellow, Philip Roth, Leslie Fielder, Bruce Jay Friedman, Herbert Gold, Jack Ludwig, Myron Kaufmann, Neal Oxenhandler, etc., reveals how much recent American fiction has dealt with marriage or the strong possibility of it between a Jew and a Gentile.[21]

Not only are all the authors listed male, but the fiction Sklare referred to involved Jewish men marrying Gentile women. Fiction anticipated reality. The JAP, not yet named, was not mentioned. Sklare, however, did speculate as to causes of intermarriage. He noted that Jewish male insider/outsider status might be appealing to some Gentile women who did "not want Bohemian husbands but rather respectable ones who are somewhat 'different'". He wrote "the old notions about the causes of intermarriage are beginning to look as outmoded as the causes themselves". What were these notions?

> Both on the folk level and in more sophisticated terms, these notions invariably involved the imputation of some defect in the contracting parties. If a Gentile girl agreed to marry a Jew, it must be because no Christian would have her, or because *she had made herself sexually available as no Jewish girl would deign to do*. Similarly, if a Jewish man married a Gentile girl, it must be because no Jewish girl would have him, or because he was a self-hater or a social climber.[22]

Sklare was thus aware of the stereotype of Jewish female sexual frigidity or restraint, but did not regard it as a significant cause of intermarriage. Of the letters written in response to the article, only one touched on gender at all, by Judith Guttman of Waltham, MA:

Mr. Sklare asks the wrong question in his article on intermarriage.... He should ask what is wrong with the Jewish girl. What Mr. Sklare ignores in his discussion of the high rate of intermarriage on the University of Illinois faculty is that no "properly" reared Jewish girl would consider a professor for a husband when she might have a lawyer or a doctor — or even a dentist! Where is that politically liberal, avant-garde Jewish student to find his mate? Among the potential officers of suburban Hadassah?[23]

Whether Guttman was being sarcastic or sincere is difficult to determine. Clearly, however, the idea that Jewish intellectual men might flee materialistic, proto-JAPs was part of the cultural consciousness, even if intermarriage rates were still quite low.

Writing decades later, Riv-Ellen Prell was clear about the effect of these stereotypes. Unmarried Jewish men and women in their twenties and thirties in the 1970s, 1980s and 1990s saw in the image of the JAP their hopes for a future wrenched from them. "To love and marry a Jew became the equivalent of being a slave of middle-class life".[24] The solution, implied but unstated in Prell's book, is intermarriage. Yet the discourse in Jewish academic and popular journals during the 1970s, 1980s and 1990s dealing with intermarriage did not blame the JAP or Jewish women particularly. Sociologists Sidney Goldstein and Calvin Goldscheider's 1966 study compared native-born Jews to immigrants and those from the suburbs to those from the cities. They noted in a terse manner that Jewish men were more likely to marry non-Jews than Jewish women, adding that this "conforms to the patterns observed in almost all other communities".[25]

Four years later, the reality of higher rates of intermarriage had begun to arrive. Marshall Sklare again wrote in *Commentary*, with a piece, "Intermarriage and Jewish Survival". He concerned himself primarily with the avoidance of discussion in the Jewish community, and then with how the Reform movement should deal with the issue. Most American Jews, he wrote, "are dimly aware that such unions after all represent the logical culmination of the quest for full equality".[26] This time, there was no talk of gender; political scientist Leonard Fein wrote a letter to *Commentary* in response, noting that "roughly two thirds of all Jews who intermarry are male", but he too made no effort explain this gender gap.[27] In the 1970 book *The Jewish Family in the Changing World,* four articles pondered intermarriage, and none emphasised gender.

197

This pattern continued through the 1970s. By the end of the decade, discussion continued, but the gender gap remained unexplained. The National Jewish Population Study of 1972-1973 led to more alarmism at the prospect of an imagined American Jewish demographic demise. Fred Massarik, scientific director of the study, displayed a more positive view in his June 1978 *Moment* magazine article "Rethinking the Intermarriage Crisis", which attempted to alleviate some of these fears. This article noted gender differences "among non-Jewish wives, nearly forty percent claim conversion to Judaism.... Conversely, among non-Jewish husbands, the rate of conversion to Judaism is not more than three percent". He also noted that "Jewish husbands with non-Jewish wives are less likely to report a 'strongly Jewish' upbringing than Jewish wives with non-Jewish husbands". Finally, he mentioned the statistical reality of the time, that "there are a good many more intermarriages where the husband is Jewish than where the wife is Jewish".[28]

In 1979, David Singer attempted to summarise the discussion in *Commentary* magazine. His article, which refers to Sklare's previous two pieces, was appropriately titled "Living with Intermarriage". Faced with a thirty-one percent intermarriage rate, Singer lamented the lack of understanding of the phenomenon. "We do not know why Jewish men tend to intermarry more than Jewish women, and whether this situation is changing as a result of the women's movement".[29] That same year, Bernard Farber, Leonard Gordon and Albert J. Mayer observed that the situation was indeed changing, writing that "the proportion of Jewish women marrying non-Jews seems to be increasing at a more rapid rate than that of men". They speculated that "the changing role of women generally" not only led to increased intermarriage among Jewish women, but also to a decline in "identity change", namely, that Jewish and Christian women who married outside their faith would be less likely to convert. They anticipated a trend where "each marital partner would abandon religious identification toward a non-religious, secular pattern".[30] They did not assign any blame, but rather attempted to observe and predict a phenomenon.

Perhaps the closest these mainstream Jewish communal magazines came to blaming Jewish women as a cause for intermarriage in the late 1970s came in an April 1977 *Moment* magazine feature: "We are Many: Our Readers Speak on

Intermarriage". This collection of responses to a January survey contained this anonymous admission:

> I am a fairly attractive Jewish boy, age 25, and I date *only* non-Jewish girls. I am sure I will marry one, but I will insist she convert first. If someone would teach Jewish girls how to use makeup and look attractive, teach them some manners and how to be feminine instead of feminist, the intermarriage rate would plummet. Since there is no chance of that happening, I'm off to see my beautiful Korean girlfriend.[31]

The frequency of this sort of view among young Jewish men of the 1970s remains difficult to gauge. With rising intermarriage rates among Jewish women, however, as well as host of other factors that could lead to intermarriage, the likelihood that this sort of reasoning proved decisive for men or women making marital decisions at this time is slim. Probably, Jewish men and women simply married who they pleased; the stigma to marrying outside the faith, while perhaps not entirely gone, was significantly diminished, as was their desire to maintain their religious heritage.

Conclusion

By the end of the 1970s, intermarriage rates rose among Jewish women, a trend that would continue to this day. The Jewish communal and academic discourse that dealt with Jewish exogamy in the 1960s and 1970s, however, did not emphasise the gender gap, or its decline. Jewish communal leaders and intellectuals did not blame Jewish women for intermarriage: if anything, they blamed Jewish men, and implicitly valorised Jewish women, who married within the fold and protected the faith in hearth and home. Pop culture texts, in contrast, implicitly blamed Jewish women for the increasing rates of Jewish male intermarriage. Specifically, the development of the JAP stereotype, a reflection of Jewish misogyny, directed fictional Jewish men toward exotic shiksas. Yet there is no evidence to suggest that these contrived scenarios actually guided the decisions of real Jewish men. Several possible explanations exist for the rising rates of intermarriage in the 1960s and 1970s, from suburbanization to spatial integration to secularization and assimilation more broadly. Deficiency on the part of Jewish women is not one of them. Communal leaders and intellectuals may not have understood why intermarriage rates were increasing, but they knew enough not to blame Jewish women. To them, intermarriage was not a gendered issue, not an expression of male anxiety or ambivalence towards assimilation: it was a reality. Explanations were less important than solutions, Rabbis were more important than JAPs.

Postscript
What happened to the JAP? More modern JAPs, like Alicia Silverstone's Cher Horowitz in *Clueless* or Princess Vespa, the Druish Princess in *Space Balls*, are not as pernicious characters as Lila Kolodny or Brenda Patimkin. The same can be said, perhaps to a lesser extent, of Fran Descher's Fran Fine in *The Nanny*. Today, the stereotype is no longer immediately associated with Jews, as in *Legally Blonde* or *Beverly Hills 90210* or *The O.C.*, where the Jappiest characters are not even Jewish. Elle Woods in *Legally Blonde* is the exact same character as Cher Horowitz in *Clueless*, only Elle is not Jewish, and Cher is, but just barely (interestingly, Elle is played by non-Jewish Reese Witherspoon and Cher by Jewish Alicia Silverstone).

Chapter Sixteen
"I'm one of the few males who suffer from penis envy": Woody Allen and the feminised Jewish male
Thomas Grochowski

While there have been books that examine Woody Allen's philosophical themes, and many others that broadly cover Allen's work, I know of no book-length treatment of Allen's Judaism — or the theme of sex. Allen's humour relies on intercourse. We must remember that "intercourse" is not limited to sex. The other main definition refers to communication, to dialogue among individuals and peoples. Language is often, as David Biale notes, a substitute for sex.[1] Allen's comic works bring out a range of multi-levelled linguistic and sexual discourses; in so doing, they not only expose the foibles of modern sexual relations, but offer us an image of intellectual eroticism unknown to American popular culture prior to the sixties.

It is not entirely possible, given the parameters of this anthology, to provide a full account of the ways that religion and sex interact in Woody Allen's *oeuvre*, which includes over forty films, three collections of prose, nearly a dozen plays of varying length, and a handful of recorded pieces of stand-up comedy. Here, I shall focus on two central issues, one ideological, the other formal. First, I wish to claim that Allen's early *schlemiel* persona is an embodiment of what Daniel Boyarin has called the "femminized Jewish male", an erotic image in contrast to pop cultural images of American masculinity as embodied by John Wayne (or, significant for Allen, Humphrey Bogart).[2] In contrast to WASPy men of action, the Allen persona is a thinker, using his considerable "street sense" to resolve conflicts (when he actually succeeds in resolving them, of course). Second, I will suggest that Allen's *formal* style creates an unstable textual and social order, one that commingles religion, language and sex for the purposes of lampooning them.

Allen's humour is based, like that of many comics, on exaggeration for effect. Allen has certainly emphasised his Jewishness, and played upon popular Jewish stereotypes, but his primary goal as a comic was to create a sympathetic character that was well-liked by the audiences.[3] This persona was pathetic, yet rooted in the surreal more than the real: mothers knit chickens and swallow mah-jong tiles; policemen, out of tear gas, perform the death scene from *Camille* in order to get kidnappers out of a house; he is given a pet ant that is passed off as a dog; elevators make anti-Semitic remarks.

Allen's jokes on romance, marriage, and sex cultivate his loser status, but also manifest identity matters for second-generation American post-war Jews. He tells of a cousin who married "a very thin girl from the neighbourhood who had her nose lifted by a golf pro". The cousin sells mutual funds and provides, among other kinds of insurance, "orgasmic insurance — if her husband fails to satisfy her sexually, Mutual of Omaha has to pay her every month". Maurice Yacowar writes that the routine, while emphasising the Allen persona's sense of inadequacy, also presents the audience with an idealised image of assimilated Jews, one Allen's character does not reach in his stand-up routines.[4] Allen's own marriage is referred to in one routine as "the Ox-Bow Incident." In another bit he claims he and his wife were married by "a Reform rabbi, a *very* Reform rabbi — a Nazi". He complains of his wife's "Nazi recipes" like "Chicken Himmler". Ultimately this marriage falls apart, and Allen runs into a conflict between his religion and the state law: in order to get a divorce, New York requires proof of adultery, but the Ten Commandments forbid it.

Allen also plays upon the incongruities of the idea of this wimpish character who gets beaten up by Quakers (as he says in *Sleeper* [1973]) and who could also be "basically... a stud". In admitting to trouble with mechanical objects, he claims that "anything I can't reason with or kiss or fondle I don't get along with". He also suggests that "there is something seductive about me when I shoot crap". He takes a girl home and, while thinking of baseball players to prolong the moment of sexual climax, the girl is already taking a shower. As Allen's career turns from stand-up material to writing, acting, and directing films, the persona turns, too. The stand-up character is likeable in part because of his willingness to expose his sexual neuroses for an audience (though this is an *appearance* of exposure). Despite the incongruity of the image of Allen and Monique Van Vooren appearing together in a vodka ad (a historical fact that Allen rewrites for comic effect in a famous monologue), "Woody Allen" does become a kind of intellectual sex symbol for a generation of postwar, college-educated "neurotic" Americans, be they Jews or not. While *Annie Hall* (1977) is regarded as Allen's best manifestation of the *schlemiel* persona, I will begin my discussion with a different character from an earlier work to show the very clear attributes of the "feminised" Jewish male who ultimately becomes an erotic masculine figure.

Play it Again, Sam was produced on Broadway in 1968, and dramatically extends Allen's sexual persona. It focusses on the troubles of Allan Felix, a Jewish film critic and recent divorcé, and is said to have been loosely based on Allen's own post-divorce dating life. Allan cannot get anywhere with women, because he's too nervous and anxious. It is in the 1972 film adaptation of Allen's play, directed by Herb Ross, where we can see the effeminate characteristics of the Allen persona, something not as apparent in the stand-up routines. Allen sets up a contrast between Allan Felix and Humphrey Bogart, who appears as a ghostly counsel to Allan. Bogart represents the tough, urban gentile masculinity Felix aspires to; after an apprenticeship playing gangsters, Bogart appeared in *The Maltese Falcon* (1941) in what would be his archetypal performance: tough, street-smart, unable to be hoodwinked by anyone, including a tricky dame. Here Bogart insists that "dames are simple" and that "somewhere along the line you got it backwards". Bogart means that it is the woman who is supposed to get pretty and smell nice for the man, that the man need "just whistle" to get the woman. When Allan tries to act tough, drinking a bourbon and soda as per his icon's advice, he chokes on the booze, unable to tolerate this initiation into manhood. At one point, when answering the door, Allan's voice is a nervous, feminine sound, saying, "yes?" Later, while at a club watching a beautiful blonde dancing, Allan shouts out, "I want to have your child!" This, as Sam Girgus points out, is another reversal of gender identification, since the linguistic convention is to say that the woman is having the man's baby.[5]

In the development of the Allen persona in the stand-up material and in the early films, we can suggest that Allen is a representation of the Jew as the effeminate male, that he is not manly enough, by the ideals set forth by Hollywood (and by a larger social order, looking not only at the Allan Felix/Bogart dyad but also the stand-up routines). But we can also see something different. The persona Allen crafted in the sixties and seventies represents what Daniel Boyarin has called the "idealised Jewish femme", an image Boyarin also refers to as "the eroticised Jewish male sissy" and the "femminised Jewish male". Boyarin, citing hundreds of years of Jewish history, recognises the anti-Semitic discourses that condemned the Jew as being unmanly, and other historians have emphasised the importance of the Jewish male's *physical* features as crucial to this discourse, especially but not limited to the circumcised penis. But Boyarin argues that there is more than mere stereotyping at work: "the Jewish ideal male as countertype to 'manliness' is an assertive historical product of Jewish culture".[6] The construction of the Jewish femme, going back to the period of the Roman Empire, is in Boyarin's view an active one by Jewish leaders seeking an alternative masculinity to that being promulgated by the Romans. Boyarin's historical analysis of Jewish history and rabbinical texts offers us Jewish men who are learned, sensitive and erotic. Allen, too, presents with an image of a Jew who is sexy in part because of the incongruity of his calling himself a sexual being, because of his willingness to expose his neurosis on a stage or screen.

As the narrative of the film unfolds, Allan's friends Dick and Linda Christie try to help him find dates, all of which end disastrously. Allan is only able to relax when with Linda, who is as neurotic and insecure as he, and when Dick goes away on a business trip "Bogart" encourages Allen to turn a dinner meeting with Linda into a romantic date. Linda, neglected by Dick's obsession with his work, spends the night, affirming Allan's attractiveness. While Allen has used the fantasy elements of the Bogart iconography to suggest that his character's trouble lies in his inability to distinguish fantasy from reality, the film's ending, which imitates the end of *Casablanca*, demonstrates that one can *use* art to make some sense of life.[7] Allan tells Bogart, "the secret isn't in being you; it's in being me". (When characters cannot tell the difference, as Cecilia the waitress cannot in *The Purple Rose of Cairo* [1985], their stories end more tragically.)

Annie Hall continues this exploration of the erotic male Jew as positive archetype rather than anti-Semitic stereotype. Alvy Singer is *not* a schlemiel in the way that Allan Felix is. Alvy discovers the opposite sex at a very young age — and also experiences rejection at that time. He considers his problem with women to be symbolised by Groucho Marx's joke about not wanting to join any club that would have him as a member. Yet despite two failed marriages, Alvy continues to date women and does not have the kind of trouble meeting them that Allan Felix has. One *Rolling Stone* reporter he dates characterises her sexual experience with Alvy thus: "sex with you is really a Kafkaesque experience... I mean that as a compliment". And in the central relationship of the film, we see a range of sexual experiences that demonstrate the joys and struggles of interpersonal relations in the wake of the Sexual Revolution. As the first Allen film to treat the characters in generally more realistic settings — as opposed to the nineteenth century Russia of *Love and Death* (1975) or the futuristic world of *Sleeper* — *Annie Hall* presents images of sex and the body in more "natural", or perhaps we should say, less fantasmic, circumstances. There are no giant breasts as in *Everything You Always Wanted to Know About Sex* (1972), and no outrageous food/sex encounters as in *Bananas* (1971). There are sex jokes of course, but there is a different tone to them. In *Sleeper*, Allen's Miles Monroe, when learning that the artist Luna got a Ph.D. in oral sex, responds, "did you take any Spanish with that?" In *Annie Hall*, Alvy comments after having had sex with the *Rolling Stone* reporter, "I think I'm starting to get some feeling back into my jaw." The body is given a more natural expression. Alvy describes Annie as "polymorphously perverse", but clearly this "perversion" is not the kind of perversion we see represented in earlier Allen films. Sex is also linked to the creative process: after they make love for the first time, Alvy says to Annie, "as Balzac said, there goes another novel".

Sex is also a locus of conflict in the film. There are a number of moments of "problematic" intimacy, as we see in scenes from Alvy's first two marriages, and in a later encounter with Annie, where Alvy refuses to let Annie smoke grass before making love. Alvy's controlling tendencies create a *Pygmalion*-like relationship for him and Annie, and once Annie begins to reject the student-teacher relationship, they cannot continue. While Kathleen Rowe has criticised Allen's persona as an anti-feminist one, who uses his "feminization to prop up [his] own authority" in order to "instruct women about relationships, romance, and femininity itself", Allen clearly presents his own subjectivity as one that is as shaky as the Coney Island roller coaster Alvy claims to have lived under.[8] The split-screen reveals the two different perspectives Alvy and Annie have about the same quantity of sex. Alvy's personality is also fuelled by his political and religious paranoia, which creates sexual neurosis: he is unable to have sex with his first wife because of his concerns over the Kennedy assassination and when Alvy argues that the country's failure to support New York City, then in the midst of a deep financial crisis that had mayor Abe Beame preparing to file for bankruptcy, he claims, "it's foreskin", emphasising the locus of the federal government's refusal to offer aid to the city right on the body of many of its Jewish inhabitants. Alvy even claims that "the rest of the country thinks we're left-wing Jewish homosexual pornographers. I think of us that way sometimes and I *live* here". In twentieth century American culture, the Jew is often characterised as urban, in images both positive and negative. In a famous monologue, Lenny Bruce claimed that to live in New York is to be a Jew, regardless of one's ethnicity — and conversely, if you live in middle America, even if you are Jewish, you are a goy.[9]

As a good patient of Freudian analysis, Allen also gives us a castration image. His mother, having been introduced in a previous flashback, now faces the camera to criticise Alvy's pessimistic and paranoid world view, while peeling a carrot. Alvy's identification with the feminine is most explicitly affirmed when he admits to Annie that he is "one of the few males" who has penis envy. The joke reinforces Alvy's sense of inferiority due to his Jewish body, but also cultivates an alternative masculine identity, as he does when he explains his refusal to shower in public places by saying "I don't like to get naked in front of other men of my gender". Allen has emphasised Alvy's outsider status from the opening monologue, and here in this exchange from his first meeting with Annie Alvy marks himself as a male but not a *masculine* one in the goyish sense.

It is easy, too easy, to see Alvy and Annie's relationship as a stereotype of the Jew/WASP Romance, with both Jewish male and WASP female indulging in fantasies about the Other. In discussing *Annie Hall* — and in some cases the off-screen romance between Allen and Diane Keaton, which had ended years before this film was shot — many writers make the comparisons to Philip Roth's *Portnoy's Complaint* (1969), where we see so explicitly the male Jew's sexual obsession with the goy female — to the point where for Alex Portnoy America itself *means* a *shiksa*. There is no question that the contrast between the Brooklyn-born Alvy and the Wisconsin-born Annie is part of the charm of the film, and that our knowledge of Allen and Keaton's romance adds to that charm. But Allen both heightens and defuses the mythic stature of that contrast, the erotic mysteries the Other holds. (Compare *Annie Hall* with Spike Lee's *Jungle Fever* [1991] and you'll see what I mean; in Lee's film, that mythic attraction is the film's focal point.) Allen and Ralph Rosenblum's editing is crucial here.

The film begins with Alvy's monologue, and after telling a series of jokes that are designed in part to set up one of the film's key themes but also to suggest the way Alvy uses humour to deflect some hard truths of life, Alvy tells us, "Annie and I broke up". We know right away that the relationship has ended, and indeed the first time Annie appears she is angry and argues with Alvy. Even when Allen shows us their first meeting, he does not idealise Annie in the way that Portnoy idealises his goyish fantasies. There is a kind of reversal of roles in that meeting, as Annie, wearing a tie, clearly is nervous and stammering as she cautiously pursues Alvy. While Alvy chides her by asking if she grew up in a Norman Rockwell painting, it is Annie who first speaks of the two's ethnic differences: "you're what Grammy Hall would call a real Jew". Since at this point in the film, Allen has also shown us scenes of his first two wives, we know that Alvy's sexual libido is not limited to gentile fantasies. Unlike the problems of his two marriages, the sex with Annie is described in highly positive ways — at first. However, later in the film, the two struggle, as she insists on smoking pot before sex and both see the same amount of sex –" three times a week" in different ways (she thinks it's too much, he not enough). But even when Alvy confesses that he fell for the Wicked Queen in *Snow White*, and casts Annie as that queen, when she speaks we are aware of the artifice of the scene when the Annie Queen says, "I don't have periods — I'm a cartoon character!" Despite the fact that the relationship ultimately fails, both Alvy and Annie have grown from the conflict — Annie has gained self-confidence, and Alvy has gained a greater understanding of the more positive aspects of his outsider status.[10]

Allen uses more than merely the Jew/WASP dynamic to express the struggles of modern lovers. One of his greatest talents is the way that he blends a range of narrative and cinematic *forms* and thus creates a social order that is textually as well as morally unstable. *Play it Again, Sam* not only mocks the Allen persona's lack of the masculine stereotype, but debunks the illusion of Bogart as masculine ideal, showing it as mere Hollywood construction. (My favourite such moment occurs when Bogart, encouraging Allan Felix to make a romantic dinner with Linda, stops him from buying the wrong candles because "those are for a Jewish holiday".) Allen places his own character into *Casablanca* in the beginning, where it almost seems that Bogart is saying his farewell lines to Allan, not just to Ingrid Bergman, and at the end, where Allan re-enacts *Casablanca*'s farewell scene with Linda and Dick (minus the shooting of Conrad Veidt).

Elsewhere Allen uses sex to send up the private eye genre. In, "The Whore of Mensa", for example, Allen's private eye, Kaiser Lupowitz, a Jewish descendant of the hard-boiled dicks (as it were) of a previous generation, breaks up an intellectual prostitution ring. Lupowitz's client, the appropriately named Word Babcock, a man who manufactures and services joy-buzzers, has been cheating on his wife not by having sex with beautiful prostitutes, but rather by having intellectual conversations with "thin" and "pale" college grads in hotel rooms. Babcock explains: "I want a quick intellectual experience, then I want the girl to leave". When Kaiser poses as a john and makes a date, he notes that the ring "really knew how to appeal to your fantasies. Long, straight hair, leather bag, silver earrings, no makeup". Even though the story ends with Kaiser in bed with a physical education major, intending to contrast pleasures of the body with those of the mind, "The Whore of Mensa" nevertheless implies a close relationship between physical and intellectual prostitution. (It is also significant that one of the reasons Word Babcock turns to Flossie, the "madam" of this ring, concerns the wife's refusal to discuss Ezra Pound or T.S. Eliot, the two Modernist poets most associated with anti-Semitism.)

In Allen's most overtly *parodic* films, which destabilise the genres being parodied, an unstable social order where sex becomes not merely a joke, but a public one, is often created. In *Bananas*, Fielding Mellish meets a politically active young woman named Nancy (played by Allen's second wife, Louise Lasser). Their relationship fails because she says there is "something missing" that she cannot identify (though she is able to note some of Fielding's shortcomings that are apparently *not* the something missing). When Fielding returns as the new leader of the banana republic of San Marcos, she is in awe of the leader, whom she finds sexually attractive — until he reveals who he is. The film ends, as it opened, with an ABC Sports broadcast featuring Howard Cosell commentating "at ringside" the "consummation" of the marriage between Fielding and Nancy. Sexual intercourse is likened to professional boxing, as terminologies from the sport are used to discuss the sex. It is the public display of sex, its transformation as spectacle, that Allen seems to be ridiculing (even as he had made a reputation discussing his private life in his stand-up monologues). If the earlier borscht belt comics told wife jokes, Allen's humour expands the range of topics to the explicit.

Allen's most notorious film concerning sex takes its title from the Dr. David Reubens sex manual. Though some of Dr. Reubens' questions are used, *Everything You Always Wanted to Know About Sex* (*But Were Afraid to Ask)* features original answers written by Allen. The film is a series of comic sketches, each one answering a question. Allen appears in four of the sketches — as a medieval court jester trying to seduce the queen (under orders from his father's ghost, making *Hamlet*'s Freudian connection explicit); as an Italian lover whose girlfriend can only find sexual pleasure in public places; as a young sex researcher who must stop a mad scientist from unleashing a giant breast upon the world; and finally, as a sperm in a sketch explaining what happens during ejaculation. While Allen is surely ridiculing the very idea of sex manuals, he is also suggesting that public talk about sex is having a dehumanising effect on the public, reducing it to cold, scientific terminology.

This is made explicit in what is considered the most outrageous and offensive sketch, an answer to the question, "What are sex perverts?" This scene has been criticised extensively for its being over the top, though that must surely be a relative term in a film that features a psychiatrist having an affair with a sheep. "What's My Perversion?" is a parody of the game show *What's My Line?* Panellists like Regis Philbin must guess the odd behaviours of contestants instead of their professions. The "blasphemous" part of the sketch occurs at the end, when an elderly rabbi from the Midwest (who must correct host Jack Barry on how to pronounce his name, Chaim) is allowed to live out his fantasy by being tied up and spanked, while his wife sits at his feet violating a food taboo by eating pork ribs.

The scene has been criticised for its blasphemous content, but what Allen really demonstrates in the sketch is the way that

209

modern society has created such a blurred line between private and public that every action, sacred and profane, can become potential fodder for entertainment. While Yacowar is right to claim that, in the context of the seventies, this sketch is Allen's way of "render[ing] openly the sexual obsessions that ...television generally deals with by coy indirection",[11] in our modern tabloid media landscape, "What's My Perversion?" seems very much a prophecy of so-called trash-TV talk shows, where people openly speak about their various sexual and emotional dysfunctions. The sketch opens not with the rabbi, but with another man, whose perversion is that he likes to expose himself on subways. The panellists must play the "What's My Line?" game in order to figure out what his perversion is. This is clearly metaphor for our modern society, where people expose their faults and failings in order to get attention on television. When we meet the rabbi, the absurd nature of his fantasy makes it almost impossible to take seriously. David Biale sees the sketch as mere farce, and weaker because of it.[12] But for all its outrageousness — both this sketch and the film as a whole — Allen's basic theme is that modern sex is not as liberating as the rhetoric of the sexual revolution would have us believe. The difference is that people's neuroses are visible for all to see.

I am not blinded to the sexism of Allen's work. As Boyarin notes, the tradition that helped to construct this femminized Jewish male ideal does contain a negative history of repression of women. One can see similar criticisms of Allen's work, from the casual, typical sexism of his early films to the outrageous misogyny of Harry Block, the title character from *Deconstructing Harry* (1995). Nevertheless, I do believe that the persona Allen created through his standup material, his writing, and his performance in his films, manifests important qualities of the eroticised Jewish male intellectual, an image that works with and strains against stereotypes.

Notes

Chapter 1

[1] Arthur A. Cohen and Paul Mendes-Flohr, eds., *Contemporary Jewish Religious Thought* (New York: Free Press, 1987), 971.

[2] Shlomo Pines, *Guide for the Perplexed* (Chicago: University of Chicago Press, 1974), I, 59. See also Moshe Idel, *Kabbalah and Eros* (New Haven: Yale Press, 2005), 8-11.

[3] Examples of such doctrinal affirmations made by modern Jewish movements include the 1937 Columbus Platform of the Reform Movement, the 1988 declaration of principles, *Emunah v'Emet*, of the Conservative Movement, and the widely-circulated *Thirteen Principles of Faith* written by Aryeh Kaplan and endorsed by the Orthodox Union.

[4] Cameron Afzal, "Early Jewish and Christian Mysticism: A collage of working definitions" (a paper presented at the 2001 Conference of the Society of Biblical Literature), 3.

[5] Yehezkhel Kauffmann, *The Religion of Israel: From its beginnings to the Babylonian Exile* (New York: Schocken Books, 1960), 21-23.

[6] Translations of this passage appear in Frank Cross, *Canaanite Myth and Hebrew Epic* (Cambridge, MA: Harvard University Press, 1973), 22-23; W. W. Hallo and K. L. Younger, eds., *The Context of Scripture*, vol. 1, (Leiden: Brill, 2000), 280-281.

[7] Hallo and Younger, eds., *The Context of Scripture,* vol. 1, 400. See also Thorkild Jacobsen, "The Battle Between Marduk and Tiamat", *Journal of the American Oriental Society* 88:1 (January-March 1968), 104-108.

[8] David Biale, *Eros and the Jews* (New York: Basic Books, 1992), 114; Howard Eilberg-Schwartz, *God's Phallus* (Boston: Beacon Press, 1994), 111.

[9] Harold Bloom, ed., *Song of Songs* (New York: Chelsea Publishing, 1988), 49-63.

[10] Idel, *Kabbalah and Eros,* 34. Notice the reiteration of the sexual commandment "be fruitful and multiply" (Gen. 1:28) in the context of the Temple.

[11] Idel, *Kabbalah and Eros*, 33.

[12] Arthur Green, *Guide to the Zohar* (Stanford: Stanford University Press), 51-52; see also Idel, *Kabbalah and Eros*, 140.

[13] Arthur Green and Barry W. Holtz, eds., *Your Word Is Fire: The Hasidic Masters on Contemplative Prayer* (Woodstock, VT: Jewish Lights Publishing, 1993).

[14] Geoffrey Dennis, *The Encyclopedia of Jewish Myth, Magic, and Mysticism,* (Woodbury: Llewellyn Worldwide), 65-67. See also Lawrence Fine, ed., *Physician of the Soul, Healer of the Cosmos: Isaac Luria and his Kabbalistic Fellowship,* (Stanford: Stanford University Press, 2003), 173-174.

Chapter 2

1 See generally Saul Olyan & Martha Nussbaum, eds., *Sexual Orientation and Human Rights in American Religious Discourse* (Oxford: Oxford University Press, 2006).

2 For example, Lot's neighbours in Sodom are not "gay" — they merely seek to gratify their desires with Lot's (male) guests, and Lot appears to think that his (female) daughters would serve as suitable replacements. Likewise the sexual partners in Leviticus 18:22; these are not "gay men" — they are men engaging in same-sex activity. See Jonathan Katz, *The Invention of Heterosexuality* (New York: Plume, 1996); Stephen D. Moore, *God's Beauty Parlor, and other Queer Spaces in and Around the Bible* (Stanford: Stanford University Press, 2001), 16; David Halperin, *One Hundred Years of Homosexuality* (New York: Routledge, 1990), 43-48.

3 Mary Douglas' *Purity and Danger: An Analysis of Concepts of Pollution and Taboo* (1966) remains the classic study on this subject. See also Ken Stone, *Practicing Safer Texts: Food, Sex, and Bible in Queer Perspective* (New York and London: T&T Clark, 2005), 46-50; Jacob Milgrom, *Leviticus 1-16: A New Translation with Introduction and Commentary* (Anchor Bible Commentary, New York: Doubleday, 1991); John Sawyer, ed., *Reading Leviticus: A Response to Mary Douglas* (Sheffield: Sheffield Academic Press, 1996). I discuss *Purity and Danger* in part two.

4 See Saul Olyan, "'And with a Male You Shall Not Lie the Lying Down of a Woman': On the Meaning and Significance of Leviticus 18:22 and 20:1", *Journal of the History of Sexuality* 5:2 (1994); Michael Satlow, "'They Abused Him Like a Woman': Homoeroticism, Gender Blurring, and the Rabbis in Late Antiquity", *Journal of the History of Sexuality* 5:1 (1994); Steven Greenberg, *Wrestling with God and Men: Homosexuality in the Jewish Tradition* (Madison: University of Wisconsin Press, 2004), 192-96; Daniel Boyarin, "Are There Any Jews in 'The History of Sexuality'?" *Journal of the History of Sexuality* 5:3 (1995), 333-35.

5 Bradley S. Artson, "Gay and Lesbian Jews: An Innovative Legal Position", *Jewish Spectator* (Winter 1990); Jay Michaelson, "How can you be gay and Jewish?", *Zeek* (September 2004).

6 Later Jewish sources also discuss procreation and family stability as rationales for the Levitical prohibition. See Greenberg, *Wrestling with God and Men*, 147-74.

7 My discussion here is primarily about sexuality, not gender. Obviously, many of the points raised in a conversation about sexual minorities apply with equal or more force to gender minorities, but my primary focus here will be on the religious significance of homosexuality.

8 Others include Theodore Jennings, *Jacob's Wound: Homoerotic Narrative in the Literature of Ancient Israel* (New York and London: Continuum, 2005); Moore, *God's Beauty Parlor*; Raymond-Jean Frontain, ed., *Reclaiming the Sacred: The Bible in Gay and Lesbian*

212

Culture (Binghamton, NY: Harrington Park Press, 2003); Robert E. Goss and Mona West, eds., *Take Back the Word: A Queer Reading of the Bible* (Cleveland, OH: The Pilgrim Press, 2000); Ken Stone, ed, *Queer Commentary and the Hebrew Bible* (Cleveland, OH: The Pilgrim Press, 2001); idem., *Practicing Safer Texts*; Gary David Comstock & Susan E. Henking, eds., *Que(e)rying Religion: A Critical Anthology* (New York and London: Continuum, 1997).

9 See David Halperin, *One Hundred Years of Homosexuality* (New York: Routledge, 1990), 43-48; Katz, *The Invention of Heterosexuality*; Eve Kosofky Sedgwick, *Epistemology of the Closet* (Berkeley: University of California Press, 1990); Gilbert Herdt, *Third Sex, Third Gender: Beyond Sexual Dimorphism in Culture and History* (New York: Zone, 1996).

10 See Emmanuel Levinas, "Diachrony and Representation", in *Time and the Other and Additional Essays* trans. Richard A. Cohen (Pittsburgh: Duquesne University Press, 1987), 45-51; Jacques Derrida, "Like the Sound of the Sea Deep Within a Shell: Paul De Man's War", *Critical Inquiry* 14:3 (Spring 1988), 590-652.

11 David Halperin, *Saint Foucault: Toward a Gay Hagiography* (New York: Oxford University Press, 1995), 61.

12 See Randy Conner, *Blossom of Bone: Reclaiming the Connections Between Homoeroticism and the Sacred* (San Francisco: Harper SanFrancisco, 1993); Toby Johnston, *Gay Spirituality: The Role of Gay Identity in the Transformation of Human Consciousness* (Maple Shade, NJ: Lethe Press, 2004); Mark Thomspon, *Gay Spirit: Myth and Meaning* (New York: St. Martin's, 1988).

13 Conner, *Blossom of Bone*, 99-125; Will Roscoe, "Priests of the Goddess: Gender Transgression in Ancient Religion", *History of Religions* 35:3 (1996), 295-330.

14 Will Roscoe, *Changing Ones: Third and Fourth Genders in Native North America* (New York: Palgrave, 2000), 222-47; Walter Williams, *The Spirit and the Flesh: Sexual Diversity in American Indian Culture* (Boston: Beacon, 1986), 17-109.

15 See Mircea Eliade, *Patterns in Comparative Religion* trans. Rosemary Sheed (New York: Sheed & Ward, 1958) claiming the "sacred was at once 'sacred' and 'defiled'"); Jeffrey Stout, *Ethics after Babel* (Boston: Beacon Press, 1988), 145-62; Greenberg, *Wrestling with God and Men*, 186-89.

16 See Stephanie Dalley, *Myths from Mesopotamia* (Oxford: Oxford University Press, 1987), 329ff; Thorkild Jacobsen, "The Battle between Marduk and Tiamat", *Journal of the American Oriental Society* 88:1 (January-March 1968), 104-108. On the gendered aspects of this myth see Tikva Frymer-Kensky, *In the Wake of the Goddesses: Women, Culture, and the Biblical Transformation of Pagan Myth* (New York: Fawcett Book Group, 1993); Luce Irigaray, *This Sex Which Is Not One* (Ithaca, NY: Cornell University Press, 1985).

17 See Douglas, *Purity and Danger*, 4-6, 59-61; Stone, *Practicing Safer Texts*, 46-50; Stout, *Ethics after Babel*, 156-61.

18 Mary Douglas, *Leviticus as Literature* (Oxford: Oxford University

Press, 1999), 19-25 (refuting much of her earlier book's theories); Stone, *Practicing Safer Texts*, 60-64.

19 Stone, *Practicing Safer Texts*, 59.

20 See Frymer-Kensky, *In the Wake of the Goddesses*, 200-202; Stone, *Practicing Safer Texts*, 58-61; Greenberg, *Wrestling with God and Men*, 177; Johanna Stuckey, "Sacred Prostitutes", *MatriFocus*, 5.1 (2005); Conner, *Blossom of Bone*, 67-81; William G. Dever, *Did God Have a Wife? Archaeology and Folk Religion in Ancient Israel* (Grand Rapids, MI: Eerdmans, 2006); Richard A. Henshaw, *Female & Male, the Cultic Personnel: The Bible and the Rest of the Ancient Near East* (Allison Park, PA: Pickwick, 1994); Saul M. Olyan, *Asherah and the Cult of Yahweh in Israel* (Atlanta, GA: Scholars, 1988).

21 It is important not to overstate the gender dimorphism of the halachic system, however, which includes multiple gender and sex categories, including *tumtum, androgynos*, and, by some counts, *avlonit, saris adam*, and *saris chama*. (The term *androginus*, for example, appears over three hundred times in the Babylonian Talmud). See Alfred Cohen, *"Tumtum* and *Androgynous"*, *Journal of Halacha & Contemporary Society* XXXVIII (Fall 1999); Elliot Rose Kukla and Reuben Zellman, "Created by the Hand of Heaven: A Jewish Approach to Intersexuality", *Torah Queeries* (21 April 2007).

22 Stone, *Practicing Safer Texts*, 64.

23 See Jennings, *Jacob's Wound*, 25-36; Gary David Comstock, *Gay Theology without Apology* (Cleveland: Pilgrim Press, 1993), 79-90; Tom Korner, *Jonathan Loved David* (Philadelphia: Westminster, 1978); Yaron Peleg "Love at First Sight? David, Jonathan, and the Biblical Politics of Gender", *Journal for the Study of the Old Testament* 30:2 (2005), 171-189.

24 Jennings, *Jacob's Wound*, 25-66.

25 Nanette Stahl, *Law and Liminality in the Bible* (Sheffield: Sheffield Academic Press, 1995), 17.

26 Jay Michaelson, "I'm Just Not That Kind of God: Queering Kabbalistic Gender Dimorphism", in Danya Ruttenberg, ed., forthcoming 2007.

27 Charles Mopsik, *Sex of the Soul: The Vicissitudes of Sexual Difference in Kabbalah*, ed. and trans. Daniel Abrams (Cherub Press 2005), 39-45.

28 See Jacob Press, "'What in the world is the sin if I thrill to your beauty'? The homosexual love poems of the medieval rabbis", *Mosaic* 7 (1989) 12-26; Greenberg, *Wrestling with God and Men*, 113-22; Raymond P. Scheindlin, *Wine, Women, and Death: Medieval Hebrew Poems on the Good Life* (Philadelphia: Jewish Publication Society, 1986).

29 See Moshe Idel, *Kabbalah and Eros* (New Haven: Yale Press, 2005), 232-233; Yehuda Liebes, *On Sabbateanism and its Kabbalah: Collected Essays* (Jerusalem: Mossad Bialik, 1995) (Hebrew), 107-109; Avraham Elqayam, "To Know the Messiah: The Dialectics of the Sexual Discourse in the Messianic Thought of Nathan of Gaza" (Hebrew), *Tarbiz* 65 (1996), 637-70; Rachel Elior, "Jacob Frank and

his Book *The Sayings of the Lord*: Anarchism as a Restoration of Myth and Metaphor", in *The Sabbatian Movement and Its Aftermath: Messianism, Sabbatianism and Frankism*, vol. 2, ed. Rachel Elior (Jerusalem: Institute for Jewish Studies, 2001), 471-547; Ada Rapaport-Alpert, "On the Role of Women in Sabbateanism", *Jerusalem Studies in Jewish Thought* 16 (2001), 143-327.

Chapter 3

I am grateful to Helen Burstin, Symcha Burstin, Sefra Burstin, Shauna Sherker and Jennifer Dowling, who read and commented on various drafts of this paper.

[1] Rebecca T Alpert, "Lesbianism", in *Jewish Women: A Comprehensive Historical Encyclopedia* (Jerusalem: Shalvi Publishing, 2006), electronic format.

[2] See for example Norma Fain Pratt, "Culture and Radical Politics: Yiddish Women Writers in America, 1890-1940", in Judith R. Baskin, ed., *Women of the Word: Jewish Women and Writing* (Detroit: Wayne State University Press, 1994), 125-126; Irena Klepfisz, "Queens of Contradiction: A Feminist Introduction to Yiddish Women Writers", in Frieda Forman, Ethel Raicus, Sarah Silberstein Swartz and Margie Wolfe, eds., *Found Treasures: Stories by Yiddish Women Writers* (Toronto: Second Story Press, 1994), 50.

[3] See for example Angus Calder with Lizbeth Goodman, "Gender and poetry" in Lizbeth Goodman, ed., *Literature and Gender* (London: Routledge, 1996), 47; Irena Klepfisz, "*Di mames, dos loshn*/The mothers, the language: Feminism, *Yidishkayt*, and the Politics of Memory", *Bridges: Journal for Jewish Feminists and our Friends* 4:1 (1994), 17.

[4] Klepfisz, "Queens of Contradiction", 25.

[5] See for example Rivke Kope, *Intim Mitn Bukh: Mekhabrim, Bikher, Meynungen* [*Intimate with the Book: Writers, Books, Opinions*] (Paris, 1973), 39.

[6] Alpert, "Lesbianism".

[7] Ibid.

[8] Dina Libkes, "Dina Libkes biography" in E. Korman, *Yidishe dikhterins antalogye* [*Anthology of Yiddish Poetesses*] (Chicago: Farlag L. M. Shteyn, 1928), 348 (translated by author).

[9] Dina Libkes, "*Fun Yener Zayt Vant*" in Korman, *Yidishe dikhterins antalogye*, 307-308.

[10] Translation by Hinde Ena Burstin.

[11] The original Yiddish would be literally translated as "A young woman sleeps beside me". There is no mention of being enthralled. This has been added for poetic effect, to maintain the rhyme sequence of the original.

[12] Sore Ayzn, *Geklibene Lider and Poemes* [*Selected Poems and Odes*] (Yohanesburg/Keyp Toun: Farlag fun der Dorem Afrikaner Yidisher Kultur Federatsye, 1965), 18.

[13] Translation by Hinde Ena Burstin.

[14] The original Yiddish uses the word *tsetrogn* meaning agitated or upset. The word "blush" was substituted to maintain the rhythm of the original.

[15] *"Tsu Mayn Boben Vos Ikh Hob Keynmol Nisht Bakent"*, "A Mother's Day Poem" and "The Spell" in Catherine Odette, ed., *The Chosen of the Chosen: Writings by Jewish Lesbian Daughters of Holocaust Survivors* (Madison: Upstream Books, 1992), 19-25, 136-138.

[16] Hinde Ena Burstin, *"Miriyam's Lid"* and "Miriyam's Song" in *Bridges: Journal for Jewish Feminists and our Friends* 5:1 (1995), 58-59.

[17] Translation by Hinde Ena Burstin.

[18] Pre-destined one, soul mate, from the belief that souls split in two before coming to Earth, and that each soul seeks her other half.

[19] Fain Pratt, "Culture and Radical Politics", 119-120.

[20] Korman, *Yidishe dikhterins antalogye*, viii, ix.

[21] Karlinsky, Simon, "Russia's Gay Literature and Culture: The Impact of the October Revolution" in Martin Bauml Duberman, Martha Vicinus and George Chauncey Junior, eds., *Hidden from History: Reclaiming the Lesbian and Gay Past* (New York: NAL Books, 1989), 358.

[22] Dina Libkes, "Dina Libkes biography" in Korman, *Yidishe dikhterins antalogye*, 348.

[23] See for example Irena Klepfisz, *Dreams of an Insomniac: Jewish Feminist Essays, Speeches and Diatribes* (Portland: The Eighth Mountain Press, 1990), 71-72.

[24] Ken Cage, *Gayle, The Language of Kink and Queens: a History and Dictionary of Gay Language in South Africa* (Johannesburg: Jacana Media, 2003), electronic format.

[25] *Yidishe Kultur* 5 (September/October 1992), 21-23.

[26] Forman, et al., *Found Treasures*, 237.

[27] Korman, *Yidishe Dikhterins Antalogye*, vii, xi.

Chapter 4

[1] Amir Sumaka'i Fink and Jacob Press, *Independence Park: The Lives of Gay Men in Israel* (Stanford: Stanford UP, 1999), 14.

[2] Quoted in Fink and Press, *Independence Park*, 14.

[3] Linda Grant, "Tel Aviv Tales", *Guardian G2* (19 November 2003), 7.

[4] Allen Ellenzweig, "Picturing the Homoerotic", in *Queer Representations: Reading Lives, Reading Cultures, A Center for Lesbian and Gay Studies Book*, ed. Martin Duberman (New York: New York UP, 1997), 57.

[5] Baruch Kimmerling, "Militarism in Israeli Society" (in Hebrew), *Theory and Criticism* 4 (1993); 123-40.

[6] Ella Shohat, *Israeli Cinema: East/West and the Politics of Representation* (Austin: University of Texas Press, 1989), 59.

[7] Ibid., 60.

[8] Roy Grundmann, *Andy Warhol's* Blow Job (Philadelphia: Temple UP,

2003), 43-44.

9 Richard Dyer, *Now You See It: Studies on Lesbian and Gay Film* (London: Routledge, 1990), 112.

10 Richard Dyer, *The Culture of Queers* (London: Routledge, 2002), 5.

11 Dyer, *Now You See It*, 91-92.

12 Ibid., 92.

13 Yosefa Loshitzky, *Identity Politics on the Israeli Screen* (Austin: University of Texas Press, 2001), 1.

14 Lee Edelman, *Homographesis: Essays in Gay Literary and Cultural Theory* (New York: Routledge, 1994), 4.

15 Ibid.

16 Dyer, *The Culture of Queers*, 163.

17 Lee Walzer, *Between Sodom and Eden: A Gay Journey through Today's Changing Israel* (New York: Columbia UP, 2000), 35.

18 David M. Halperin, *One Hundred Years of Homosexuality and Other Essays on Greek Love* (New York: Routledge, 1990), 78-79.

19 Thomas Waugh, "The Third Body: Patterns in the Construction of the Subject in Gay Male Narrative Film", in *Queer Looks: Perspectives on Lesbian and Gay Film and Video*, ed. Martha Gever, Pratibha Parmar and John Greyson (New York: Routledge, 1993), 145.

20 Raz Yosef, "The Military Body: Male Masochism and Homoerotic Relationships in Israeli Cinema" (in Hebrew), *Theory and Criticism* 18 (2001): 26

21 The colonel's remark is an allusion to the famous sequence in Francis Ford Coppola's *Apocalypse Now* (1979), in which American helicopters fire missiles and drop mustard yellow smoke bombs while Colonel Kilgore, played by Robert Duvall, announces: "I love the smell of napalm in the morning". This reference suggests that the IDF actions in Lebanon were comparable to the American army's actions in Vietnam, a comment that stands as one of the very few in the film made against war and its implications.

22 Ellis Hanson, ed., *Out Takes: Essays on Queer Theory and Film* (Durham: Duke UP, 1999), 4.

Chapter 5

1 David Biale, *Eros and the Jews: From Biblical Israel to Contemporary America* (Berkeley: University of California Press, 1997), 181.

2 Ibid., 183-203, especially on asceticism in the service of the nation (192–193).

3 Michael Gluzman, "Longing for Heterosexuality: Zionism and Sexuality in Herzl's *Altneuland*", *Theory and Criticism — An Israeli Forum*, 11 (Winter 1997), 145-163 (Hebrew).

4 Daniel Boyarin, *Unheroic Conduct: The Rise of Heterosexuality and the Invention of the Jewish Man* (Berkeley: University of California Press, 1997), 274.

5 Nurith Gertz, *Holocaust Survivors, Aliens and Others in Israeli Cinema and Literature* (Tel-Aviv: Am Oved Publishers and The Open

University of Israel, 2004), 17 (Hebrew).

6 See Raz Yosef, *Beyond Flesh*: *Queer Masculinities and Nationalism in Israeli Cinema* (New Brunswick, NJ and London: Rutgers University Press, 2004), 144-63.
7 Sigmund Freud, "Fetishism" (1927), in *Freud, Sexuality and the Psychology of Love*, ed. Philip Rieff, trans. Joan Riviere (New York: Collier, 1963), 215-18.
8 Biale, *Eros and the Jews*, 179.
9 Sandra Meiri, "Masquerade and Bad Faith in *Peeping Toms*", *Shofar* 24:1 (2005), 107-24.
10 Ella Shohat and Robert Stam, *Unthinking Eurocentrism: Multiculturalism and the Media* (New York and London: Routledge, 1994); Raz Yosef, "Homoland: Interracial Sex and the Israeli-Palestinian Conflict in Israeli Cinema", *GLQ: A Journal of Lesbian and Gay Studies* 8:4 (2002), 553–79.
11 Teshome H Gabriel, "Third Cinema as Guardian of Popular Memory: Towards a Third Aesthetics", in *Questions of Third Cinema*, ed. Jim Pines and Paul Willemen (London: BFI, 1989), 53–64.

Chapter 6

1 It appears that in Orthodox Judaism these contradictory thoughts seem to be reconciled. As Blu Greenberg argues, "Jewish women, on the whole have been treated well by Jewish men, with strong cultural values... as a result, they have been content to live within the traditional religious and social roles that have been assigned to them. In addition, as Orthodox scholars like Greenberg have argued, men are thankful to God for not making them women as they have less *mitzvoth* to carry out then women, which allows them more time to focus on Torah study. Blu *Greenberg, On Woman and Judaism: A View from Tradition* (Philadelphia: Jewish Publication Society of America, 1998), 4-5.
2 Cited in Joan Dupont, "Directors Eye on Hidden World of Jerusalem", *The International Herald Tribune*, 15 May 1999, http://www.iht.com/articles/1999/05/15/cannes.2.t_0.php. Last consulted in July 2007.
3 Stephanie Wellen Levine, *Mystics, Mavericks, and Merrymakers: An Intimate Journey Among Hasidic Girls* (New York: New York University Press, 2003), 45.
4 Lynne Schreiber, *Hide and Seek: Jewish Women and Hair Covering* (New York: Urim Publications, 2003), 11.
5 Carole Delaney, *The Seed and the Soil: Gender and Cosmology in Turkish Village Society* (Berkley: University of California Press, 1991), 88.
6 Schreiber, *Hide and Seek*, 12.
7 Ibid., 13
8 Howard Eilberg-Schwartz, "Introduction — The Spectacle of Female Hair", in *Off with her Head!: The Denial of Women's Identity in Myth, Religion, and Culture*, ed. Howard Eilberg-Schwartz and Wendy

Doniger (Berkeley: University Of California Press, 1999), 1.

9 Ibid., 2.
10 Karen Lang, "Shaven Heads and Loose Hair: Buddhist Attitudes toward Hair and Sexuality", in *Off with her head!*, ed. Eilberg-Schwartz and Doniger, 33.
11 Delaney, *The Seed and the Soil*, 87.
12 Schreiber, *Hide and Seek*, 47-49.
13 Tehilla Abramov, *The Secret of Jewish Femininity: Insights into The Practice of Taharat HaMishpachah* (South Field: Targum/ Feldheim, 1988), 55-56.
14 Griselda Pollock, "What's Wrong with Images of Women?", *Screen Education* 24 (1977), 26.
15 Karen McCarthy-Brown, "Fundamentalism and the Control of Women", in *Fundamentalism & Gender* (New York: Oxford University Press, 1994), 188.

Chapter 7

1 Antje Ascheid, "Safe Rebellions: Romantic Emancipation in the 'Woman's Heritage Film", *Scope: an online journal of film studies* 4 (Feb. 2006) http://www.scope.nottingham.ac.uk/article.php?issue= 4&id=124. Last consulted in July 2007.
2 Jackie Byars, "Gazes/Voices/Power: Expanding Psychoanalysis for Feminist Film and Television Theory", in *Female Spectators: Looking at Film and Television*, ed. E. Deidre Pribram (New York: Verso, 1988), 122.
3 Alfred Rubens, "Jews and the English Stage, 1667-1850", *Transactions of the Jewish Historical Society of England* 24 (1974), 164, 154.
4 Susan Levin, "The Gipsy is a Jewess: Harriett Abrams and Theatrical Romanticism", in *Romantic Women Writers: Voices and Countervoices*, ed. Paula Feldman and Theresa Kelley (Hanover, NH: University Press of New England, 1995), 240.
5 Ibid., 236.
6 Ibid., 240.
7 Juliet Barker, *The Brontës: A Life in Letters* (New York: Viking, 1997), 325-8.
8 Levin, "The Gipsy is a Jewess", 249.
9 Edward P. Harris, "From Outcast to Ideal: The Image of the Actress in Eighteenth-Century Germany", *The German Quarterly* 54:2 (1981), 185.
10 Jeannette Jakubowski, "Vierzehtes Bild: >> Die Jüdin<<", *Antisemitismus*, ed. J. Schoeps and J. Schlör (Munich: Piper, 1995), 196.
11 Janis Bergman-Carton, "Negotiating the Categories: Sarah Bernhardt and the Possibilities of Jewishness", *Art Journal* 55:2 (1996), 57-58.
12 Cited in Lynette Felber, "Capturing the Shadows of Ghosts: Mixed Media and the Female Gaze in *The Women on the Roof* and *The Governess*", *Film Quarterly* 54:4 (2001), 37 n21.

[13] Cited in Leslie Camhi, "Loving a Dark Idea: The Jewess is Back", *Forward* (31 July 1998), 1.

[14] Aviva Kempner, "Finally: Jewish Women Have Sex on the Screen", *Lilith* (31 Mar. 1999), 38.

[15] Sander Gilman, "Salomé, Syphilis, Sarah Bernhardt and the 'Modern Jewess'", *The Jew in the Text*, ed. Linda Nochlin and Tamar Garb (London: Thames and Hudson, 1996), 97-120.

[16] Sander Gilman, *The Jew's Body* (London: Routledge, 1991), 96-7.

[17] Gilman, "Salomé", 108.

[18] *Ibid.*, 98.

[19] G. William Beardslee, "The 1832 Cholera Epidemic in New York State: 19th Century Responses to Cholerae Vibrio", *Archiving Early America*. http://earlyamerica.com/review/2000_fall/1832_cholera_part1.html. Last consulted in July 2002.

[20] Ibid.

Chapter 8

[1] Bryan Cheyette, *Constructions of "the Jew" in British Literature and Society: Racial Representations* (Cambridge: Cambridge University Press, 1993), 8.

[2] The contradictory nature of Jewish stereotypes and images has also been highlighted by other scholars. See Albert Memmi, *Portrait of a Jew* (London: Eyre and Spottiswoode, 1963), 168.

[3] Michel Foucault, *The History of Sexuality, Volume 1: An Introduction* (London: Allen Lane, 1979), 103.

[4] Ibid., 39.

[5] Paul Hoch, *White Hero Black Beast: Racism, Sexism and the Mask of Masculinity* (London: Pluto, 1979), 51.

[6] Gavin Schaffer, "'Like a baby with a box of matches': British scientists and the concept of 'race' in the interwar period", *British Journal of the History of Science* 38:3 (2005), 307-324 and "'Scientific' Racism Again?: Reginald Gates, the *Mankind Quarterly* and the question of 'race' in science after the Second World War", *Journal of American Studies* 41:2 (2007), 253-278.

[7] Robert Rentoul, *Race Culture or Race Suicide? (A Plea for the Unborn)* (New York: Walter Scott, 1906), xiii, 5.

[8] Thurman Rice, *Racial Hygiene: A practical discussion of eugenics and race culture* (New York: Macmillan, 1929), 14, 350.

[9] Anthony M. Ludovici, *The Quest of Human Quality: How to Rear Leaders* (London: Rider, 1952), 162; Parkes Weber in the Parkes Weber MSS, Wellcome Archive, London, PP/FPW/C.8/2, Note on the effect of the war on the Jewish race, 1940.

[10] Redcliffe Salaman, "Heredity and the Jew", *Journal of Genetics* 1:3 (1911), 4-21.

[11] Redcliffe Salaman MSS, Cambridge University Central Library, Box 19, Salaman's "Presidential Lecture", 1911.

[12] Joseph Jacobs, *Studies in Jewish Statistics* (London: Nutt, 1891),

xxiii.

13 Reginald Gates MSS, King's College London, File 11/102, Notes on N. Bentwich, "The Jews in our time", 1960.

14 Mary Davies and Arthur G. Hughes, *An investigation into the comparative intelligence and attainments of Jewish and non-Jewish school children* (Cambridge, Cambridge University Press, 1927). This report was commissioned by the Jewish Health Organisation of Great Britain (JHOGB) of which Salaman was a leading member. It was intended to serve as a foil to a previous study by Margaret Moul and Karl Pearson, which had argued that Eastern European Jewish immigrant children were inferior to their British peers (see below).

15 Arthur G. Hughes, "Jews and Gentiles: their intellectual and temperamental differences", *Eugenics Review* 18 (1928), 94.

16 Salaman MSS, Box 13, Lecture to the JHOGB, "Heredity: A factor in Public Health", 5/12/25.

17 Rice, *Racial Hygiene*, 14.

18 Jacobs, *Studies in Jewish Statistics*, vii.

19 Rentoul, *Race Culture*, 124.

20 Sidney Dark, *The Jew Today* (London: Ivor Nicholson and Watson, 1933), 59.

21 Hughes, "Jews and Gentiles", 92.

22 J. Rumyaneck, "The comparative psychology of Jews and non-Jews: A survey of the literature", *British Journal of Psychology* 21:4 (1931), 414.

23 Cheyette, *Constructions of the "Jew"*, 140, 6; Sander Gilman, *The Jew's Body* (London: Routledge, 1991), 122-125; Memmi, *Portrait of a Jew*, 116.

24 Freeman, *Social Decay* p.266.

25 R. Austin Freeman, *Social Decay and Regeneration* (London: Constable, 1921), 267, 266.

26 Eugenics Society MSS, Wellcome Archive, London, News Sheet: "Alien Reform of the Tariff", 30/10/1930, SA/EUG/19, (Box 62).

27 Joseph Banister, *England under the Jews* (London: Private, 1901), 36, 39.

28 George Bernard Shaw, *The Revolutionist's Handbook* cited in Cheyette, *Constructions of "The Jew"*, 107.

29 Arnold White, *The Modern Jew* (London: Heinemann, 1899), 144-5.

30 Anthony Goldwin Smith, "Can Jews be Patriots", *Nineteenth Century* 3 (1878), 884.

31 Margaret Moul and Karl Pearson, "The problem of alien immigration into Great Britain illustrated by an examination of Russian and Polish alien children", *Annals of Eugenics* (1925-6), 45-6, 127, 18, 124-5.

Chapter 9

1 Linda Grant, *Sexing the Millennium* (London: HarperCollins, 1994), 14, 99, 140.

2 Ibid., 137, 227.
3 Sigmund Freud, *On Sexuality: Three Essays on the Theory of Sexuality and Other Works* (London: Penguin, 1981), 109.
4 Grant, *Sexing the Millennium*, 227, 259.
5 Ibid., 242, 236.
6 Ibid., 192.
7 Linda Grant, *When I Lived in Modern Times* (London: Granta, 2000), 130, 146.
8 Ibid., 197, 203, 200.
9 Linda Grant, *Still Here* (London: Little, Brown, 2002), 185, 149, 150.
10 Howard Jacobson, *Who's Sorry Now?* (London: Vintage, 2003), 9-10.
11 Ibid., 44, 58, 237, 232.
12 Ibid., 66, 60.
13 Ibid., 292, 259.
14 Ibid., 126, 171, 172, 305, 324.
15 Howard Jacobson, *Kalooki Nights* (New York: Simon & Schuster, 2006), 277, 22, 23, 398, 283.
16 Ibid., 171-2.
17 Ibid., 162, 178, 432, 450.
18 British Council Arts Website on Adam Thirlwell's *Politics*, http://www.encompassculture.com/results/?qs=Adam+Thirlwell. Last consulted in July 2007. Thirlwell's second novel, *Miss Herbert*, with a publication date of July 2007, was unavailable at the time of writing.
19 Adam Thirlwell, *Politics* (London: Vintage, 2004), 3, 160.
20 Ibid., 12, 88, 151.
21 Ibid., 97, 171, 213.
22 Ibid., 59, 7, 14, 194.
23 Ibid., 75, 79, 251.
24 Naomi Alderman, *Disobedience* (London: Viking, 2006), 121, 133, 55, 247.
25 Ibid., 256, 246, 256,
26 See, for example, Rod Mengham and Philip Tew (eds.), *British Fiction Today* (London: Continuum, 2006) and Philip Tew, *The Contemporary British Novel: From John Fowles to Zadie Smith* (London: Continuum, 2004).

Chapter 10

1 Rhonda Lieberman, "Jewish Barbie", reprinted in Norman Kleeblatt, ed., *Too Jewish: Challenging Traditional Identities* (New York and New Brunswick, NJ: The Jewish Museum and Rutgers University Press, 1996), 108-9.
2 Ibid., 109.
3 M. Plante, ed., *Deborah Kass: The Warhol Project* (New York: Distributed Art Publishers, 1999), 30.
4 Monica Bohm-Duchen and Vera Grodzinski, "Gender, Religion and Ethnicity: Jewish Women in Visual Culture", in *Issues in Architecture Art and Design* (1996), 20.

5   Ibid., 21.
6   Amelia Jones, "The Undecidability of Difference: The Work of Rachel Garfield", in the *Focal Point Gallery Monograph on Rachel Garfield*, 2005.
7   Rachel Garfield, "Towards a Re-Articulation of Cultural Identity: Some Tropes of Artistic Practice or Problematizing the Jewish Subject in Art", *Third Text* 20:1 (January 2006), 99-108.

Chapter 11

1   Henry Roth, *Mercy of a Rude Stream, volume 1: A Star Shines Over Mt. Morris Park* (New York: St. Martin's Press, 1994), 160.
2   Mary Gordon, "Confession, Terminable and Interminable", *New York Times Book Review,* 26 Feb. 1995, 5.
3   Ibid, 6.
4   David Bronsen, "A Conversation with Henry Roth", *Partisan Review* 36:2 (1969), 265.
5   John S. Friedman, "On Being Blocked and Other Literary Matters: An Interview", *Commentary* 64 (Aug. 1977), 28.
6   Bronsen, "A Conversation with Henry Roth", 266.
7   Roth, *A Star Shines*, 3.
8   Hana Wirth-Nesher, "Facing the Fictions: Henry Roth's and Philip Roth's Meta-Memoirs", *Prooftexts: A Journal of Jewish Literary History* 18.3 (Sep. 1998), 266.
9   Hana Wirth-Nesher, "*Call It Sleep*: Jewish, American, Modernist, Classic", *Judaism: A Quarterly Journal of Jewish Life and Thought* 44:4 (Fall 1995), 396.
10 Roth, *A Star Shines*, 59.
11 Henry Roth, *Mercy of a Rude Stream, volume 2: A Diving Rock on the Hudson* (New York: St. Martin's Press, 1995), 379.
12 Ibid.
13 Ibid., 382.
14 Ibid., 378.
15 Ibid., 47.
16 Ibid.
17 Roth, *Diving Rock*, 190.
18 Ibid., 243.
19 Henry Roth, *Mercy of a Rude Stream, volume 4: Requiem for Harlem* (New York: St. Martin's Press, 1998), 14.
20 Ibid., 170.
21 Ibid., 139.
22 Roth, *Diving Rock*, 377.
23 Henry Roth, *Mercy of a Rude Stream, volume 3: From Bondage* (New York: St. Martin's Press, 1996), 331.
24 Roth, *Diving Rock*, 371.
25 Ibid., 71.
26 Laurie Vickroy, *Trauma and Survival in Contemporary Fiction.* (Charlottesville: University of Virginia Press, 2002), 30.

27 Ibid, 31.
28 Roth, *Diving Rock*, 145.
29 Ibid., 213.
30 Ibid., 34.
31 Ibid., 340.
32 Ibid., 333.
33 Ibid., 179.
34 Stacy S. Mulder, "'*Tikkun* and *Teshuvah*': Continuity in the Novels of Henry Roth". Diss. Ball State University, Indiana, 2002, 268.
35 Jonathan Rosen, "Lost and Found: Remembering Henry Roth", *New York Times Book Review*, 10 Dec. 1995, 47.
36 "Confession, Terminable and Interminable", 5.
37 Steven G Kellman, "'The Midwife of His Rebirth': Henry Roth and Zion", *Judaism: A Quarterly Journal of Jewish Life and Thought* 49.3 (Summer 2000), 346.
38 Roth, *Diving Rock*, 285.

Chapter 12

1 Lous Dupré, *The Enlightenment and the Intellectual Foundations of Modern Culture* (New Haven: Yale University Press, 2004), xi.
2 Joel Berkowitz and Jeremy Dauber, *Landmark Yiddish Plays: A Critical Anthology* (Albany, NY: SUNY Press, 2006), 1.
3 Nina Warnke, "God of Vengeance: The 1907 Controversy Over Art and Morality", in Stahl, ed., *Sholem Asch Reconsidered*, 63-77.
4 See Edward J. Bristow, *Prostitution and Prejudice: The Jewish Fight Against White Slavery, 1870-1939* (New York: Schocken, 1983).
5 Ellen Schiff, "Introduction", in *Awake and Singing: 7 Classic Plays from the American Jewish Repertoire* (New York: Mentor/Penguin, 1995), xxvi.
6 Exceptions include two plays in which pregnancies resulting from pre-marital sex are major issues: Clifford Odets's *Awake and Sing!* and in S.N. Behrman's *The Cold Wind and the Warm*, both plays with strong Jewish content. In the former, an immigrant is tricked into marrying the newly pregnant woman and only learns later that he is not the baby's father. In the latter, Willie sleeps with one girl, Leah, when he is in love with another, Myra, who is marrying another man. When her new husband dies shortly thereafter, family members pressure Myra to accept a levirate marriage to his younger brother Aaron. She refuses to remarry at all, referring vaguely to sexual difficulties she encountered on her wedding night. Willie learns he is the father of Leah's purportedly adopted baby, and he kills himself.
7 Andrea Most, *Making Americans: Jews and the Broadway Musical* (Cambridge, MA: Harvard UP, 2004). See especially 436-63. Two exceptions are characters that appear in 1920s Broadway musicals *Whoopee* (1929) and *Girl Crazy* (1930) whose ambiguous sexuality parallels their Jewish-outsider status.
8 Alisa Solomon, "How *Fiddler* Became Folklore", *Forward* (2 and 9

September, 2006).

9   See John M. Clum, *Acting Gay: Male Homosexuality in Modern Drama* (New York: Columbia University Press, 1994), 265-270.

10 William Finn, *The Marvin Songs: Falsettoland, March of the Falsettos, In Trousers* (Garden City, NY: Fireside Theatre, 1989), 215.

11 Peter F. Cohen, "Strange Bedfellows: Writing Love and Politic in *Angels in America* and *The Normal Heart*", *Journal of Medical Humanities* 19:2/3 (1998), 197-219.

12 Quoted in Norman J. Cohen, "Wrestling with Angels", in *Tony Kushner in Conversation* ed. Robert Vorlicky (Ann Arbor, MI: University of Michigan Press, 1998), 217-230; Eve Kosofsky Sedgwick, *The Epistemology of the Closet* (Berkeley, CA: University of California Press, 1990).

13 Wendy Wasserstein, *The Heidi Chronicles* (New York: Vintage, 1991).

Chapter 13

1   Simone Baird, "The A-Z of Burlesque", *Time Out*, 1 May 2007 [online] http://www.timeout.com/london/clubs/features/2874/The_A-Z_of_burlesque.html. Last consulted August 2007.

2   See the Carnesky productions website [online] www.carnesky.com. Last consulted in October 2007.

3   Lyn Gardner, Review of *the Girl from Nowhere* and *Jewess Tattooess* in *The Guardian*, 27 June 2003.

4   Reviews of Duckie productions can be read on their website [online] www.duckie.co.uk. "Bite-size burlesque" was a term used by *Observer* critic Susannah Clapp, 22 December 2003.

5   Judith Palmer, "Expensive Thrills", *The New Statesman*, 14 June 2004 [online] http://www.newstatesman.com/200406140036. Last consulted in May 2007.

6   San Francisco Featured Event: Smut Fest page [online] http://www.eros-zine.com/articles/2006-07-25/smutfest0725/. Last consulted in May 2007. Over a decade later, new episodes of *Real Sex* are still being made and Smut Fests, MCed by Jennifer Blowdryer, are still taking place in San Francisco. Blowdryer's real surname is Waters.

7   C. Carr, *On Edge: Performance at the End of the Twentieth Century* (Hanover and London: University Press of New England, 1993), 174-76.

8   See, for instance, Danielle Willis's account in a 1995 interview with Alexander Laurence [online] http://www.neitherday.com/danielle_willis/interviews_articles_an_interview.html. Last consulted in May 2007.

9   Blowdryer, quoted in Annie Sprinkle, *Annie Sprinkle's Post-Modern Pin-Ups Bio Booklet To Accompany the Pleasure Activist Playing Cards* (Richmond, VA: Gates of Heck, 1995), 57.

10 Sprinkle featured in the following HBO broadcasts: *Real Sex 2* (1994), *Real Sex 3* (1995), and *Wild Cards* (1996).

11 Sprinkle, *Annie Sprinkle's Post-Modern Pin-Ups Bio Booklet*, 13.

12 Marisa Carnesky, telephone conversation with the author, 6 August 2007. See *Annie Sprinkle's Post-Modern Pin-Ups Bio Booklet*, p. 17.

13 *Annie Sprinkle's Post-Modern Pin-Ups Bio Booklet*, 8-9.

14 Carr, *On Edge*, 176.

15 Geraldine Harris, *Staging Femininities: Performance and Performativity* (Manchester: Manchester University Press, 1999), 37.

16 Annie Sprinkle, *Post-Porn Modernist: My 25 Years as a Multimedia Whore* (San Francisco: Cleis Press, 1998), 117.

17 Ibid., 12.

18 Annie Sprinkle, telephone conversation with the author, 13 April 2005.

19 Harris, *Staging Femininities*, 43.

20 Roberta Mock, *Jewish Women on Stage, Film, and Television* (New York & Basingstoke: Palgrave Macmillan, 2007). This book details the historic contexts in which I am situating Sprinkle and Carnesky below.

21 Gilman, "Salomé, Syphilis, Sarah Bernhardt, and the Modern Jewess", source has already appeared (note 133).

22 Sarah Bernhardt, *The Art of Theatre*, trans. H.J. Stenning (New York and London: Benjamin Blom, 1969), 146.

23 Gilman, "Salomé, Syphilis, Sarah Bernhardt", 115.

24 Email from Annie Sprinkle to author, 10 April 2005. While lists of Jewish male directors and performers far outnumbers women, there were indeed other Jewish women working in porn films at this time. One was Sprinkle's friend Gloria Leonard who appeared with her in *Deep Inside Porn Stars*, a performance art event presented in a festival organised by New York feminist art collective Carnival Knowledge in 1984. Nina Hartley made her porn debut in the early 1980s while Sprinkle was still very active.

25 Ann Pellegrini, *Performance Anxieties: Staging Psychoanalysis, Staging Race* (London & New York: Routledge, 1997), 28.

26 Renée Sentilles, *Performing Menken: Adah Isaacs Menken and the Birth of American Celebrity* (Cambridge: Cambridge University Press, 2003).

27 Annie Sprinkle, "We've Come A Long Way — And We're Exhausted!" *Whores and Other Feminists*, Ed. Jill Nagle (New York and London: Routledge, 1997), 66.

28 Sprinkle, *Post-Porn Modernist*, 162.

29 Harris, *Staging Femininities*, 164.

30 See Sprinkle, *Post-Porn Modernist*, 18-21.

31 Judith Butler, *Gender Trouble: Feminism and the Subversion of Identity* (New York: Routledge, 1990), 147.

32 Carnesky quoted in Naomi Pfefferman, "Staging a Body of Work", *Jewish Journal*, 26 September 2003 [online] http://www.jewish journal.com/home/print.php?id=11130. Last consulted in July 2007.

Chapter 14

1 See for example Gloria Cowan and Robin R. Campbell, "Racism and sexism in interracial pornography: A content analysis", *Psychology of*

Women Quarterly 18:3 (September 1994), 323-38; Constance Penley, "Crackers and Whackers: The White Trashing of Porn", *Pornography: Film and Culture*, ed. Peter Lehman (New Brunswick, NJ and London: Rutgers University Press, 2006), 99-117; Daniel Bernardi, "Interracial Joysticks: Pornography's Web of Racist Attractions", in ibid., 220-43; and José B. Capino, "Asian College Girls and Oriental Men with Bamboo Poles: Reading Asian Pornography", in ibid., 206-19.

2   Linda Williams, "Porn Studies: Proliferating Pornographies On/ Scene: An Introduction", in *Porn Studies*, ed. Linda Williams (Durham and London: Duke University Press, 2004), 6.

3   Luke Ford, "Jews", http://www.lukeford.com/subjects/content/ jews_in_porn.html. Last consulted in June 2007. Where no reference is provided all subsequent references to Ford are from this website.

4   Sheldon Ranz, "Nina Hartley", *Shmate: A Journal of Progressive Jewish Thought* 21/22 (Spring 1989), 26.

5   Phil Goldmarx, "Letters", *The Forward* (20 June 2003), 8.

6   Nathan Abrams, "Triple Exthnics", *The Jewish Quarterly* (Winter 2004/05), 27-30.

7   David Hebditch and Nick Anning, *Porn Gold: Inside the Pornography Business* (London: Faber & Faber, 1988), 368.

8   Ibid.

9   Luke Ford, *The History of X: 100 Years of Sex in Film* (New York: Prometheus Books, 1999).

10 Ibid., 21.

11 Ibid., 167.

12 Ibid., 31.

13 Daniel Shocket, "Did You Know Most Male Porn Stars Are Jewish", *Shmate* 21/22 (Spring 1989), 34.

14 Susan Faludi, *Stiffed: The Betrayal of Modern Man* (London: Chatto & Windus, 1999), 536.

15 Ibid., 546.

16 http://www.the7thfire.com/new_world_order/zionism/jewish_ dominance_in_porn.htm. Last consulted in February 2007.

17 http://www.fpp.co.uk/BoD/origins/porn_industry.html. Last consulted in February 2007.

18 David Duke, "Jewish Anti-Gentile Hatred Present in Porn Industry", http://www.davidduke.com/general/jewish-extremist-anti-gentile-hatred-present-in-porn-industry_400.html. Last consulted in February 2007.

19 Jonathan Freedman, "Miller, Monroe and the Remaking of Jewish Masculinity" in Enoch Brater, ed. *Arthur Miller's America: Theater and Culture in a Time of Change* (Ann Arbor: The University of Michigan Press, 2005), 137.

20 Ibid.

21 Adolf, 18 August 2001, http://www.ronjeremy-themovie.com/board. htm. Last consulted in February 2007.

22 Daniel Bitton daniel660@hotmail.com, 31August 2001, ibid.

23 Steve Almond, "To Each His Own Fetish", *Nextbook* (4 January 2007), http://www.nextbook.org/cultural/feature.html?id=491. Last

consulted in June 2007.

[24] Abraham H. Foxman, http://www.lukeford.com/subjects/content/jews_in_porn.html. Last consulted in June 2007.

Chapter 15

[1] Cited in Charlotte Baum, Paul Hyman and Sonya Michel, *The Jewish Woman in America* (New York: New American Library, 1977), 259.

[2] Ibid., 237-238.

[3] David Zurawik, *The Jews of Primetime* (Hanover, NH: Brandeis University Press/University Press of New England, 2003), 35-36.

[4] Ibid., 36.

[5] Herman Wouk, *Marjorie Morningstar* (Boston, MA: Back Bay Books, 1955, 1983), 11.

[6] Riv-Ellen Prell, "Why Jewish Princesses Don't Sweat", in *Too Jewish? Challenging Traditional Identities,* ed. Norman L. Kleebatt (New York: The Jewish Museum and New Brunswick, NJ: Rutgers University Press, 1996), 78.

[7] Philip Roth, "Goodbye, Columbus", in *Goodbye, Columbus and Five Short Stories* (New York: Vintage, 1959, 1987), 13.

[8] Ibid., 26.

[9] This article is referred to in Riv-Ellen Prell, *Fighting to Become Americans: Jews, Gender and the Anxiety of Assimilation* (Boston: Beacon Press, 1999), 185.

[10] Julie Baumgold "The Persistence of the Jewish American Princess", *New York* (22 March 1971), 25.

[11] Leslie Tonner, *Nothing But The Best: The Luck of the Jewish Princess,* (New York: Coward, McCann and Geoghegan, 1975), 83.

[12] Alan Dundes, "The JAP and the JAM in American Jokelore", *Journal of American Folklore* 98 (1985), 462-464.

[13] Ibid., 471-472.

[14] Frederic Cople Jaher, "The Quest for the Ultimate Shiksa", *American Quarterly* 35 (1983), 538.

[15] Ibid., 535.

[16] Tonner, *Nothing But The Best*, 85-86.

[17] Jaher, "The Quest for the Ultimate Shiksa", 531.

[18] Ibid., 540.

[19] Ibid., 537-539.

[20] Marshall Sklare, "Intermarriage & the Jewish Future", *Commentary* 37:4 (April 1964), 47.

[21] Ibid.

[22] Ibid., 51; emphasis added.

[23] Judith Guttman, "Letters", *Commentary* 38:3 (September 1964), 10.

[24] Prell, *Fighting to Become Americans,* 208.

[25] Sidney Goldstein and Calvin Goldscheider, "Social and Demographic Aspects of Jewish Intermarriages", *Social Problems* 13:4 (Spring 1966), 390.

[26] Marshall Sklare, "Intermarriage and Jewish Survival", *Commentary*

49:3 (March 1970), 52.

27 Leonard Fein, "Letters", *Commentary* 49:6 (June 1970), 6-8.

28 Fred Massarik, "Rethinking the Intermarriage Crisis", *Moment* (June 1978), 33.

29 David Singer, "Living with Intermarriage", *Commentary* 68:1 (July 1979), 49.

30 Bernard Farber, Leonard Gordon, and Albert J. Mayer, "Intermarriage and Jewish Identity: the implications for pluralism and assimilation in American society", *Ethnic and Racial Studies* 2:2 (April 1979), 227-228.

31 Anonymous, "We are Many: Our Readers Speak on Intermarriage", *Moment* (April 1977), 37.

Chapter 16

1 David Biale, *Eros and the Jews: From Biblical Israel to Contemporary America* (Basic Books, 1992), 2.

2 Daniel C. Boyarin, *Unheroic Conduct: The Rise of Heterosexuality and the Invention of the Jewish Man* (Berkeley: University of California Press, 1997).

3 Eric Lax, *Woody Allen: A Biography* (New York, Knopf, 1991), 158. See 156-64 for a full discussion of Allen's stand-up persona.

4 Maurice Yacowar, *Loser Take All* (New York: Continuum, 1991), 20.

5 Sam B. Girgus, *The Films of Woody Allen* (New York: Cambridge University Press, 1993), 21.

6 Boyarin, *Unheroic Conduct*, 4.

7 See Mary P. Nichols, *Reconstructing Woody* (Lanham, MD: Rowan and Littlefield, 1998).

8 Kathleen Rowe, *The Unruly Woman: Gender and the Genres of Laughter* (University of Texas Press, 1995). 197. I respond at greater length to Rowe's characterization of the Allen persona as a "medlodramatised male" in my article "Neurotic in New York: The Woody Allen Touches in *Sex and the City*", in *Reading Sex and the City*, ed. Janet McCabe and Kim Akass (London: I. B. Tauris, 2004).

9 See Biale, *Eros and the Jews*, 216.

10 Mark E. Bleiwess, "Self-Deprecation and the Jewish Humor of Woody Allen", in *Perspectives on Woody Allen*, ed. Renee R. Curry (New York: Prentice Hall, 1996), 211.

11 Yacowar, *Loser Take All*, 145.

12 Biale, *Eros and the Jews*, 206.

About the Authors

Nathan Abrams is a Lecturer in Film Studies and Director of Graduate Studies at Bangor University. He has written widely on Jewish-American history, politics, popular culture and film, including four books, *Struggling for Empire: Norman Podhoretz and the Rise and Fall of the Neo-Cons* (forthcoming); *Commentary Magazine 1945-1959: 'A journal of significant thought and opinion'* (London and Portland, OR: Vallentine Mitchell, 2006); *Studying Film* (co-authored with Ian Bell and Jan Udris; London: Arnold, 2001) and *Containing America: Production and Consumption in Fifties America* (co-edited with Julie Hughes; Birmingham: Birmingham University Press, 2000). He is also currently working on a project that examines the new and changing depictions of Jews in Anglo-American film.

Lisa Bloom is the author of *Gender on Ice: American Ideologies of Polar Expeditions* (University of Minnesota Press, 1993), which is the only critical book to date on the Arctic and Antarctic written from a feminist perspective, and an edited anthology entitled *With Other Eyes: Looking at Race and Gender in Visual Culture* (University of Minnesota Press, 1999). She recently completed a third book (Routledge: London, 2006) titled, *Jewish Identities in U.S. Feminist Art: Ghosts of Ethnicity*. Her interdisciplinary research and pedagogical interests cut across numerous fields including feminist studies, media and film studies, cultural studies, visual culture and the history of art. She has both an M.F.A. from the Visual Studies Workshop and Rochester Institute of Technology (1985), and a PhD from the History of Consciousness Board at the University of California, Santa Cruz (1990). Bloom is currently a visiting associate professor in the Dept. of Communication at the University of California, San Diego.

Hinde Ena Burstin is a Research Associate in the Department of Hebrew, Biblical and Jewish Studies at the University of Sydney, Australia. She is an internationally published bilingual (Yiddish and English) writer and an award-winning Yiddish poetry translator. She teaches Yiddish and Yiddish literature, and has been an invited presenter on Yiddish literature, in Europe, North America, South Africa and around Australia. She is currently researching radical themes in Yiddish poetry. Hinde Ena Burstin is also a lesbian activist.

Nir Cohen is currently a Post Doctoral Fellow at the Department of Jewish and Hebrew Studies, University College London. He completed his PhD in Film Studies there in 2006. He also holds an MA in Cultural Studies from Goldsmiths College, University of London and a BA (Hons) from the General and Interdisciplinary Studies Programme in the Faculty of Humanities, Tel Aviv University.

Jyoti Sarah Daniels is currently pursuing an L.L.B. (Bachelor of Law) degree at the University of Saskatchewan. In 2004 she graduated from the University of Saskatchewan with a BA in Religious Studies and Sociology and went on to pursue a MA in Religious Studies at the University of Regina which she completed in 2006. The focus of her thesis work was on the representation of the Hasidic female body in film as presented through the mediums of myth and ritual. She remains interested in the intersection between religion, gender, culture, and film.

Geoffrey Dennis is a rabbi and university lecturer. He has degrees in Education and Nursing besides his ordination. He is an energetic and engaging speaker and has been a popular lecturer in congregations, universities and national conferences. Articles by him appear in periodicals like *Parabola: The Magazine of Myth and Tradition* and *Healings Ministries*. He is a major contributor to *Encyclopedia Mythica*, an online resource devoted to world myth and folklore and author of *The Encyclopedia of Jewish Myth, Magic, and Mysticism*, (Woodbury: Llewellyn Worldwide). He is currently teaching and practicing Judaism (until he gets it right) in North Texas, where he lives with his wife and two sons.

Ben Furnish holds a PhD in theatre and film studies from the University of Kansas and is currently managing editor of BkMk Press at the University of Missouri-Kansas City, where he also teaches in the English Department. He is author of *Nostalgia in Jewish-American Theatre and Film, 1999-2004* (Lang) and has contributed to such books as *Holocaust Literature* (Routledge),

Jewish-American Poets and Dramatists: A Bio-critical Source-book (Greenwood), *Novels into Film* (Facts on File), and *The Sixties in America* (Salem). He also has work soon to appear in *Studies in Jewish Civilization, Dictionary of Literary Biography*, and *Encyclopedia Judaica*.

Alan Gibbs is a Lecturer in American Literature at University College, Cork, Ireland. He received his BA and MA from the University of the West of England, Bristol and his PhD from the University of Nottingham. His research on Henry Roth encompassed editing an issue of *The Journal of the Short Story in English* on the work of Roth, which included editing a previously unpublished story of Roth's. His monograph, *Henry Roth's Mercy of a Rude Stream: Fragments Shored against His Ruin* will be published by Mellen in early 2008.

Thomas Grochowski is Assistant Professor of English at St. Joseph's College of New York. He is a longtime admirer of Woody Allen's films and has taught courses on Allen for New York University and for Purchase College of the State University of New York. His contribution to the anthology *Reading Sex and the City* (IB Tauris, 2004) assessed the influence of Allen's work on the popular HBO sitcom. He has recently contributed to the anthologies *Mediated Deviance and Social Otherness* and *A Century of the Marx Brothers*, both from Cambridge Scholars Publishing (UK). He has published work on media and the O.J. Simpson murder case and contributed to *Routledge's Encyclopedia of the Documentary Film*. He regularly teaches a course in Rock and Roll Films for Queens College of the City University of New York. He also holds an MFA in Creative Writing from Brooklyn College, studying under Allen Ginsberg. A Native New Yorker, he lives in Brooklyn with his wife and children.

Peter Lawson is the author of *Anglo-Jewish Poetry from Isaac Rosenberg to Elaine Feinstein* (Vallentine Mitchell, 2006). He has also edited an anthology, *Passionate Renewal: Jewish Poetry in Britain since 1945* (Five Leaves, 2001). Currently, Lawson is researching ghosts and bodies in diasporic fiction. He teaches English Literature at the University of Tampere, Finland.

Judith Lewin is an Associate Professor in the English Department at Union College, where she also teaches on the Women's and Gender Studies programme. Her publications are concerned with the issue of gender and representation, especially of the Jewish woman in nineteenth-century literature. She has two book projects in progress, *Literary Jewesses and Nineteenth-Century Jewish Women: A Dynamics of Identification* and *Jewish Women's Fiction: From Glikl to Goodman*.

Sandra Meiri is a lecturer at the Open University of Israel. She has published articles on transsexuality, gender and film. Her book *Any Sex You Can Do I can Do Better* (*Min She'Eino Mino*) is forthcoming from Migdarim, Tel Aviv: Ha-kibbutz Ha-Meuhad).

Jay Michaelson (www.metatronics.net) is a visiting professor at Boston University Law School and a doctoral candidate in Jewish Thought at the Hebrew University of Jerusalem. The chief editor of *Zeek: A Jewish Journal of Thought and Culture* (www.zeek.net), and the director of Nehirim: GLBT Jewish Culture and Spirituality (www.nehirim.org), Jay writes and teaches frequently on issues of sexuality and religion; his work has appeared on NPR, and in *Tikkun*, the *Forward*, *Blithe House Quarterly*, the *Jerusalem Post*, and anthologies including *Mentsh: On Being Jewish and Queer* (Alyson, 2004), and he is a recent finalist for the Koret Young Writer on Jewish Themes Award. His chapter is part of a longer work in progress entitled "The Religious Significance of Homosexuality". Other books include *God in Your Body: Kabbalah, Mindfulness, and Embodied Spiritual Practice* (Jewish Lights, 2006) and *Another Word for Sky: Poems* (Lethe Press, 2007).

Roberta Mock is Reader in Performance and Associate Dean (Research) in the Faculty of Arts at the University of Plymouth. Her books include *Jewish Women on Stage, Film, and Television* (Palgrave Macmillan, 2007) and, as editor, *Performing Processes: Creating Live Performance* (Intellect, 2000) and *Walking, Writing and Performance: Autobiographical Texts* (Intellect, forthcoming 2008). She has written articles for *New Theatre Quarterly*, *Studies in Theatre & Performance*, *Contemporary Theatre Review*, *Body Space & Technology*, *Feminist Review*, and *Women's Studies*. She is currently preparing a solo performance exploring food and

Jewishness through the re-enactment of 1960s nightclub performances.

Yael Munk is a lecturer at the Open University of Israel and the Sapir College. Her research deals with post-colonial views of Israeli cinema, women and gender studies.

Dr Gavin Schaffer is Senior Lecturer in European history at the University of Portsmouth. He has published widely on the history of racial science in Britain and the racialisation of immigrants and minorities in British society.

David Weinfeld was born and raised in Montreal, Canada. He attended college at Harvard University in Cambridge, Massachusetts, where he graduated cum laude in History. He is currently a doctoral student at New York University in Hebrew and Judaic Studies and History. His interests include modern European and American Jewish history, especially intellectual and cultural history.

Also available from Five Leaves

Secret Judaism and the Spanish Inquisition
Michael Alpert
£14.99

The World is a Wedding
Bernard Kops
£9.99

Bernard Kops' East End
Bernard Kops
£9.99

Reporting from Palestine 1943-1944
Barbara Board
£9.99

If Salt Has Memory: Jewish exiled writers from Europe, Africa, the Middle East and Latin America
Ed. Jennifer Langer
£10.99

Rock'n'Roll Jews
Michael Billig
£7.99

The Art of Blessing the Day: poetry on Jewish themes
Marge Piercy
£7.99

East End Jewish Radicals 1875-1914
William Fishman
£14.99

www.fiveleaves.co.uk

Also available from Five Leaves

Passionate Renewal: Jewish poetry in Britain since 1945
Ed. Peter Lawson
£14.99

For Generations: Jewish Motherhood
Ed. Mandy Ross and Ronne Randall
£9.99

Gardens of Eden Revisited (poetry)
Michelene Wandor
£7.99

When Joseph Met Molly: a reader on Yiddish film
Ed. Sylvia Paskin
£14.99

All My Young Years: Yiddish poetry from Weimar Germany
A.N. Stencl
£7.99

The London Years
Rudolf Rocker
£14.99

www.fiveleaves.co.uk

Jewish fiction from Five Leaves

The Hiding Room
Jonathan Wilson
£7.99

A Palestine Affair
Jonathan Wilson
£7.99

An Ambulance is on the Way
Jonathan Wilson
£7.99

A Year of Two Summer
Sean Levin
£7.99

Magnolia Street
Louis Golding
£9.99

Lindmann
Frederic Raphael
£9.99

The Slow Mirror and other stories: New fiction by Jewish writers
Ed. Sonja Lyndon and Sylvia Paskin
£9.99

www.fiveleaves.co.uk